Translating Euclid

Designing a Human-Centered Mathematics

Synthesis Lectures on Human-Centered Informatics

Editor
John M. Carroll, *Penn State University*

Human-Centered Informatics (HCI) is the intersection of the cultural, the social, the cognitive, and the aesthetic with computing and information technology. It encompasses a huge range of issues, theories, technologies, designs, tools, environments and human experiences in knowledge work, recreation and leisure activity, teaching and learning, and the potpourri of everyday life. The series publishes state-of-the-art syntheses, case studies, and tutorials in key areas.

How We Cope with Digital Technology
Phil Turner
2013

Translating Euclid: Designing a Human-Centered Mathematics
Gerry Stahl
2013

Adaptive Interaction: A Utility Maximization Approach to Understanding Human Interaction with Technology
Stephen J. Payne and Andrew Howes
2013

Making Claims: Knowledge Design, Capture, and Sharing in HCI
D. Scott McCrickard
2012

HCI Theory: Classical, Modern, and Contemporary
Yvonne Rogers
2012

Activity Theory in HCI: Fundamentals and Reflections
Victor Kaptelinin and Bonnie Nardi
2012

Conceptual Models: Core to Good Design
Jeff Johnson and Austin Henderson
2011

Geographical Design: Spatial Cognition and Geographical Information Science
Stephen C. Hirtle
2011

User-Centered Agile Methods
Hugh Beyer
2010

Experience-Centered Design: Designers, Users, and Communities in Dialogue
PeterWright and John McCarthy
2010

Experience Design: Technology for All the Right Reasons
Marc Hassenzahl
2010

Designing and Evaluating Usable Technology in Industrial Research: Three Case Studies
Clare-Marie Karat and John Karat
2010

Interacting with Information
Ann Blandford and Simon Attfield
2010

Designing for User Engagement: Aesthetic and Attractive User Interfaces
Alistair Sutcliffe
2009

Context-Aware Mobile Computing: Affordances of Space, Social Awareness, and Social
Influence
Geri Gay
2009

Studies ofWork and theWorkplace in HCI: Concepts and Techniques
Graham Button andWes Sharrock
2009

Semiotic Engineering Methods for Scientific Research in HCI
Clarisse Sieckenius de Souza and Carla Faria Leitão
2009

Common Ground in Electronically Mediated Conversation
Andrew Monk
2008

Translating Euclid: Designing a Human-Centered Mathematics
Gerry Stahl

ISBN: 978-3-031-01072-9   print
ISBN: 978-3-031-02200-5   ebook

DOI 10.1007/978-3-031-02200-5

A Publication in the Springer series
SYNTHESIS LECTURES ON HUMAN-CENTERED INFORMATICS
Lecture #17
Series Editor: John M. Carroll, Penn State University

Series ISSN   1946-7680 Print   1946-7699 Electronic

Translating Euclid

Designing a Human–Centered Mathematics

Gerry Stahl
The iSchool & the Math Forum, Drexel University

SYNTHESIS LECTURES ON HUMAN-CENTERED INFORMATICS #17

ABSTRACT

Translating Euclid reports on an effort to transform geometry for students from a stylus-and-clay-tablet corpus of historical theorems to a stimulating computer-supported collaborative-learning inquiry experience.

The origin of geometry was a turning point in the pre-history of informatics, literacy, and rational thought. Yet, this triumph of human intellect became ossified through historic layers of systematization, beginning with Euclid's organization of the *Elements* of geometry. Often taught by memorization of procedures, theorems, and proofs, geometry in schooling rarely conveys its underlying intellectual excitement. The recent development of dynamic-geometry software offers an opportunity to translate the study of geometry into a contemporary vernacular. However, this involves transformations along multiple dimensions of the conceptual and practical context of learning.

Translating Euclid steps through the multiple challenges involved in redesigning geometry education to take advantage of computer support. Networked computers portend an interactive approach to exploring dynamic geometry as well as broadened prospects for collaboration. The proposed conception of geometry emphasizes the central role of the construction of dependencies as a design activity, integrating human creation and mathematical discovery to form a human-centered approach to mathematics.

This book chronicles an iterative effort to adapt technology, theory, pedagogy and practice to support this vision of collaborative dynamic geometry and to evolve the approach through on-going cycles of trial with students and refinement of resources. It thereby provides a case study of a design-based research effort in computer-supported collaborative learning from a human-centered informatics perspective.

KEYWORDS

Computer-Supported Collaborative Learning (CSCL), Design-Based Research (DBR), Virtual Math Teams (VMT), group cognition, dynamic geometry, post-cognitive philosophy, interaction analysis, creative discovery, multi-user software, interactional resources.

Contents

Figures

Tables

Logs

Acknowledgments

The effort reported here to develop a contemporary approach to the learning of collaborative dynamic geometry has itself been a collaborative learning experience. The interdisciplinary, international VMT research team from 2003–2009 is documented in (Stahl, 2009, esp. pp. xix-xxi). In its current phase from 2011–2016, the project is a collaboration among the iSchool at Drexel, the Math Forum at Drexel, the School of Education at Drexel, and the Department of Urban Education at Rutgers-Newark.

Since the conception of the Virtual Math Teams (VMT) Project in 2002, the project has been a major research effort at the Math Forum, a pioneer online resource for math education. Stephen Weimar, the Director of the Math Forum, has contributed generously of his deep understanding of math education and collaboration practices, participating in the weekly project meetings for a decade.

The recent project team includes HCI faculty from the iSchool: Sean Goggins, Michael Khoo, Andrea Forte, and Jennifer Rode. Professional development of mathematics teachers is conducted by Arthur Powell (Urban Education at Rutgers-Newark), Loretta Dicker (Rutgers), Jason Silverman (Director, Graduate Programs in Mathematics Learning and Teaching at Drexel's School of Education), and Annie Fetter (Math Forum). In addition, Dragana Martinovic (Windsor University, Canada) and Diler Öner (Bogazici Universitesi, Turkey) are visiting researchers on the project.

Carolyn Rosé (HCI Institute, Carnegie-Mellon University) and her students have collaborated in experiments with software discourse agents in VMT. Math Forum programmers Baba Weusijana and Jimmy Xiantong Ou developed the VMT software in 2009 and 2010. Since then, Math Forum programmer Anthony Mantoan has been the VMT software developer. Drexel iSchool students contributing to the project include Nora McDonald, Rachel Magee, Christopher Mascaro, and Robert Hedges-Goettl; Alan Black is developing learning analytics and visualization tools.

During the past year, the Project offered a ten-week teacher professional-development course on Collaborative Dynamic Mathematics to 24 math teachers to prepare them to use the VMT software in their schools. Twelve of the teachers then formed small online groups of students, who each engaged in eight hour-long sessions of dynamic mathematics. The teachers and students provided the Project with invaluable experiences, thoughtful reflections and rich data. They confirmed in many ways that the translation of Euclid is promising, inspiring and productive.

The VMT Project has been supported by the following grants from the US National Science Foundation and the Office of Naval Research:

- 2003-2006: "Collaboration Services for the Math Forum Digital Library." DUE 0333493.

- 2003-2009: "Catalyzing & Nurturing Virtual Learning Communities." IERI 0325447.

- 2005-2008: "Engaged Learning in Online Communities." SBE-0518477.

- 2007-2009: "Exploring Adaptive Support for Virtual Math Teams." DRL0723580.

- 2009-2012: "Dynamic Support for Virtual Math Teams." DRL-0835383.

- 2009-2012: "Theories and Models of Group Cognition." ONR CKI.

- 2011-2016: "Computer-Supported Math Discourse Among Teachers and Students." DRL-1118773.

Although the VMT Project has been a collaborative effort, the author is solely responsible for the views expressed in this book.

Gerry Stahl, VMT Project Director and PI
Philadelphia, March 16, 2013

CHAPTER 1

Vision: The Cognitive Potential of Collaborative Dynamic Geometry

Chapter Summary

This opening chapter provides an overview of the book. It suggests that an approach to collaborative dynamic geometry can be designed to transform the teaching of Euclidean geometry from a rigidified procedural approach, based on memorization of authoritative texts, to a human-centered exploration of a foundational source of informatics and rigorous thinking. It introduces a research project to explore the proposed translation of geometry education. This example of the redesign of a subfield of human-centered informatics involves multiple inter-related dimensions, including cognitive history, contemporary philosophy, school mathematics, software technology, collaborative learning, design-based research, CSCL theory, developmental pedagogy, and scaffolded practice.

How should one translate the classic-education approach of Euclid's geometry into the contemporary vernacular of social networking, computer visualization, and discourse-centered pedagogy? The birth of geometry in ancient Greece and its systematization by Euclid played an important role in the development of deductive reasoning and science. As it was translated and refined over the centuries, however, geometry lost some of its cognitive power and its very nature became obscured. Recently, computer-supported versions of dynamic geometry have been developed, which afford visualization, manipulation, exploration, conjectures about constraints, and construction of dependencies. Particularly within a context of computer-supported collaborative learning, a dynamic-geometry environment may be able to facilitate the experience of mathematical insight and understanding that was traditionally the hallmark of geometry.

> How should one translate the classic-education approach of Euclid's geometry into the contemporary vernacular of social networking, computer visualization, and discourse-centered pedagogy?

The Virtual Math Teams (VMT) Project is pursuing a research-based approach that integrates design of technology and pedagogy with research into their effectiveness in actual practice. Focusing on the core elements of collaborative dynamic geometry that are now within reach, it operationalizes social networking as online collaboration, computer visualization as exploration through dynamic dragging and dynamic construction, and pedagogy as discourse about dynamic dependencies.

The effective path for translating Euclidean geometry is not apparent. The original inspiration of the geometric enterprise is lost behind layers of distortion and concealment, and cannot be retrieved in its historical form. The path of reinvention—following a design-based research approach—involves countless cycles of trial and error, with evolution of a new model guided by careful analysis of intermediate effects and bursts of technological invention. Above all, students must be supported in the disruptive learning process that can break them free of the restrictive practices of traditional schooling. They will need a variety of learning resources to aid them in developing new collaboration practices and math practices.

This book presents an argument about computer-supported collaborative learning of mathematics that has grown out of an on-going research agenda. It incorporates a number of specific investigations written during the current research phase and extends them as part of an integrative reflection that became much more than the sum of its individual contributions.

The purpose of this volume is to set out an argument that was too complex to be spelled out persuasively in a conventional conference paper, journal article, or book chapter. The argument builds on historical and philosophical backgrounds as well as empirical evidence and analysis. It requires the reader to be transported along a path of imaginative vision and conceptual discovery, leading to a new perspective on educational research. The turns of this path have only recently emerged from the work reported in this publication.

In particular, the argument for the importance of teaching students to design their own dynamic-geometric constructions translates the focus on dependencies from mathematical theory to classroom practice, and the analysis of interactional resources supports that by providing a conceptual perspective on how to present collaborative dynamic mathematics. Spanning both of these themes, the ontology of creative discovery points the way to transform our thinking into a human-centered informatics.

Much focus and clarity about these themes was achieved in the translation from focused discussions, reports on individual trials, or topical essays into the genre of a more integrative volume.

1.1   TRANSLATION

The term "translate" has multiple meanings. Within geometry, it is a technical term meaning to move an object a certain distance and direction, perhaps indicated by a vector of a given length and orientation (see Figure 1.1). As a form of rigid transformation, the translation of an object should result in an object precisely congruent with the original object—that is retaining the same length and angle measurements.

Figure 1.1: Translating from the era of the clay tablet to the age of the digital tablet.

Within linguistics, translation moves a text from one language into another, presumably without changing the message. As geometry has been transported through the epochs of history, its texts have been translated from language to language. In these translations, the social practice of geometry and the understanding of its texts have, however, changed—with weighty intellectual consequences.

The principles of hermeneutics (Gadamer, 1960/1988)—which study the effects on interpretation of shifting historical horizons and linguistic reformulations—teach us that we cannot hope to remove bias and misunderstanding by returning to some purported original meaning, but must reinterpret within our own situation, taking into account the history of a text's effects. Therefore, we must return to the murky origins of geometry and trace the broad outlines of the subsequent evolving traditions of geometry study. Then we must carefully design a revised approach, based on findings of research specifically targeted to this aim.

The attempt discussed in this book to work out a vision of geometry education that is human centered has been underway for a decade. It follows an iterative, evolving approach of design-based research, which never really reaches an end-point. Along the way, it involves many collaborators, a variety of disciplines and an assortment of concepts. Necessarily interdisciplinary, the project implicates many dimensions, corresponding to various academic fields, addressed in the different chapters of this book. Moving between chapters, the discussion is translated from one conceptualization to another. Table 1.1 may help to keep track of the key terminology used in each chapter. The terms in different rows generally indicate distinctions between levels of analysis.

Following an overview of the argument in Chapter 1, the historical origins of the discipline of geometry—as defined in school mathematics—is reviewed in Chapter 2. Here we see that the discoveries of geometry were conceived as involving objects and truths from a Platonic realm of Ideas, rather than as results of human creative inventiveness. This was further reified into a

Table 1.1: Dimensions of translations from chapter to chapter

	Ch 2 historical era	Ch 3 cognitive level	Ch 4 mode of creation	Ch 5 resource	Ch 6 unit of analysis	Ch 7 activity	Ch 8 meaning	Ch 9 technique	Ch 10 mode of learning	Ch 11 mode of being
	platonic idea	individual cognition	visualize	dynamic dragging	individual	explore	interpretation	inquiry	observation	presence
	learner co-creation	group cognition	represent	dynamic costruction	small group	make sense	intersubjective shared understanding	design	discourse	co-presence
	systematic procedural corpus	social practice	define	dynamic deendencies	community	establish definition	member methods, math practices, resources	proof	knowledge building	math content

systematic corpus of propositions and procedures to be memorized. A review of philosophical reflections on this history in Chapter 3 indicates that, in parallel with this reification, an ideology of individualism held sway, which focused on mental phenomena of individuals to the exclusion of cognitive processes at the group level and of social practices at the community level. Collaborative learning is viewed as an antidote to the traditional fixation on the individual.

The approach of dynamic geometry suggests a focus on dependencies among geometric objects as a key to learning and understanding geometry. This is presented in Chapter 4, where one can see the importance of visualizing geometric configurations, representing relationships among the constituent parts and defining dependencies among objects. Then Chapter 5 describes the dynamic-geometry software in terms of its three primary functions: dynamic dragging, dynamic construction and dynamic dependencies.

In order to support a collaborative-learning approach to the use of dynamic geometry, the GeoGebra (www.geogebra.org) software application was integrated into the Virtual Math Teams (VMT) collaboration environment. As described in Chapter 6, this involved significant technical changes to make GeoGebra multi-user, so teams of online students could work together on the same constructions and discuss what they were doing. Rather than geometry tasks being done by individuals, they could now be accomplished by small groups; the results of the group work could then be shared in a larger classroom and be compared with accepted results in the school-math community. Chapter 7 provides several interaction analyses of such work: Individuals on a team each explore a problem by dragging points; the group makes sense of what is observed; and they are then able to explore dependencies through construction and to relate their group understanding to canonical definitions.

Chapter 8 proposes a theory of how the levels of individual cognition, group cognition, and social practices can be connected by boundary-spanning resources: linguistic expressions, graphical representations, software tools, mathematical objects, etc. The primary resources for dynamic geometry involve the practices of dragging, construction, and determining dependencies. These resources may take the form of social practices that are taught, group practices that emerge during collaboration or individual skills that develop through guidance and collaboration with others. While individuals must interpret for themselves what takes place in the group, the centerpiece of collaborative learning is the creation of intersubjective shared understanding at the small-group level.

Given the math content, collaborative technology and theory of resources, how can effective pedagogy be designed? Chapter 9 reviews the multiple dimensions that have to be kept in mind for supporting teams of students, who must simultaneously deal with learning dynamic geometry, interacting online with peers and using new technologies. This includes supporting student inquiry, the design of geometric figures, and the explanation or the proof of results. Then Chapter 10 presents sample topics to guide virtual math teams in exploring the basics of collaborative dynamic geometry. In the current phase of the VMT Project, this approach is being tried in a number of schools, in collaboration with teachers who received professional development training for this. Analysis of student interactions looks at how groups are observing dynamic figures, engaging in productive mathematical discourse and building geometric knowledge. As Chapter 11 discusses, this is part of the design-based research process in which multiple stakeholders engage in frequent trials to advance technology, theory, pedagogy, analysis, and other aspects of the research. Integration of the manifold aspects is important. The activities designed for students must balance maintaining their individual presence as involved in the mathematics, supporting their co-presence in working collaboratively and relating to valuable content of the field of geometry.

That is the book in a nutshell. The rest of this chapter foreshadows each chapter in somewhat more detail.

1.2   THE CLASSIC POTENTIAL

A small community of geometers in ancient Greece established a set of discourse practices and inscription methods that defined subsequent literate rational thought in the West. Since the golden age of Greece, geometry and rationality have gone through many transformations. To approach the question of what form mathematics education should take in the 21st century, it is helpful to first understand what took place historically to allow geometric reasoning to unfold as an early form of rational thinking.

A cognitive history of this accomplishment is documented in Netz (1999). Latour (2008) reviewed Netz' analysis and suggested some of its significance. According to Netz, the discourse of the early geometers involved innovations in:

1. physical inscription technology;

2. specialized textual forms; and

3. the communication and memory of propositions.

These emerged within the intellectual ferment of ancient Greece, although somewhat at the periphery of that society.

The inscriptions. Using very primitive technology—ephemeral sketches in the sand and more persistent and portable diagrams inscribed on papyrus, wood, wax, or clay tablets—Euclid's predecessors constructed intricate geometric figures using just straightedge and compass. The diagrams (graphical drawings representing the ideal geometric figures) consisted of points, line segments, and arcs or circles. Construction sequences were used to establish dependencies among the components of constructed figures. Importantly, components were labeled with letters. The labels allowed accompanying texts to reference specific components, thus providing a clear visible connection between the elements of the inscription and specific statements in the text.

The texts. The textual discourse of the early geometers consisted of a highly stylized, formulaic language. The language of geometry was derived from everyday written Greek, but required specialized training to be used. The language was geared to stating parts of propositions and proofs, such as the statement of given conditions, or well-known propositions that contributed to the proof, or steps of construction and of proof conclusions. Presentations of geometric propositions consisted primarily of proofs with their accompanying labeled diagrams.

The propositions. In addition to mastering the inscription and discourse practices, a mathematician had to be very familiar with the corpus of established propositions. The knowledge of these propositions was probably passed down through apprenticeship in small, distributed communities of geometers. Only later, Euclid compiled the theorems systematically, providing a persistent and literate basis for this knowledge, which spread around the world for thousands of years. Originally, geometry was a hobby of aristocrats with the time to concentrate on the mastery of a challenging task.

The content of geometry—definitions of basic geometric objects, common notions, logical equivalencies, postulates, and previous propositions—was assumed in the presentation of proofs. Also, implicit in the geometric texts was a practice of rational thought, which made the proof persuasive as necessarily true. That is, for instance, that the truth of a theorem was not dependent upon the particularities of the diagram, construction process, set of referenced theorems, or text of the proof. Rather, the diagram, construction, propositions, and argumentation were merely means for bringing the reader to a transcendent mathematical truth. Geometry invented the sense of "apodictic" or deductive truth: a form of truth that was evidenced by the procedure of the geometric proof.

While we know very little about the people who developed geometry in the 5th and 4th centuries BCE, we can try to imagine the intellectual effort that was required. Geometry was probably practiced by a small number of aristocrats scattered around the Mediterranean. Although individual proofs were circulated with labeled diagrams and proof texts, the comprehension of each new proof required accurate memory of a growing corpus of previous proofs, which the new proof relied upon in various ways. The text of the proofs was in Greek, but in an arcane written version of the everyday spoken language. Proofs could be quite involved and demanding, but the written language made them even harder to parse, as written words were not then separated by spaces. The language of geometry was a spin-off of the early stages of written language using an alphabet. It is striking that the use of the alphabet to label geometric objects was so powerful that mathematicians still use Greek letters in their diagrams.

"At the age of eleven, I began Euclid, with my brother as my tutor. This was one of the great events in my life, as dazzling as first love. I had not imagined that there was anything so delicious in the world." – Bertrand Russell

Geometry represented a towering intellectual accomplishment in the history of human society and has provided a profound inspiration ever since. It defined and epitomized logical argumentation and rational thinking—even providing the template for the earliest philosophic reasoning. Throughout history, mathematicians and philosophers have cited their first experiences with geometry as pivotal for their intellectual careers. The study of geometry long provided a cornerstone of a classic education: a training ground for rigorous thinking. In particular, the experience of the Eureka moment of insight into the key connection in a geometric proof seems to have inspired people for millennia.

1.3   THE FAILED POTENTIAL

Unfortunately, geometry is not so often experienced as an exhilarating activity by most students today. Many people say that they dislike mathematics, they are not good at it and they prefer to avoid the challenges that it presents. They have either not had the experience with geometry that mathematicians praise or they have not valued it in the same way. Of course, the fascination with geometry as an exciting way of thinking has probably never been widespread in the population at any time. However, it seems that the way that it is commonly presented in school misses much of the impetus that was there at the start. Let us see how that could have come about and consider how we might regain the original excitement in a way that is appropriate for our times.

A major watershed in the history of geometry was the organization, systematization, and cataloging of the propositions and their proofs. As long as the core knowledge of the known propositions relied on word-of-mouth apprenticeship and the circulation of occasional documents, access to this knowledge was limited to a small number of people who had the time and passion to devote to this study. Eventually, there were attempts to support the learning of geometry by compiling volumes of proofs and organizing them so that they built on each other sequentially. The most important of these efforts was Euclid's *Elements* (300 BCE/2002). His set of volumes began with a list of important terms and assumptions, making explicit some of the tacit knowledge that had been passed down among the early geometers through personal demonstration.

By reading a sequence of the assembled proofs, one could gain proficiency in the geometric practices. This facilitated the dissemination of geometry. Consequently, the compilation by Euclid was widely circulated through the centuries and translated into various languages. In the process, the presentation was reinterpreted in keeping with the different cultures (e.g., Roman) and languages (e.g., Latin). It became increasingly formalized and procedural.

Reading an edition of Euclid's *Elements* was considered a cornerstone of a classic education until the era of public education. Throughout Western history, more people have read Euclid's book than any other book, except the Bible. Contemporary geometry textbooks for high school can still be seen as variations on Euclid. During the intervening 2,300 years of codification, the practices of geometric discourse, inscription, labeling, construction, and proof have lost much of their cognitive freshness. Not all students of geometry still experience the sense of rational necessity as an exhilarating discovery.

A number of prominent philosophers of the 20th century have identified broad intellectual changes, of which what happened with geometry could be seen as symptomatic. One tendency is for the products of creative human effort to be treated as eternal, unchanging objects that are not connected to human needs and activities. Another is to reduce all cognitive phenomena to mental contents of individuals. Together, these result in an ahistorical and individualistic view of knowledge and learning. It becomes impossible to consider geometry as an historical product of a creative community; instead, this perspective pictures geometry as a set of fixed facts associated with the individual mathematician, Euclid. The implication for learning is that individual students have to accept and be able to give back verbatim the propositional and procedural knowledge of geometry, based on acceptance of traditional authorities (Euclid, teachers, textbooks). Even proof—which was a major development of Greek geometry and which should put the path to determining validity into every student's hands—becomes a non-creative procedure to be followed dogmatically.

1.4   THE VISION OF POTENTIAL

To mathematicians since Euclid, geometry represents the archetype of creative intellectual activity. Its methods set the standard throughout Western civilization for rigorous thought, problem solving, and argumentation. Many educators teach geometry in part to instill in students a sense of deductive reasoning. Yet, too many students—and even some math teachers—end up saying that they "hate math" and that "math is boring" or that they are "not good at math" (Boaler, 2008; Lockhart, 2009). They have somehow missed the intellectual math experience—and this may limit their life-long interest in science, engineering, and technology.

Perhaps it is time to re-invent the practices of geometry in the computer age. This would involve reformulating each of the practices of discourse, inscription, labeling, construction, and proof. This would not be the first time that the presentation of geometry has been reinterpreted, but could be a decisive opportunity for rejuvenating it.

> "*Euclid alone has looked on Beauty bare.*" – Edna St. Vincent Millay

The vision behind attempting this is that geometry can be turned back into a creative enterprise. A number of developments have taken place recently that can contribute to achieving this potential. One is the appearance of dynamic-geometry software. This software lends itself to a constructivist approach, like that of Logo (Papert, 1980) in the recent past. Another is the practice of computer-supported collaborative learning or CSCL (Stahl, Koschmann & Suthers, 2006), using networked digital devices, which are gradually becoming broadly available even in schools.

A look at how Euclid's propositions can be translated into dynamic geometry reveals that geometric findings do not have to be seen as eternal verities from some otherworldly realm. They can be seen as the product of visualizing the problem by exploring it through dragging points of a figure around the screen, representing relationships among objects by construction and designing the proper dependencies into the construction. If such a tool is put into the hands of groups of students working together, perhaps what took place on the shores of the Mediterranean 2,500 years ago can be duplicated around the networked globe now.

With the development of dynamic-geometry and dynamic-mathematics software environments like Geometer's Sketchpad, Cabri, Cinderella and GeoGebra, there has been a resurgence of interest in basic geometry around the world. The free availability of open-source GeoGebra has resulted in a burgeoning user community, primarily of math teachers. Although dynamic mathematics encourages active learning and student construction of meaning, these technologies have not been designed to support collaboration.

While the importance of collaborative learning for online education may be obvious to CSCL researchers and its possible advantages have been well documented in cooperative-learning (Johnson & Johnson, 1989; Slavin, 1980) and CSCL research for decades (Sawyer, 2006), support for collaboration is still not always designed into new educational platforms. For instance, the latest hot approach to university instruction—massive open online courses or MOOCs—are generally based on the lecture paradigm, where students passively watch talking-head videos of famous professors and are not given any sanctioned opportunities for interaction with peers. Similarly, the acclaimed Khan Academy offers thousands of YouTube videos explaining detailed topics in school mathematics, but students have no support for interactively exploring the topics themselves or discussing them with other students. These technological opportunities are generally not designed to incorporate constructivist learning principles (Bransford, Brown & Cocking, 1999).

As noted above, the primordial math experience around Greece in 5th and 4th century BCE was based on the confluence of labeled geometric diagrams (*shared visualizations*) and a language of written mathematics (*asynchronous collaborative discourse*), which supported the rapid evolution of math cognition in a small community of math discourse, profoundly extending mathematics and Western thinking. Can this Greek model of asynchronous collaborative communities be translated into a vision of computer-supported collaborative learning?

What if one could today foster stimulating *communities of math discourse* in networks of math teachers, in classrooms of K-12 math students and in online communities? Is it possible to leverage the potential of networked computers and dynamic math applications to catalyze groups of people exploring math and experiencing the intellectual excitement that Euclid's colleagues felt—refining and testing emerging 21st century media of *collaborative math discourse* and *shared math visualization* to support math discourse in both formal and informal settings and groupings.

Educators who teach math teachers—and others—have found that many people teaching K-12 math have had little experience themselves participating in processes of mathematical exploration and discovery (Krause, 1986; Livingston, 1999; Silverman & Thompson, 2008). It is necessary to provide teachers with first-hand experiences and to mentor them in guiding their students to engage in rich math discourses that go beyond generating numeric answers to supply math reasoning and to draw conceptual connections.

The learning sciences have transformed our vision of education for the future (Sawyer, 2006). New theories of mathematical cognition (Bransford, Brown & Cocking, 1999; Brown & Campione, 1994; Greeno & Goldman, 1998; Hall & Stevens, 1995; Lakatos, 1976; Lemke, 1993; Livingston, 1999) and math education (Boaler, 2008; Cobb, Yackel & McClain, 2000; Lockhart, 2009; Moss & Beatty, 2006), in particular, stress collaborative knowledge building (Bereiter, 2002; Scardamalia & Bereiter, 1996; Schwarz, 1997), problem-based learning (Barrows, 1994; Koschmann, Glenn & Conlee, 1997), dialogicality (Wegerif, 2007), argumentation (Andriessen, Baker & Suthers, 2003), accountable talk (Michaels, O'Connor & Resnick, 2008), group cognition (Stahl, 2006), and engagement in math discourse (Sfard, 2008; Stahl, 2008). These approaches place the focus on problem solving, problem posing, exploration of alternative strategies, inter-animation of perspectives, verbal articulation, argumentation, deductive reasoning, and heuristics as features of significant math discourse (Maher, Powell & Uptegrove, 2010; Powell, Francisco & Maher, 2003; Powell & López, 1989).

To learn math is to participate in a mathematical discourse community (Lave & Wenger, 1991; Sfard, 2008; Vygotsky, 1930/1978) that includes people literate in and conversant with topics in mathematics beyond basic arithmetic. Learning to "speak math" is best done by sharing and discussing rich math experiences within a supportive math discourse community (Papert, 1980; van Aalst, 2009). By articulating thinking and learning in text, students make their cognition public and visible. This calls for a reorientation of the teaching profession to facilitate dialogical student practices. It also requires the development of content and resources to guide and support the student discourses. Teachers and students must learn to adopt, appreciate and take advantage of the visible nature of collaborative learning. The emphasis on text-based collaborative learning can be well supported by computers with appropriate computer-supported collaborative-learning software.

1.5   THE KEY DEPENDENCY

The key to understanding dynamic geometry is not the memorization of terminology, procedures, propositions or proofs. It is *dependencies*. This is not a well-recognized fact. Dependency is built into dynamic-geometry software at its most fundamental technical and conceptual levels. However, research on the use of this software barely mentions it and rarely discusses its key role. Both the research literature and the practitioner research stress the ability to move—or "drag"—points and other objects around the screen to observe variations in geometric figures. For instance, Scher (2002), Healy et al.

> The key to understanding dynamic geometry is not the memorization of terminology, procedures, propositions, or proofs. It is dependencies.

(1994), and Hölzl (1996) focus on dragging, as do most articles on dynamic geometry written for teachers. There are exceptions, such as Noss et al. (1994) and Jones (1997), which are concerned with construction, while Jones (1996) and Hölzl et al. (1994) are among the very few who discuss dependencies. There are also reflections on how dynamic geometry can support thinking about proofs (deVilliers, 2003; deVilliers, 2004; Hoyles & Jones, 1998; Laborde, 2000). For a broader review of the literature, including trade-offs on the different approaches, see Powell and Dicker (2012) and Sinclair (2008).

Dynamic geometry can be understood in terms of three important activities that it supports:

1. dynamic dragging;

2. dynamic construction; and

3. dynamic dependencies.

Problem solving in this medium generally involves an integration of these activities. One should explore a problem through dragging to observe dynamic behavior as objects are varied. Then one should investigate new arrangements through construction of new geometric figures. The construction should be guided by the attempt to build in certain dependencies among the objects, such as that the second and third leg of an equilateral triangle should be constructed in a way that their lengths are dependent upon the length of the base side—even when the length of the base changes through dragging.

Experience dynamic geometry

To understand this book, it is necessary to have personal experience with dynamic geometry. Take a few minutes now at a computer to try GeoGebra. If you can do this collaboratively, discussing each step with a friend, that would be ideal.

1. First, watch a two-minute video on constructing an equilateral triangle in GeoGebra, such as the one at **www.youtube.com/watch?v=ORIaWNQSM_E**.

2. Then download GeoGebra from **www.GeoGebra.org** and open it up.

3. Try the basic geometry tools. Construct a point with the point tool. Use the move tool to drag it around. Construct a line segment with the segment tool and drag it. Construct a circle with the circle tool. Construct a new point on your line segment and one on your circle; drag these points. What happens? Move your line to cross your circle and construct a new point where they intersect (see point H in **Figure 1.2**). Can you move your new point directly or indirectly?

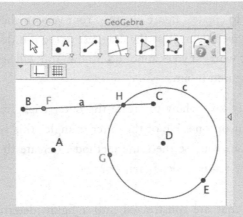

Figure 1.2: Free, constrained, and dependent points.

4. Try to construct an equilateral triangle yourself. Use the "File" | "New" menu item to clear the work area. Start with a base side AB. Then draw circles of radius AB centered on endpoints A and B, respectively. Construct point C at an intersection of these circles. Use the polygon tool to construct triangle ABC. Drag the vertices—this is the "drag test." Do you see why the triangle remains equilateral dynamically? The position of point C is dependent upon the circles, which are dependent upon the segment AB.

5. Now download the file inscribe.ggb from **www.GerryStahl.net/vmt/inscribe.ggb** or from **www.geogebratube.org/material/show/id/43056**. Follow the directions (as in **Figure 1.3**.) Drag points A and D to explore the figure and discover its built-in dependencies. How would you describe the geometry of this figure?

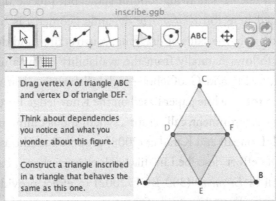

Figure 1.3: The inscribe challenge problem.

6. The challenge is to create a figure like this. Your version should behave dynamically the same as the given figure. Use the drag test to see if it does. This is a challenging problem. Do not worry if you cannot do it now. You will see later in the book how various groups figured it out.

7. Hint: You already know how to create the outer triangle, ABC. Start with that. Construct a point on one side of the outer triangle. This will be one vertex of the inner triangle. Can you use the same method to create the inner triangle? Try it. Does it satisfy the required dependencies?

The dependencies that are constructed into a figure determine its characteristics. These characteristics hold even under dragging. Sometimes a figure might look like it has certain characteristics: a triangle may look equilateral. However, when a vertex is dragged, it will not remain equilateral-looking unless the proper dependency was constructed in it. That is why students are taught to use the "drag test" to make sure that an apparent characteristic is dynamically valid.

Dragging is easy and fun for students. By comparison, proper construction can be tricky and frustrating. Designing a figure to have the right dependencies can be particularly straining. Learning to do dynamic geometry requires time, concentration and guidance. Many teachers decide that they do not have the time in their classroom to help students develop the skills in construction and dependencies. In fact, often the teachers may not have the time to develop such skills themselves. Therefore, it is common practice to provide students (and teachers) with ready-made constructions. Then the students can just drag points and observe the behaviors. Taking it a step further, teachers might do the dragging themselves and project it for the students to watch passively. In such cases, dynamic geometry is largely reduced to illustrating facts from Euclidean geometry. It may even be restricted to serving as a teacher's drawing tool for static, but precise figures.

The vision pursued here for *collaborative* dynamic geometry is one in which students work together to develop and apply the skills of dragging, constructing, and designing dependencies. This is not a new vision. It follows naturally from the availability of dynamic-geometry software—like Geometer's Sketchpad, Cabri and GeoGebra—and collaborative-learning software. For instance, Gadanidis et al. (2002) wrote a white paper based on the Knowledge Forum asynchronous collaborative knowledge-building environment, calling for a synchronous online math environment. Reis and Karadag (2008) and McDougall and Karadag (2008) proposed methods for tracking student learning in such a system. The effort described in this book pursues those goals in a comprehensive way.

Read today, Euclid's *Elements* (300 BCE/2002) in effect provides instructions for dynamic-geometry constructions. The "elements" of geometry are not so much the points, lines, circles, triangles and quadrilaterals, but the basic operations of constructing figures with important relationships, such as congruence or symmetry. Just as Euclidean geometry contributed significantly to the development of logical, deductive, apodictic cognition in Western thought and in the formative minds of many prospective mathematicians, so collaborative experiences with dynamic geometry may foster in students ways of thinking about dependencies in the world.

1.6   VIRTUAL MATH TEAMS

The Virtual Math Teams (VMT) Project was conceived in 2002 as a way of providing through the Math Forum an online environment for the collaborative learning of mathematics. It started out simply using a commercial text-chat (AOL chat) system and asking small groups of students to work on the Math Forum's Problem of the Week together. It has been growing from that ever since. By 2009, the VMT environment was quite complex, with Java chat rooms including shared whiteboards, web browsers, a wiki and social-networking functions. It could thereby support work by individuals, small groups and whole classes. Information could be moved back and forth between these levels. The approach to VMT grew out of research reported in (Stahl, 2006). A collection of research reports on the project by team members and international collaborators was then published in (Stahl, 2009).

The VMT Project is motivated by a belief in the power of collaborative learning. This belief is founded on a variety of theoretical and empirical findings:

- Collaborative learning is a foundational mode of learning generally. Toddlers learn from interacting with members of their immediate family and with peers—imitating and starting to communicate with others. Vygotsky (1930/1978) documented how the acquisition of most human cognitive skills typically takes place first through collaboration, and only later they become individual mental faculties.

- When one carefully investigates knowledge building, it often takes place in small-group interactions in which participants build on each other's contributions in ways that the resultant knowledge cannot be attributed to any individual, but only to the group.

- Collaborative interactions often serve to train the perceptions of individuals to see something as others see it, that is, in new ways. This is related to the larger point that collaboration brings together different perspectives on a topic. The confrontation of different perspectives may cause productive "cognitive conflict" or otherwise stimulate innovative resolutions or syntheses.

- Community practices are disseminated and revised as they are taken up in the concrete collaborative interactions of small groups within the community.

- In general, collaborative interactions frequently confront problems and respond to questions, negotiating differences and producing resolutions.

- In these ways and others, interactions at the small-group level contribute to making the problem-solving power of a small group more than the sum of its parts.

After the first trials of the VMT Project with the simple chat tool, it was apparent that collaborative mathematics required a shared graphical space that participants could point to. While a generic whiteboard with simple drawing tools facilitated some impressive collaboration among students, the drawings were quite primitive. It took too long to make some of the drawings and it was sometimes hard for the other students to interpret them.

Meanwhile, mathematics software was being widely used in schools. In particular, many teachers were starting to use Geometer's Sketchpad or GeoGebra in geometry classes. Thus, the idea arose to integrate dynamic-geometry software into VMT in order to provide increased mathematical functionality.

The integration of two rather complex pieces of software—VMT and GeoGebra—turned out to be possible, but challenging. GeoGebra had originally been designed from the ground up for single-users. Creating a multi-user system involved not only re-thinking the software architecture, but also re-designing how dynamic geometry should work for groups.

1.7   GROUP COGNITION

The VMT Project was closely associated with the theory of group cognition. That is an approach to the study of collaborative learning and knowledge building that focuses methodologically on the small-group unit of analysis. It uses techniques of interaction analysis to follow group processes of problem solving and joint meaning making. It takes analytic tools of video analysis and Conversation Analysis from face-to-face informal conversation among dyads and adapts them to online, computer-mediated communication about mathematics in small groups.

Because the VMT Project proceeds by means of constant iterations of trial and analysis, it was necessary to carry out relatively quick case studies. The purpose of the case studies was to see what took place in the chat rooms, how successful interactions were carried out and what problems arose. In order to design effective software for supporting the kind of interactions that were desirable in the project, it was important to understand the nature of such interactions and the variety of problems that could get in the way. Reliance on established theories from psychology and education was unreliable, since they were generally based on face-to-face interaction or on models of individual learning. The design-based research approach of the VMT Project—which never reaches a final end-state—is driven by on-going formative assessments, rather than being confirmed by a summative assessment. The focus is on understanding how the group interactions and knowledge building are mediated by the latest version of technology and pedagogy, rather than on comparing individual learning outcomes before and after interventions.

1.8   RESOURCES THEORY

Taken within the context of other theories popular in CSCL, the theory of group cognition implied a view of learning, problem solving, and knowledge building as taking place on three primary units of analysis: individual, small-group and community. It appeared that some phenomena of importance to CSCL took place on one of these levels and some on the others. Different methods of analysis were applied at the different levels. However, it was also clear that these three levels were intimately intertwined and influenced each other in essential ways. For instance, concepts from the highest socio-cultural-historical levels of mathematical knowledge could be introduced into group discussions, play a creative role in the meaning making there, and eventually be internalized into individual skills.

A problem for the project was, on the one hand, to introduce content from the community level into group-collaborative activity and, on the other hand, to see that shared intersubjective understanding developed at the group level resulted in learning at the individual level. One way to think about this was in terms of resources (or artifacts or practices), which could traverse the different levels and thereby provide connections between them.

For teaching dynamic geometry, among the most important resources are the practices of dragging objects, constructing figures and building dependencies. These practices are acquired at the group unit through guided collaboration. Community-level math content, the culture of doing mathematics and the effective practices of mathematics are introduced into group activities, for instance in the form of scaffolded resources defining topics of discussion and exploration. Through participation in group practices, individuals can then develop the corresponding personal skills.

1.9   DESIGN OF RESOURCES

A set of principles for the design of dynamic-geometry resources was compiled based on experience through many iterations of trials in the VMT Project, a long history of resource development for math teachers and math students at the Math Forum, training materials for different dynamic-geometry systems, textbooks, governmental learning standards and Euclid's *Elements*. These principles enunciated several dimensions that had to be considered and balanced.

The goal was to design resources to improve the following skills in math teachers and students.

- Collaboration: To work effectively together to explore dynamic geometry.

- Dragging: To explore mathematical phenomena by varying visual representations.

- Construction: To construct mathematical figures embodying relationships.

- Dependencies: To notice, wonder about, and form conjectures about mathematical dependencies, using them to justify, explain, and prove mathematical findings.

- Math content: To understand core concepts, relationships, theorems, and constructions of basic high-school geometry.

- Discourse: To engage in significant mathematical discourse.

1.10   INTRODUCTORY RESOURCES

The principles of resource design evolved through formulating topics for group work, creating activities and instructions around the topics. As new resources were developed, they were tried out: first by the developers, then by groups of research-team members, then by volunteers and teachers, and finally by groups of students. Every year, sets of resources would be designed and would evolve through many versions.

The current set of resources for dynamic geometry gradually introduces students to the elementary objects of the field: points, lines, circles, triangles, and polygons. It guides them in how to effectively drag objects, construct figures and build dependencies in collaborative GeoGebra. There are topics devoted to standard content in high-school geometry, like congruent triangles, but also open-ended mini-worlds and challenge problems to encourage creativity.

1.11   DESIGN-BASED RESEARCH

Human-centered informatics is about treating the sources of information, software, logic, and mathematics as products of human creative discovery. Collaborative dynamic geometry can provide a model for this, just as geometry provided a model for compelling argumentation during the birth of Western civilization. However, to do so, students must begin to see the objects, constructions, and dependencies of dynamic geometry as creations of their own collaborative efforts and discoveries of their joint explorations.

> Students must begin to see the objects, constructions, and dependencies of dynamic geometry as creations of their own collaborative efforts and discoveries of their joint explorations.

Equilateral triangles, constructions of parallel lines and dependencies among centers of triangles are not otherworldly mysteries that must be accepted on authority, but products of people working, inquiring, and talking together—products of their joint creativity, design and investigation. The basic modes of dynamic-geometry activity—dragging, constructing and dependencies—can together form a model of *creative discovery*, illustrating the general interplay between human agency and reality's resistance. The discovery of geometric propositions through the creation of geometric dependencies can stand as a metaphor for the interplay of people and data in human-centered informatics.

To effectively convey this experience to students involves a combination of theory (about collaborative learning, dynamic geometry, resources), design (of pedagogy and geometry activities), technology (to support collaborative dynamic geometry), research (into how students enact resources), and practice (to see what works and what does not over time and in various contexts). Balancing these multiple dimensions requires an interdisciplinary team engaged in design-based research. This book reports understandings gained from the design-based research of the VMT Project during the period 2010–2012.

CHAPTER 2

History: The Origin of Geometry

Chapter Summary

Geometry started out as an evolving creation of a creative intellectual community. However, over time, the objects and practices of geometry have come to be understood as otherworldly ideals to be accepted on authority, rather than as elements of human imagination and exploration. The history of geometry from the early Greeks, to Euclid's systematization, to modern axiomatic systems, and to contemporary schooling can be seen as a process of the successive obscuring of the origin of geometry in human activity.

To understand the plight of geometry education today, it is informative to go back to its origins in ancient Greece. Geometry is solidly rooted in the history of Western civilization. It developed at the same time as some of the most important cultural developments: the beginnings or high points of written history, philosophy, drama, logic, and sculpture.

2.1 FOLK GEOMETRY

Ever since people stopped wandering and settled down on patches of land, they have probably had ways to measure out the land ("geo-metric"), build structures in various shapes, and conceive of various visual forms. Look at the intricate patterns woven into fabrics or carved into rocks, pottery, and jewelry in pre-literate cultures. Here, the designed objects carried aesthetic and social values. They had not yet been quantified and made comparable based on a universal system of equivalences—see the literature of ethno-mathematics and Alexander (1964).

Throughout history, there have always been developments in practical mathematics, which interact with the pure or academic mathematics of professional mathematicians. The practical approach to geometry as techniques for dividing plots of land or calculating distances goes back at least to Egypt. It dominated textbooks in the Middle Ages, following the lead of Fibonacci's *Practica Geometriae* published in 1220. For instance, the practical navigational needs of ship captains in the era of global exploration, colonization and world trade drove the invention of complex algorithms, detailed numeric tables, and computational instrumentation (Hutchins, 1996). As an example, a 15th century Venetian method for correcting a ship's bearings after being blown off course by the wind provided tables based on a drawing (see Figure 2.1) and trigonometric computations (Long, McGee, & Stahl, 2009). This, in turn, pushed the development of logarithms in mathematics and even the design of early computers (Gleick, 2011).

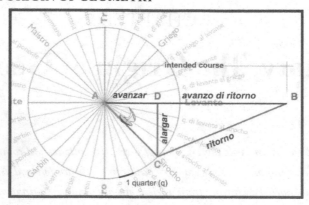

Figure 2.1: Course correction via the *marteloio* method. Reproduced from http://brunelleschi.imss.fi.it/michaelofrhodes/navigate_toolkit_basics.html.

Formal, systematic geometry first emerged from common practice in the pre-Socratic days of Greece, from which few artifacts survive to tell the story. It developed the method of deductive reasoning and helped to transform the nature of literacy, science, and human cognition (Husserl, 1936/1989; Netz, 1999).

2.2 THE FIRST GEOMETERS

In the 5th and 4th centuries BCE, a small, distributed network of members of the Greek upper class developed a highly formalized version of geometry. Theirs was one of the first specialized applications of writing using an alphabet. They combined a formalized subset of written Greek with related line drawings. Significantly, the endpoints and intersections of the lines and arcs of the drawings were labeled with letters, which were used to reference them in the text. They created a genre combining text and diagram that spanned oral and literate worlds—incorporating the urge to persuade using words while pointing to objects—with the tools of the literate minority.

We barely know a few names of these early geometers; surviving copies of their work are reproductions, translations, or interpretations from hundreds of years later. Although their work was not particularly highly valued in the mainstream Greek culture, the "hobby" of doing geometry employed impressive intellectual skill. The tightly argued texts—circulated around the Mediterranean on parchment scrolls and clay tablets—were written in a minimalist style that was hard to follow. The newly invented discourse of proofs relied on an abstraction of geometric configurations to formal abstractions, such as that "a line is breadthless length"—i.e., a line has no thickness or any other characteristics other than its measurable length. To follow the argument of a proof—let alone to formulate a new proof—one had to be able to recall and understand an extensive corpus of previous definitions, postulates, and propositions.

In order to structure their proofs effectively as self-contained and incontestable arguments, geometers had to reduce their subject matter to purely formal aspects, such as the length of lines. In addition, they laid out the proofs themselves in a clearly structured order, which made explicit the goal of the argument and the fact that the goal was achieved in the end. Each proof consisted of several discrete steps—sometimes as many as 40. The steps of a proof were restricted to formal relationships, such as that one line or angle was equal in measure to another.

The argument uniting the steps to arrive at the stated goal unfolded through reliance upon a small set of transitive connections, such as that if A=B and C=B then A=C and A, B, and C are all equal. These connections were accepted from the start as part of the geometry enterprise. The standardization of the minimal language of geometry made it clear that only these established connections were being used to make the deduction. Their transitive nature ensured that a proof that followed the conventionalized rules would be a valid, convincing deduction.

The frequent reliance on the transitive property of equality in Euclid's presentation is striking. The first item in his list of "common notions" is, "Things which are equal to the same thing are also equal to one another" (Euclid, 300 BCE/2002, p. 2). The strategy which frequently occurs in his proofs is to show that two magnitudes such as the lengths of two line segments are both equal to the same thing like the length of a third line segment. For instance, in his very first proposition, on the construction of an equilateral triangle, Euclid argues that since the lengths of each of the legs of the triangle are equal to the length of the base (because the respective leg and the base are radii of the same circle by construction and all radii of a circle are equal by definition of a circle), all the sides are equal to each other (p. 3).

The transitive property of equality is valid in mathematics. Its use provides much of the glue that allows Euclid to build up complex proofs. As long as each element of the proof (i.e., that A=B and that C=B) is valid then the conclusion of the large proof (that A=C or that A, B and C are all equal) will also be "apodictically" valid as long as the argument is connected by logical principles like the transitivity of equality.

Geometry is confined to a system of objects and procedures for which such validity is maintained. Of course, in the broader social life, one cannot count on this kind of validity. For instance, in interpersonal relationships like a romantic triangle, if person A loves person B and C also loves B, it is not often true that A loves C. Love is not transitive; it is more complicated.

The history of mathematics can be viewed as an on-going process of defining math objects and rules in ways that produce elegant, consistent, rigorous proofs (Lakatos, 1976); Greek geometry is a prime example of this. The definitions of abstract points, lines and circles allowed one point to stand for any point and one line to be equivalent to any other, except for length and the points that it passed through. Furthermore, the rules of deduction were simple and easily combined to build up deductions that are more complicated without introducing problems. As long as one restricted one's discourse to this small, carefully crafted, well-defined and orderly domain of geometric objects, a controlled vocabulary and transitive rules, one's proofs could be unassailable and universally persuasive.

The early Greek geometers proved propositions about geometric objects that go far beyond today's high-school geometry in insight and complexity. This would surely have been impossible without the use of diagrams. Even the simplest geometric arguments are difficult to follow without studying diagrams. The human mind is severely limited in its ability to handle long sequences of utterances and to keep track of many inter-related objects within short-term memory. The diagrams allow people to take advantage of their powerful visual analytic skills. The lettered labels on the objects in the diagram provide deictic references to the objects intended by specific written phrases, effectively integrating the visual situation and the linguistic deduction. Through the coordination of formal proof discourse with labeled diagrams, the Greeks could prove and communicate rather involved propositions.

2.3   PLATO'S ACADEMY

The cognitive importance of geometry was well recognized from the beginning. Plato (428 to 348 BCE) certainly felt that the study of mathematics was good training for philosophy. Above the entrance to Plato's Academy was inscribed the phrase "Let none but geometers enter here." Plato's mentor, Socrates, is shown in one of Plato's early dialogs demonstrating a geometric proof to a servant named Meno (Plato, 350 BCE/1961). Plato's successor, Aristotle, made original contributions to geometry, as well as conceptualizing deductive logic.

> Above the entrance to Plato's Academy was inscribed the phrase *"Let none but geometers enter here."*

The Socratic dialog with Meno is instructive about Plato's epistemology. In the dialog, Socrates walks an unschooled servant boy through the steps of a geometric proof, eliciting the boy's assent at each logical move. Socrates' conclusion is that since the boy never saw the proof before in his life and was never taught about it yet understood and agreed with it in detail, he must have remembered this knowledge from before he was born. While Plato developed a sophisticated theory of knowledge in his later dialogs, this principle remained. There was no source of new knowledge in the world (like experience or creativity). All people are born with complete knowledge. However, they do not remember almost any of it. All learning is a process of remembering. Education is a matter of reminding; the word 'education' is derived from "leading forth," e.g., from memory. Therefore, the source of knowledge is neither discovery in the world or creation through human activity and interaction, but in some otherworldly source that is dimly recalled. It is like people living in a cave amongst shadow memories of a forgotten world that exists outside in the sunshine (Plato, 340 BCE/1941). Human knowledge consists of faulty memories of Ideas, which exist outside our world in an eternal, ideal form. The prototypes of such Ideas are the concepts of mathematics, like numbers, points, π.

While Plato did not engage directly in the practice of geometry in his surviving writings, there seems to be a complex interaction between his philosophy and the nature of Greek geometry. Latour (2008) argues that Plato wanted to use the deductive power of geometry to support his philosophic claims. Plato was in intellectual competition with the Sophists, who used rhetoric to convince their audience, and with the political leadership, who called upon established authority and the gods. Plato questioned authority, brought his audience to a sense of *aporia* (awe, based on puzzlement in the face of an impasse in the usual approach to a topic), and then tried to convince through logical argument, modeled to some extent on the new deductive style of the geometers.

However, Latour claims that Plato could not succeed at adopting the geometry model because the success of geometry's deductive power flows from its formalism, its rejection of all content, whereas Plato needed to retain the content because he was interested in content-full topics like the Good, the True and the Beautiful. These topics are based on the richness of everyday language and cannot be reduced to well-defined meanings, relations of equivalence, and limited language.

Perhaps Plato was pushed in the direction of his doctrine of Forms or Ideas by the model of geometry. If he could say—as he certainly did in his early dialogs—that he was not talking about a specific just act, but about the concept of justice itself, which applies to all just acts without having any of the specifics of any one such act, then perhaps he could formalize his concepts so that his arguments about them would have the deductive power of geometry: the characteristic that they cannot be doubted and are self-evidently true. Unfortunately for Plato, he was determined to discuss broad, complex topics based on vague terms of everyday language, whereas the success of geometry relied upon radically restricting its discourse. Plato wanted his deductions to apply to life, not to be confined to abstract objects like ideal points.

As Heidegger puts it, the philosophic experience that follows awe is intended to change one's view. Philosophy has aims and methods that differ essentially from those of mathematics:

> In philosophy, propositions never get firmed up into a proof. This is the case, not only because there are no top propositions from which others could be deduced, but because here what is "true" is not a "proposition" at all and also not simply that about which a proposition makes a statement. All "proof" presupposes that one who understands—as he comes, via representations, before the content of a proposition—remains unchanged as he enacts the interconnection of representations for the sake of proof. And only the "result" of the deduced proof can demand a changed way of representing, or rather a representing of what was unnoticed up until now. (Heidegger, 1938/1999, p.10)

Following a proof step-by-step involves the manipulations of formal components, re-presenting things in terms of abstract symbols, illustrative diagram elements, standardized terminology, and transitive comparisons. However, a philosophic argument cannot reduce its topic to a representation of the topic, like a geometer can reduce a line to a labeled diagram of a line. Even the idea, form, or concept of justice is not a representation of justice, but a rich understanding of what all just acts are about. Further, the point of a philosophic argument is not simply to deduce a truth, but to persuade the audience about how they should live a good, just and beautiful life by gradually transforming their thinking and actions.

2.4   EUCLID'S ELEMENTS

It is assumed that Euclid lived shortly after Plato, c. 323 to 283 BCE. It is possible that Euclid studied in Plato's Academy in Athens and it is likely that mathematics was studied in the Academy. In one of the few surviving references to Euclid, it is noted that Apollonius (developer of the theory of conics and irrational numbers) "spent a very long time with the pupils of Euclid at Alexandria, and it was thus that he acquired such a scientific habit of thought." By "scientific," we can assume Apollonius primarily meant systematic. Not much else is known of Euclid as a person, other than this indirect reference.

It is not known if Euclid actually proved any new propositions or if he just compiled well-known proofs, working in the great library of Alexandria, an early gathering place of the world's knowledge. There had been some previous attempts to compile the propositions of geometry, but none were considered of comparable power to Euclid's. Euclid published 13 volumes of geometry, in which the propositions were not only organized based on their subject matter, but built on each other systematically.

Euclid's presentations of the propositions all followed a similar template from statement of goal to declaration of conclusion, and they were apparently all accompanied by clear, labeled diagrams corresponding to the steps of the proof. Although the inter-relationships among the propositions were implicit in their individual original proofs, it must have taken a deep understanding and overview to put together all the propositions so systematically and to preface them with a clear statement of the assumed definitions, postulates and common notions. Euclid's presentation of geometry has since then stood up to scrutiny for 23 centuries and has inspired and influenced scientific and mathematical thought in the Western world more than any other text.

2.5   ROMAN AND ENGLISH TRANSLATIONS

Unfortunately, we have no extant copies of the *Elements* as written by Euclid. We must rely on translations of translations and copies of copies of those. Each translation is necessarily an interpretation, and many copyists tried to "improve" the presentation. The standard English version now is a recent republication (Euclid, 300 BCE/2002) of Heath's 1908 translation of Heiberg's 1883 scholarly Greek version. The earliest printed Greek version is from 1533, predated by a printed Latin version from 1482.

Each edition made different changes: eliminating whole sections from each proof to avoid redundancies, adding clarifying phrases, etc. For instance, the introductory list of definitions, postulates, and common notions was not originally broken down into numbered lists (as it is now), or even into separate sentences. It provided a general introduction to the terminology, rather than a set of axioms that could be referenced in the proof (as they are now). In addition, translations—most significantly from the original Greek to the Roman way of thinking, which strongly influenced Western scientific thinking when Latin was the lingua franca—transformed syntax and changed tenses and ways of referencing. It is particularly unfortunate that we have no exemplars of ancient diagrams, only medieval and modern versions.

Organization and systematization seem to be inherent in the practice of geometry. The notion of rigor in proof entails meticulous step-by-step procedures, precisely formulated and carefully built upon one another. In classical education, training in geometry was considered a means of disciplining unruly minds. Moreover, the birth of geometry may have contributed significantly to the rationalization of the Western mentality.

The historical development of geometry following its birth further refined its systematic nature. Where Socrates was a free spirit intellectually and Plato sought after the essences, their follower, Aristotle was more of a systematizer, initiating a tendency that led to the great system builders in philosophy and the hierarchical thinking of the Neo-Platonist church, which dominated the medieval mentality. The library of Alexandria, where Euclid presumably assembled the *Elements* of geometry, was an historic effort to compile and categorize written knowledge. Such efforts were part of the strivings of secular and religious state leadership (like Alexander the Great) to establish, manage, and control increasingly large and complex civilizations. This was an early effort at informatics and the management of "big data." The formalization, systematization and bureaucratization of knowledge paralleled that of the military, politics, faith and the economy. Geometry provided a model for the other fields, and it was itself, in turn, transformed further in that direction by the general tendency in society, which it fostered.

Pappus of Alexandria (340, Book VII) was an organizer of mathematical knowledge—like Euclid, but 600 years later. Perhaps the last major classical Greek mathematician, Pappus drew the important distinction between analysis and synthesis. Analysis is Euclid's method. It starts from "what is sought as if it were existent and true" and works back to the given conditions and previous propositions. It then reverses the sequence to present a deductive proof derivation. Synthesis is a form of exploration that begins from the given conditions and previous propositions and investigates their implications. As Livingston (1999) argues, the process of proving is a winding synthetic discovery process, later disguised in a linear analytic presentation. The nature of work in dynamic geometry—which we will characterize below as a creative-discovery process—is more naturally a synthetic approach as contrasted with a classical Euclidean paradigm of analytic proof.

2.6   AXIOMATIC GEOMETRY

People—including many mathematicians—tend to think of mathematical objects as some kind of "otherworldly" abstractions, as mental constructs that have no physical characteristics but obey logical rules (axioms and their corollaries). This view may be indirectly derived from Plato's doctrine of Ideas as a realm of essences divorced from the physical world—a view furthered in philosophy by Descartes (with his strict separation of mind and body, the mental and the physical), and perhaps motivating the formal axiomatization of mathematics. As mentioned previously, Plato may have been influenced by early geometry; now the influence is fed back from his philosophy to mathematics. One consequence is that the geometric diagram is now viewed as a rather arbitrary and secondary illustration

> The geometric diagram is now viewed as a rather arbitrary and secondary illustration of the abstract ideas discussed in a proof.

of the abstract ideas discussed in a proof. This may be an unfortunate distortion of the central role of the figure in the work of the first geometers. It may also obscure the important role of diagrams in the learning, exploration, and understanding of geometry in schools today (Livingston, 1999).

By the 20th century, mathematics was viewed as an axiomatic system. This began in a vision of systematic logic by Leibniz and was worked out by Frege and other logicians, culminating in Russell and Whitehead's detailed system. Although Gödel's and Turing's work established surprising limits to this vision, the influence on geometry was significant. Euclid's proofs are now read as axiomatic procedures. Over the centuries, the prevailing paradigms of hierarchy, logic and axiomatization have ineluctably continued the interpretive transformations of Euclid's texts.

The historical development of reason, in which geometry has played a key role, can be considered from many perspectives. In terms of individual personal development, Piaget (1990) identified the child's transition from concrete to abstract stages of thinking as pivotal. The educational role of geometry (and algebra) has always been seen as an important means for the training of abstract thinking. On a societal level, the movement from orality to literacy (Ong, 1998) can be seen as a primary watershed in human cognition. As discussed, the origin of geometry was an integral part of the emergence of literacy, including practices in visual representation, mathematics, and deduction.

The rise of rationality has brought problems as well as progress (see Chapter 3). Philosophic analyses as different as those of Heidegger (1979) and Adorno and Horkheimer (1945) trace the origin of totalitarian fascism in the Second World War all the way back to the early Greeks. The tendency to reduce the richness of nature and interpersonal living to quantifiable representations is not only empowering, but also distorting of healthy human relationships. This historic tendency includes the emphasis on quantification and calculation in the rise of capitalism and bourgeois organizational management, rational planning, and the exploitation of nature or human labor as disposable resources (Swetz, 1987). The emergence and development of geometry has been an integral element of the historical development of rational reason—although it has not often been analyzed in this context. The view dominating contemporary thought—for instance in cognitive science and artificial intelligence—has been attributed by Hutchins (1996, p. 370) to "a nearly religious belief in the Platonic status of mathematics and formal systems as eternal verities rather than as historical products of human activity."

2.7 CHANGING APPROACHES TO TEACHING GEOMETRY

In recent decades, the teaching of geometry in public schools has moved away from the presentation of proofs in bureaucratized Euclidean style in an attempt to make the basic concepts of the field more accessible. However, the underlying mathematics has changed very little.

The major innovation in American educational philosophy was that of Dewey (1938/1991). He argued that education should be based less on the transfer of facts and more on processes of inquiry. Recent research in the learning sciences (Sawyer, 2006) has expanded this approach, arguing for the importance of helping students to construct knowledge themselves through processes of active meaning making. However, the institutions of schooling are highly resistant to fundamental changes. While they often take on the trappings and instruments of reform efforts, they integrate them into the established practices, undermining the core intention. Thus, teacher-centric classrooms and teaching to tests of factual information counteract the impact of inquiry or constructivist learning.

Within mathematics, the most radical attempt at educational reform in the U.S. was the "new math" movement. This was an attempt by mathematicians to revise the traditional math curriculum, which was largely based in medieval approaches, with foundational concepts of 20th century mathematics, such as set theory. One approach along similar lines within geometry was to foreground transformational geometry as a central conceptualization (Morris, 1986). For instance, rather than defining an isosceles triangle in terms of equal sides or angles, to define it as having one leg the result of a reflection transformation of the other leg about a line of symmetry. Of course, the new math experiment was publically perceived in the U.S. as a colossal failure, resulting in a strong "back-to-basics" backlash. Although techniques like transformations were subsequently included in the geometry curriculum, they were reduced to yet another topic of factual and procedural knowledge, rather than a foundational inquiry approach.

Somewhat later, dynamic geometry was developed and offered as a new approach to geometry learning. It, too, has an interesting history of acceptance and adaptation within schools. While it offered the promise of a radically different, inquiry-based, constructivist approach, it was largely integrated into the classroom in ways that dulled its reformist impact.

The history of geometry education in public schooling is complicated, with various initiatives and tensions reflected in educational policies, textbooks, and teaching in different countries. For a review of this history in the United States, see Sinclair (2008). Our concern in the current book is focused on the role that a human-centered approach using dynamic geometry can play within this larger picture—which is certainly not to deny that this focus and its context are intricately intertwined.

The development of a computer-based approach to geometry had a logic of its own. The graphical user interface of personal computers allows one to create objects and move them around. This takes advantage of certain technological developments, such as the difference between a "draw" program that uses vector graphics and may be programmed in an object-oriented way, as opposed to a "paint" program that uses pixel graphics. In a paint program, when the user draws something, the affected points or pixels on the drawing surface are simply colored to show where the user indicated. There is no representation of objects, which could be subsequently manipulated, such as the area now colored purple. In a draw program, the user specifies an object, such as a circle, and indicates its size and position on the surface. This information is stored internally for the draw program in terms of an object with variable properties (e.g., shape=circle, center at x=14/y=-5, radius=3, fill-color=red, line-color=black). The user can change these properties by dragging the object or selecting from menus. Given this capability of software on personal computers, geometry environments could be developed that allowed students to explore visual geometric relationship by dragging objects around the screen. For instance, one could see what happens when one drags a circle to make its radius longer.

The problem that immediately arose for someone programming a system for dynamic geometry was that of changing all the related objects when one object changed. For instance, when a user changes the radius of a circle, what happens to a chord that crosses the circle, a line that is tangent to it or a triangle that is inscribed inside it? They must all have their properties changed in very specific ways because their positions and sizes are dependent upon the circle's position and size. The whole idea of dragging is to observe how the relationship of the circle to its chord, tangent or inscribed figure is valid for range of circle sizes and positions, not just for the particular circle first drawn. The solution for the programmer is to create an internal representation of dependencies among the objects created. For instance, the positions (x and y coordinates) of the endpoints of a chord are dependent on the center and radius of the circle, such that the endpoints are always located somewhere on the circle's circumference. Similarly, the defining points of a tangent line or an inscribed triangle are dependent on the circle's center and radius: those defining points must all be automatically adjusted by the software whenever the circle changes. In a complex geometric figure, this leads to a whole hierarchy of dependencies; various objects can be dependent upon the chord that is dependent on the circle, and so on.

> Dependencies are at the core of dynamic geometry. They must be defined when objects are created. They must be maintained when objects are dragged.

Dependencies are at the core of dynamic geometry. They must be defined when objects are created. They must be maintained when objects are dragged. Without the dependencies, dynamic-geometric constructions would not make sense. Without the dependencies, dragging would not reveal anything of interest.

Yet, dependencies are not always emphasized in classrooms that use dynamic-geometry software. The dependencies lie hidden in the software. They are an obscured mystery, invisible to the students. This is largely because learning to construct figures in the software and to think about how to construct the appropriate dependencies into one's own dynamic-geometry figures takes time. Teachers often feel they cannot devote the required classroom time to something that is not directly related to required content and standardized tests. The teachers themselves may not have time to engage in the necessary learning. Furthermore, learning to do constructions and to design dependencies is a trial-and-error process, which involves failures. Teachers may feel that their students will become frustrated with such failure experiences. As a result, the use of the software in classrooms is generally reduced to observing figures being dragged. Often, the students do not even drag the objects themselves, but passively observe the teacher dragging, projected on a screen or smartboard. Frequently, the students do not see the construction taking place—it is pre-constructed.

We will explore the potential of dynamic geometry at length in this book. We will try to formulate a way of presenting dynamic geometry—including its incorporation of transformational geometry—to teachers and students that will retain its potential by involving the students in construction and dependencies as well as dragging. This may help to translate the experience from one of passively accepting already existing geometric truths to one of the creative discovery of geometric phenomena through actively constructing them based on their own designs of dependencies.

CHAPTER 3

Philosophy: The Obfuscation of Geometry

Chapter Summary

The wellsprings of human creativity and logical thinking that flowed forth in the origins of Greek geometry were progressively covered over and transformed into regulated procedures and otherworldly objects. 20th century philosophy frames this cover-up as a paradigmatic example of the over-reach of rationalization. In the sequence of world-historic epochs, successive reification of phenomena of geometry and more generally of the being of objects altered the relation of people to reality. These transformations are associated with the rise of rationalism and an ideology of individualism. Although these changes brought powerful advantages, they now need to be balanced by an approach of human-centered informatics, which guides students to understand the principles of geometry as products of human creative-discovery.

Having reviewed the history of geometry, we now put this history into a larger perspective, which is concerned with the unintended negative consequences associated with historical progress.

3.1 EPOCHS OF ONTOLOGICAL TRANSLATION

In this chapter, we reconsider the history of geometry in terms of the story told by the philosopher Heidegger in his later writings (e.g., Heidegger, 1979). According to his analysis of the history of philosophy, the early Greeks had a keen sense of the world around them, as articulated in their language. Unfortunately, through the development of Plato's philosophy and its influence on subsequent thought—as it was successively translated into different languages and cultures (e.g., Roman bureaucracy, medieval theology, modern technology)—this experience of reality was increasingly covered over. Rather than things appearing the way they did for the Greeks, they later appeared as, for instance, products of artisanship, of God or of technology. If we apply this view to the objects of geometry, we can see that although they were originally creative products of communities of geometers—resulting from their collaborative interaction mediated by labeled drawings and written propositions—the elements of geometry took on different appearances. They became objects of Platonic Ideas, Roman rules, medieval dogma, or modern logic.

In the field of human-computer interaction (HCI), Heidegger is known for his analysis of tools (e.g., of the hammer as being handy, not just spatially present) and of the phenomenon of breakdown (as revealing the nature of the tool as useful for certain projects)—(see, e.g., Dourish, 2001; Dreyfus, 1991; Ehn, 1988; Winograd & Flores, 1986). But the analysis of tools is really just a detail within his much more encompassing early phenomenology of human existence in *Being and Time* (Heidegger, 1927/1996), where he lays out an analysis of human being-in-the-world with other people and tools. (We will discuss this again in Chapter 8 on the theory of resources.)

The point about breakdown is that when tools are being used unproblematically, our understanding of them and of how to comport ourselves with them in the service of our projects is an implicit or tacit kind of knowledge. When there is a breakdown of some kind in this smooth functioning, then we become aware in the sense of developing a more explicit and developed interpretation of the tool as a resource to be used for our projects… and we become aware of the fact that it is not working that way. We only need to develop our awareness up to the point where we can fix the problem and get on with the work. In this way, the breakdown serves to uncover something of the nature of the tool, which was previously not apparent. The tool is brought out of its disclosure and made visible *as* a tool usable for doing such and such. Its significance is established within a network of significance that is projected by our life goals.

Heidegger's philosophy has a strong temporal dimension. We are strongly oriented to the future. That opens up new possibilities, structures our understanding of our situation and our resources and provides meaning. The future is always a finite one, with significant temporal limitations, ultimately established by our eventual death. Within this temporal dimension, we find ourselves at any particular moment already thrown into an existing, complex, meaningful, and shared world. That is the past, which constrains us, provides resources for us and delimits our possibilities. Stretched between past and future, we are situated in the present, in which we care for things and people within the limitations of our understanding.

The fact that the characteristics and uses of tools are uncovered in breakdown situations is important for research—hence its interest to HCI. It means that computer systems, curricula and other resources—which have been designed to be enacted by students—can be studied by looking at problematic occurrences. Take, for instance, a curricular activity that is intended to teach a student how to construct a perpendicular line. If we observe an individual student doing the activity without any difficulty, we learn little as researchers. However, if we observe a group of students trying to accomplish the activity and discussing what they are trying to do when they run into various challenges, then we can learn much. We see how the students are taking the designed resources, how they are enacting them, how they are trying to use them and what is going wrong with all of this (at least from the designer's perspective). The breakdown discloses the tool as what it is, i.e., how it is used.

> If we observe a group of students trying to accomplish the activity and discussing what they are trying to do when they run into various challenges, then we can learn much.

This is an argument for design-based research (DBR) (Barab, 2006; Brown, 1992). To design effective resources, we must intervene in realistic use situations with our prototypes, run trials, analyze results (especially in breakdown cases), revise the prototypes accordingly, and iterate this process many times. DBR integrates the design of an educational technology or intervention with research about how learning takes place with various versions of that resource. Such integration involves vision, theory, implementation, experimentation, creativity, working with teachers, domain knowledge and pedagogy—and it evolves over time, in iterative cycles.

The theory of breakdown is also an argument for students having to dis-cover knowledge themselves through usage—hands-on exploration. This is probably a large part of what is going on in "productive failure" (Kapur & Bielaczyck, 2012; Kapur & Kinzer, 2009), an important recent discovery within CSCL research. Failure often appears to occur when a group of students does not succeed in solving a challenging problem. Their approach breaks down and in response they develop their understanding further. While they may not have time in a classroom or test setting to put this new understanding to use in time to avoid failure in the short term, they now have the increased understanding that other student groups have not developed, so that they can achieve more in the long run.

Heidegger's view of disclosure in the life of a person is part of his historical theory of un-concealment (*Unverborgenheit*). He develops an ontological history, a temporal analysis of Being. Just as the nature of a tool is concealed for an individual using the tool in the smooth pursuit of his or her goals, so the nature of reality more generally is obscured within the way reality is perceived during each historical epoch. Heidegger's early analyses were focused on the individual. Although he conceptualized human existence as a social being-there-with-others in a shared meaningful world, Heidegger cut short the analysis of the shared world, reduced it to a politically conservative critique of popular culture and focused on the individual's being toward its own finitude. In his later work, Heidegger took a more world-historical view, although he still clung to an impoverished concept of history and methodology for historical analysis (Nancy, 2000; Stahl, 1975a; 1976). This had tragic consequences for his own political action.

Whatever the faults, limitations, and dead-end paths his thinking may have had, Heidegger succeeded in uncovering some questionable assumptions and perspectives that have held sway at least from Plato to well beyond Descartes. His writings influenced most of the creative, critical thinkers since his publications. He problematized many of the prevailing distinctions and assumptions, which over the eons have congealed into our common sense. One of these sets of suppositions concerns causation or the proposition that everything must have a reason. For instance, Descartes argued that he must exist because to question if he exists is to think, and "if I think, therefore I must exist" ("*cogito, ergo sum*"). This assumes that if a thought exists, there must be a thinker who caused the thought to exist. Similarly, medieval theologians argued that if there is a universe, there must have been a creator. Our sense of causality derives from the model of mechanical causation (pulling and pushing by ourselves or by machines) and personal agency. Our sense that there must be a cause or reason derives from our experience of craftspeople producing useful products and our bodies exerting influence in our physical surroundings.

Heidegger developed a radically new way of looking at how things influence each other and how history unfolds. Artifacts like shoes, bridges, paintings, poems and buildings each have their own appropriate ways of being in which they appropriate aspects of the physical, spiritual and human world. On a world-historical scale, these ways of being themselves evolve as the defining character of the epoch changes. Heidegger has some detailed analyses of the historical changes in the history of philosophy and some descriptions of artifacts as world-revealing and world-concealing actors (Stahl, 1975b; 1976). This is not the place to go into detail about Heidegger's view, which is notoriously difficult to articulate.

3.2   THE DIALECTIC OF REIFICATION

Heidegger's teacher, Husserl, was concerned in the 1930s with the philosophy of science and mathematics, which were both considered to be in crisis then. Perhaps in response to some of Heidegger's ideas, Husserl wrote an essay on "*The Origin of Geometry*" (Husserl, 1936/1989). Here he coined the term "sedimentation" to describe how an informally used word or phrase could coalesce into an established technical term. In this essay, Husserl imagined the early Greek geometers as engaging in investigations, details of which became accepted mathematical practices through repetition over time.

Husserl's metaphorical term itself became sedimented as a technical term to describe how a casual discourse move could become a routinized social practice. For instance, in his recent study of collaborative learning in the Navy, Hutchins (1996) analyzed the discourse during a breakdown situation and identified a phrase by one person that was picked up on and used repeatedly in the discourse and took on a fixed meaning and role. He said that that phrase could have been sedimented into an established technical term within the large corpus of procedures and practices in naval navigation. Similarly, Hutchins and Palen (1998) show how aspects of the instrumentation used by airplane pilots and gestures associated with them can take on specific, sedimented meanings over time.

Like the moves of Husserl's geometers or Hutchins' sailors and pilots, common words, tools, and actions can become resources with significance and influence far beyond their original, immediate context. Latour and his colleagues have described many examples of mundane objects and unselfconscious practices participating in what he calls actor networks (Latour, 2007). In his view, historical change does not take place as the result of causation by large social institutions acting under rational choices, but rather as the unintended consequences of networks of innumerable mundane actors of all kinds—not primarily people or institutions—exerting constraints on one another. Latour's actor networks have interesting parallels to dynamic geometry's dependency networks and collaborative learning's discourse networks—which are also not to be conceptualized as logical deductions of rational individual minds.

The concept of sedimentation is closely connected to that of reification. In the sedimentation process, independent grains of sand are compressed into hard rock. In reification, something relatively fluid, abstract or amorphous is transformed into a tangible object, or a thing (Latin: *rei*), as though it were material.

In her theory of the history and the learning of mathematics, Sfard (Sfard, 2000; 2008; Sfard & Linchevski, 1994) discusses the role of reification. She sees it playing a central role in the history of mathematics, much like what Husserl attributed to the early development of geometry. Actions in local contexts become reified: tried, repeated, refined and fixated. A risky creative attempt becomes transformed into a valued discovery, eventually taken as a pre-existing truth (for examples, see Lakatos, 1976). Perhaps a long-shot attempt by an individual or small group to solve a tricky problem or to deal with a seeming contradiction is catapulted into an historical advance for humanity. This is how mathematics expanded, for instance with the addition of complex numbers, infinitesimals, or non-Euclidean geometries. Then ontogeny recapitulates phylology; the individual student learning follows the steps of the field's development.

For Sfard, reification is a helpful and necessary process. A concrete instance of a math object, the naming of something or a procedure followed becomes a significant new mathematical element or practice. Something that was closely tied to a specific context becomes generalized, freed from its situation of origin. Henceforth, it is available for everyone, applicable to a range of problems. It gains status and acceptance. It is taken as the discovery of something that must have always been true in the otherworldly realm of mathematics; we just had not seen it and had to have someone discover it (or uncover it for Heidegger, or remember it for Plato).

While reification drives forward progress in mathematics, it has its down side as well. It obscures the origin of new concepts and procedures in the creative work of people. Although there are some traces of human creation in names like the "Pythagorean Theorem" or the "Euler segment," these are taken as nods to the discoverers of eternal geometric objects or relationships inherent in geometric objects, rather than as products of creative human work.

This is the "dialectic of enlightenment" (Adorno & Horkheimer, 1945): progress in rational thinking brings with it the danger that important phenomena become obscured, misunderstood, forgotten, and repressed. Rationalization of society can lead to fascism, totalitarianism or mindless bureaucracy. In mathematics, it can lead to deadening memorization in place of insight—in the name of efficient training.

> Progress in rational thinking brings with it the danger that important phenomena become obscured, misunderstood, forgotten, and repressed.

If we assume that the first geometers—of whom we have no historical record because they predated written history—experienced some form of primordial intellectual fascination as they created geometry and discovered its principles, then we might wonder why students encountering geometry today do not share that experience. Of course, some of the answer is the setting. The Greeks may have been sipping a jug of fresh wine with their friends on the sun-drenched shores of the Aegean Sea while sketching triangles in the warm sand. The students in schools may be feeling deprived of sleep, food, music, video, fresh air, and free interaction with their peers while being required to step through meaningless procedures, which they will be tested on. But, in addition, the nature of the enterprise and the experience has changed essentially through processes internal to the subject matter, such as the ancient reification, which turned adventures in imagination into propositions of geometry, and the layers of scholarly translation that followed.

Geometry is a social product. The processes of reification take place primarily at the community level, where something that arose in small-group interactions—or in the internalized voices of an individual's mind—is made available more widely. The reification of geometric elements, terms, practices and symbols are part of the dialectic of enlightenment. They contribute to intellectual progress while simultaneously obscuring their origins.

Adorno and Horkheimer (1945) showed that this dialectic is pervasive in Western culture, with its roots in ancient Greece. Central to this culture is an ideology of individualism. In the ancient Greek epic tales of Ulysses and other mythic heroes, one can already see the emergence of the individual out of the earlier focus on nature and the tribe. In the early period of capitalism, the individual took on the form of the rational thinker and entrepreneurial actor. In the subsequent industrial age, knowledge—including knowledge of geometry, considered key to rational thinking by individuals—became a commodity to be consumed by a future workforce. The nature of mathematics, knowledge, learning, and thought went through a series of translations, reflected in the theories and philosophies of the times. The ideology of individualism was central to these historic transformations.

3.3   BEYOND THE IDEOLOGY OF INDIVIDUALISM

The history of theory can be tracked in terms of the following issue: At what unit of analysis should one study thought (*cognition*)? For Plato (340 BCE/1941), in addition to the physical objects in the world, there are concepts that characterize those objects; philosophy is the analysis of such concepts, like goodness, truth, beauty or justice. Descartes (1633/1999) argued that if there is thought, then there must be a mind that thinks it, and that philosophy should analyze both the mental objects of the mind and the material objects to which they refer, as well as the epistemological relation between them. Following Descartes, rationalism focused on the logical nature of mental reasoning, while empiricism concentrated on the analysis of observable physical objects. Kant (1787/1999) re-centered this discussion by arguing that the mechanisms of human understanding provided the source of the apparent spatio-temporal nature of observed objects and that critical theory's task was to analyze the mind's constructivist structuring-categorization efforts. Up to this point in the history of theory, cognition was assumed to be an innate function of the individual human mind.

Hegel (1807/1967) transcended that individualist assumption. He traced the logical/historical development of mind from the most primary instinct of a living organism through stages of intentional-consciousness, self-consciousness, and historical-consciousness to the most developed trans-national spirit of the times (*Zeitgeist*). To analyze cognition henceforth, it is necessary to follow through its biological unfolding and go beyond to the ultimate cultural understanding of a society. Figure 3.1 identifies Hegel's approach to theory as forming the dividing line—or watershed—between philosophies or theories based on the individual and those oriented to a larger unit of analysis.

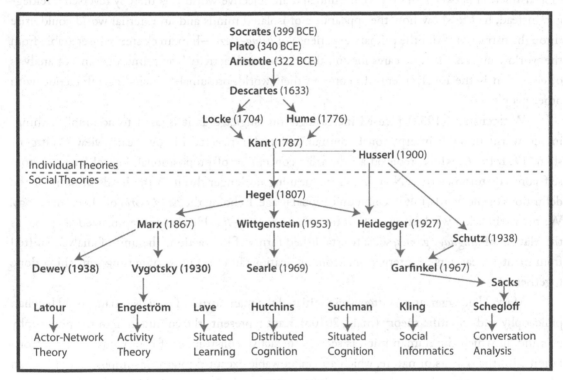

Figure 3.1: The historical dividing line between individualistic and social theories. Adapted from (Stahl, 2006, p. 289, Fig. 14-1).

Philosophy after Hegel can be viewed as forming three mainstreams of thought, following the seminal approaches of Marx (critical social theory), Heidegger (existential phenomenology), and Wittgenstein (linguistic analysis). As taken up within HCI, one can trace how these approaches established extended units of analysis.

Marx (1867) expanded upon Hegel's recognition of the historical self-generation of mankind and analyzed this historical process in terms of the dialectical co-development of the *social relations of production* and *the forces of production*. His analysis took the form of historical, political, and economic studies of the world-historical processes by which human labor produces and reproduces social institutions. Here, the study of the human mind and its understanding of its objects becomes reformulated at the epochal unit of analysis of social movements, class conflicts and transformations of economic systems.

Heidegger (1927/1996) radicalized the Hegelian dialectic between man and nature by starting the analysis of man from the unified experience of *being-in-the-world*. The Cartesian problem of a distinction between an observing mind and an objective world was thereby reversed. Heidegger, instead, had to show how the appearance of isolated minds and an external world could arise through abstraction from the primary experience of *being-there*—human existence inseparable from the worldly objects that one cares for and that define one's activity. The primordial unit of analysis of cognition is the involvement of people in their world, presumably including interaction with other people.

Wittgenstein (1953) focused increasingly on language as it is used to accomplish things in the world through interpersonal communication. He rejected his own early view (Wittgenstein, 1921/1974), which reduced a rationalist conception of propositional, logical language to a self-contradictory position. Now, linguistic meaning no longer dwelt in the heads of users or the definitions of the words, but in communicational usage. Echoing the *lived world* of phenomenology, Wittgenstein acknowledged the role of the human *form-of-life*. He also conceptualized language as the playing of *language games*, socially established forms of interaction. The unit of analysis shifted from mental meanings to interpersonal communications in the context of getting something done together.

Marx, Heidegger, and Wittgenstein initiated the main forms of post-Kantian, post-Hegelian philosophy and scientific theory (Stahl, 2010b). Kant represents the culmination of the philosophy of mind, in which the human mind is seen as the active constructor of reality out of its confrontation with the objects of nature, which are unknowable except through this imposition of human structuring categories. With Kant—over 200 years ago—the human mind is still a fixed unit consisting of innate abilities of the individual person, despite how much his philosophy differs from naïve realist folk theories, which accept the world as fundamentally identical with its appearance to the human observer.

Hegel overthrows the Kantian view of a fixed nature of mind by showing how the mind has itself been constructed through long sequences of processes. The Hegelian construction of mind can be understood in multiple senses:

1. as the biological development of the brain's abilities as it grows from newborn to mature adult;

2. as the logical development from simple contrast of *being* and *non-being* to the proliferation of all the distinctions of the most sophisticated understanding; or

3. as the historical development from primitive *homo sapiens* to modern, civilized, technological and cultured person.

After Hegel, theory shifted from philosophy to science, to explore the biological, logical, and historical processes in more detail and to verify them empirically. Followers of Marx, Heidegger, and Wittgenstein adopted approaches to this that can be characterized as *social, situated* and *linguistic*, respectively. They are all constructivist, following Kant's insight that the structure of known objects is constructed by the knowing mind. However, they all focus on a unit of analysis broader than the isolated individual mind of Descartes and Kant.

The social, situated, and linguistic theories of Marx, Heidegger, and Wittgenstein entered the discourse of HCI literature with researchers coming from the various scientific traditions that went into forming these research domains, including psychology, education, social science, design studies, computer science, and artificial intelligence (e.g., Dourish, 2001; Ehn, 1988; Floyd, 1992; Schön, 1983). Although these fields each introduced various theoretical perspectives, we can see the major philosophic influences largely through several seminal texts, the most important of which for issues of learning was *Mind in Society* (Vygotsky, 1930/1978).

Mind in Society is an edited compilation of Vygotsky's writings from the early 1930s in post-revolutionary Russia, which has been influential in the West since it appeared in English in 1978. Critiquing the prevailing psychology as practiced by behaviorists, Gestalt psychologists and Piaget, Vygotsky did not try to fit psychology superficially into the dogmatic principles of Soviet Marxism, but rather radically rethought the nature of human psychological capabilities from the developmental approach proposed by Hegel and Marx. He showed how human perception, attention, memory, thought, play, and learning (which others conceived of as mental faculties) were all products of developmental processes—in terms of both maturation of individuals and the social history of cultures. He proposed a dynamic vision of the human mind in society, as opposed to a fixed and isolated function.

> Vygotsky proposed a dynamic vision of the human mind in society, as opposed to a fixed and isolated function.

The Hegelian term, *mediation*, was central for Vygotsky, as it is to HCI. Even in his early years still talking about stimulus and response, Vygotsky asked how one stimulus could mediate the memory of, attention toward or word retrieval about another stimulus (Vygotsky, 1930/1978, p. iii). In Hegelian terms, this is a matter of mediating (with the first stimulus) the relation (memory, attention, retrieval) of a subject to an object (the second stimulus). This is fundamental to HCI because in human-computer interaction, the learning of students or the work of professionals is mediated by computers.

Another popular term from Vygotsky is the *zone of proximal development* (Vygotsky, 1930/1978, pp. 84-91). This is the learning distinction and developmental gap between what individuals can do by themselves (e.g., on pre- and post-tests) and what they can do in collaboration (e.g., situated in a small group). A group of children may be able to achieve cognitive results together that they will not be able to achieve as individuals for a couple more years. This is consistent with Vygotsky's principle that people develop cognitive abilities first in a "social" context—supported or mediated by peers, mentors, or cognitive aids like representational artifacts—and only later are able to exercise these cognitive abilities as individuals. Vygotsky's theory, if carried beyond where he had time to develop it, implies that collaborative learning provides the foundation upon which all learning is built. Methodologically, it argues against judging the outcomes of collaborative learning by evaluating or assessing individuals outside of their collaborative settings.

Vygotsky used the term *social* in an ambiguous way when he said that learning takes place socially first and then later individually. Almost everyone else treats the term ambiguously as well. The word "socially" can refer to two people talking, as well as to transformations of whole societies. For the sake of distinguishing levels of description or units of analysis in HCI, it seems important to make clear distinctions. Table 3.1 suggests sets of different terms for referring to phenomena at the individual, small-group, and societal levels. The distinction of these three levels has previously been argued for in (Rogoff, 1995), (Dillenbourg et al., 1996), (Stahl, 2006), and elsewhere. We start with these three levels, which seem particularly central to much HCI work, although other levels might also usefully be distinguished, such as "collective intelligence" at the classroom level or "collective practices" at the school level (Guribye, 2005; Jones, Dirckinck-Holmfeld & Lindström, 2006; Looi et al., 2011). Perhaps consistent usage of such terminological distinctions would lend clarity to the discussion of theories. Table 3.1 includes many of the terms and categories that will play important roles in this book.

Table 3.1: Terminology for phenomena at the individual, small-group and community levels of description. Adapted from (Stahl, 2010a, p. 27, Table 2.1).

Level of description	Individual	Small group	Community
Role	Person/student	Group participant	Community member
Adjective	Personal	Collaborative	Social
Object of analysis	Mind	Discourse	Culture
Unit of analysis	Mental representation	Utterance response pair	Socio-technical activity system, mediating artifacts

Form of knowledge	Subjective	Intersubjective	Cultural
Form of meaning	Interpretation	Shared understanding, joint meaning making, common ground	Domain vocabulary, artifacts, institutions, norms, rules
Learning activity	Learn	Build knowledge	Science
Ways to accomplish cognitive tasks	Skill, behavior	Discourse, group methods, long sequences	Member methods, social practices
Communication	Thought	Interaction	Membership
Mode of construction	Constructed	Co-constructed	Socially constructed
Context of cognitive task	Personal problem	Joint problem space	Problem domain
Context of activity	Environment	Situation	Society
Mode of Presence	Embodiment	Co-presence	Contemporary
Referential system	Associations	Indexical field	Cultural world
Form of existence (Heidegger)	Being-there (Dasein)	Being-with (Mitsein), Being-there-together at the shared object	Participation in communities of practice (Volk)
Temporal structure	Subjective experiential internal time	Co-constructed shared temporality	Measurable objective time
Theory of cognition	Constructivist	Post-cognitive	Socio-cultural
Science	Cognitive and educational psychology	Group cognition theory	Sociology, anthropology, linguistics
Tacit knowledge	Background knowledge	Common ground	Culture
Thought	Cognition	Group cognition	Practices
Action	Action	Inter-Action	Social praxis

The theoretical priority of collaborative learning is the philosophic motivation for insisting that geometry education emphasize mathematical discourse in small groups of students who are creating and discovering together, dragging, and constructing as a group.

3.4 DYNAMIC GEOMETRY AS HUMAN-CENTERED

In order to translate geometry into a form appropriate for the current age, we propose to re-focus the study of geometry on *dependencies* in collaborative dynamic geometry. This requires a coordinated shift of an entire worldview, or *Weltanschauung* as Heidegger called it. Rather than treating geometry as a matter of shapes (young children), mysticism (Pythagoras), ideal objects (Plato), propositions (Euclid), axioms (formalized math), proof (school textbooks), or logic (Frege), we treat it as centrally concerned with dependencies. This focus is associated with corresponding shifts in cognitive history, contemporary philosophy, school mathematics, software technology, collaborative learning, design-based research, CSCL theory, developmental pedagogy, and scaffolded practice—as presented in the chapters of this book.

Above all, however, the focus on dependencies emerged from the author's exploration of dynamic geometry. Dependencies increasingly seemed central to this form of mathematics. The fact that looking at reality in terms of dependencies seems more appropriate to the contemporary world than authority, mechanical causation, or rational deduction led to the human-centered characterization.

Dependencies involve the core dimensions of dynamic geometry: dragging and constructing. Dynamic dragging *discovers* dependencies and dynamic construction *creates* dependencies. The integration of discovery and creation in human-geometric creative-discovery produces dynamic geometry. In order to grant a semblance of universality to this production, it is important for the creative-discovery to be a collaborative process, involving mathematical discourse and intersubjective meaning making. The group-level work has to be integrated with individual-level and community-level processes. Group practices, individual interpretations, community institutions, and interactional resources serve to ground virtual math teams in the real world.

While it is ultimately necessary to integrate individual learning, group cognition, and community knowledge building, our project focuses on the *group level*, because attention has been aimed mostly at the other levels for the past 2,000 years. In a school setting, textbooks and paper exercises serve the individual learners, and teacher-orchestrated class discussions serve the local community. Sometimes the VMT Project provided teacher professional development in collaborative dynamic mathematics to stimulate activity in classrooms. In subsequent trials with student groups, we found that teachers often quite naturally engage in preparation and debriefing sessions about the virtual-math-team work with their classes. However, the missing collaborative experience of geometry takes place primarily in the small-group interaction in the VMT chat rooms, as we will see above all in Chapter 7.

In the previous chapter, we caught a glimpse of how our common sense about the nature of geometric objects and the reasons for their relationships evolved over the centuries. Let us now consider how the notions of creation and discovery apply to geometry in different eras.

What is a geometric point? It is not a pencil mark, a blob of ink, a small set of pixels. Is it a location on a two-dimensional grid, the limit of a circle as its area goes to zero, or an undefined term in a set of axioms? These are all modern mathematical or logical conceptions, not something the ancient Greeks could have conceived of. They are the results of a long historical development and corresponding series of conceptual translations from then until now. Why are the sides of an equilateral triangle the same length? Why do the three bisectors of a triangle's angles all meet at one point? Why does the Euler segment have the characteristics it has? These are questions central to geometry. One potential answer is that we constructed things that way; another is that we can prove the result logically; another is that certain dependencies determine it—that that is simply the way the world of mathematics is and we must discover its true character.

Dynamic geometry can involve experiences of *creative-discovery*—creativity through construction and discovery through dragging—resulting in insight about dependencies. The concept of creative-discovery overcomes the traditional distinction between idealism and realism: whether the world is created through our imposition of meaning or discovered as it is given by brute reality. Already in the philosophy of Kant (1787/1999), there is a notion that one cannot know things apart from the way they are structured by our minds, involving time, space, and causality. Recent debates in HCI have refined this interaction between how people discover affordances (Dohn, 2009) and create instrumental genesis of tools (Rabardel & Beguin, 2005).

> Dynamic geometry can involve experiences of creative-discovery—creativity through construction and discovery through dragging—resulting in insight about dependencies.

Acts of creation involve discovery; they butt up against the strictures of reality. For instance, no one could realize that the Euler segment would exist and have such interesting properties just from thinking about the dependencies in a triangle. It is something that one has to discover as one drags different triangle centers. As long as one encapsulates construction processes in custom tools for constructing the different centers, one is not aware of the constraints introduced by the construction into the Euler segment. However, once one explores by dragging the triangle and discovers the invariances in the segment, one can go back and identify dependencies. Then one can create figures that exploit and explore the phenomenon, essentially building the basis of a proof of the segment's properties It is not that the Euler segment lies implicit in the nature of the simple triangle, waiting to be discovered in its eternal essence. Rather, the carefully designed construction of the various "centers" and other points that define the Euler segment creates the dependencies that are reflected in Euler's conjecture and that are apparent in the dragging of those specially constructed points.

A philosophy of creative-discovery can provide an appropriate perspective for a human-centered mathematics. Fields of math are human products. They even have strong roots in the nature of the human body (Lakoff & Núñez, 2000). Nevertheless, a field like geometry also has surprises that do not follow in an obvious way from the definitions; they must be discovered as unanticipated consequences of the creative initiative. While dynamic geometry is a human creation—with a long history—it is also the result of rigorous discovery. Students should understand geometry as a human-centered product of this historical process of creative-discovery.

CHAPTER 4

Mathematics: Demythologizing Geometry

Chapter Summary

This chapter considers several geometric phenomena that are typically presented as Platonic ideals of otherworldly origin and reinterprets them as human creations that can be discovered through human construction. For instance, equilateral and isosceles triangles are not special phenomena to be memorized, but simply two possible combinations of constraints for triangles. Similarly, the existence of an incenter of a triangle is not a mysterious occurrence, but a straightforward consequence of its construction. These reinterpretations can be structured as activities for students of collaborative dynamic geometry.

4.1 HIERARCHIES OF TRIANGLES AND QUADRILATERALS

Children are brought up to recognize the shapes of certain prototypical geometric figures. From infancy onward, they are taught to recognize and name triangles, squares, rectangles, and circles. In school, they are presented with special three-sided or four-sided shapes: equilateral, isosceles, and right triangles or square, rectangular, trapezoidal, rhomboid, and parallelogram quadrilaterals.

However, these different shapes are not arbitrary graphical forms to be handed down through cultural traditions and memorized. Rather, they can be understood as part of the set of results from considering all the possibilities of three- and four-sided figures. Given, for instance, three line segments, there are different constraints that one can impose on them, resulting in different kinds of triangles.

- None of the lengths of the segments are equal, yielding a scalene triangle.

- The lengths of two of the segments are equal, yielding an isosceles triangle.

- The lengths of all three segments are equal, yielding an equilateral triangle.

- None of the angles at the vertices are equal, yielding a scalene triangle.

- Two of the angles at the vertices are equal, yielding an isosceles triangle.

- The angles at all three vertices are equal, yielding an equilateral triangle.

- The angle at one of the vertices is a right angle, yielding a right triangle.

- No angle is larger than a right angle, yielding an acute triangle.

- One angle is larger than a right angle, yielding an obtuse triangle.

- One angle is a right angle and the other two are equal, yielding a right isosceles triangle.

- One angle is larger than a right angle and the other two are equal, yielding an obtuse isosceles triangle.

Similarly, one can generate a set of different kinds of quadrilaterals by considering all the possible figures generated by allowable constraints on number of equal sides, number of equal angles, number of right angles, number of parallel pairs of lines. It is also possible to specify constraints in other ways, such as in terms of lines of symmetry and characteristics of side or angle bisectors.

The point is that the variety of polygon shapes can be understood in terms of constraints imposed in the construction of the figures. This provides logical insight into what would otherwise be a rather arbitrary collection of forms with obscure Greek names, which has to be memorized and taken on authority. In general, geometry makes much more sense when one understands it in terms of the constraints that are introduced through geometric constructions.

Euclid's proofs can be understood as instructions for imposing constraints on constructions of figures. For instance, Proposition 1 is entitled "On a given finite straight line to construct an equilateral triangle." The reason that the resultant triangle has equal length sides is that the two legs of the triangle are constructed with the constraint that they be the same length as the base of the triangle (the "given finite straight line"). This is accomplished by drawing a circle around each endpoint of the base (say, A and B) with a radius equal to the length of the base (AB). The legs (say, AC and BC) are then constructed to also be radii of the circles, thus having the same length as the base. The intersection of the two circles is a point that is constructed to be equidistant from the two endpoints of the triangle's base. The construction ensures that the lengths of the constructed legs (AC and BC) will be dependent upon the length of the base. As Euclid argues, AC=AB and BC=AB, so AC=BC and the three sides are all equal.

> Understanding the constraints designed into the construction process makes the proof of the equality of all three sides of the triangle obvious.

Understanding the constraints designed into the construction process makes the proof of the equality of all three sides of the triangle obvious. A student can be encouraged to memorize the construction of an equilateral triangle. Alternatively, a student can take the proposition as a lesson in the construction of new segments constrained to be the same length as the given segment. In the procedural approach, the student is likely to find the exercise meaningless and can easily forget the procedure. In the construction approach, the student may comprehend what Euclid was doing and may thereby acquire a cognitive tool that can be used in subsequent geometry problems. That Euclid treated Proposition 1 as a lesson in construction is confirmed by the fact that Propositions 2 and 3 continued this approach, demonstrating how to copy a given segment length to another point and then on to another line.

4.2   THE MYSTERY OF THE TRIANGLE INCENTER

Perhaps it is clear in the case of Euclid's first proposition that one is imposing constraints through the construction that account for the result of the sides being equal length. However, are there not some geometrical relationships that just inhere to certain shapes and are not built into figures by the dependencies of our constructions?

What about the surprising fact that the three bisectors of the angles of any triangle all meet at one point? It does not seem like we have built this property in through some construction constraints—it is simply a property of any plain triangle (see Figure 4.1). Furthermore, the point of concurrency of the angle bisectors—called the "incenter" of the triangle—happens to be exactly equidistant from the three sides of the triangle. It turns out interestingly that the incenter is always inside the triangle, for any kind of triangle (unlike some other special points of triangles). Moreover, if one constructs a circle inscribed in the triangle, it will happen that the center of the triangle is precisely at the incenter (see Figure 4.1). These all seem to be mysterious properties of the ideal geometric object, triangle; it is assumed that they must be deductively proven from axioms and other propositions to convince us of the generality of these relationships, their Platonic truth.

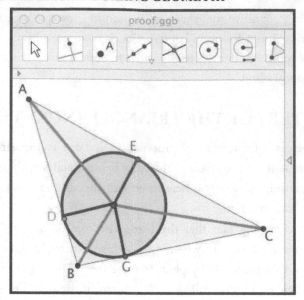

Figure 4.1: A triangle ABC with incenter and angle bisectors meeting at the incenter. The incenter is equidistant from the three sides and is the center of a circle inscribed in the triangle.

Let us investigate—using dynamic geometry—the standard belief that the relationships associated with the incenter are inherent characteristics of triangles that are not imposed by constraints designed into the construction, but are properties of triangles to be discovered, whose validity is to be deductively proven. Rather than starting from the completed figure, let us instead proceed through the construction step by step.

As our first step, we construct one of the angle bisectors (see Figure 4.2). We actually construct the angle bisector by constructing a ray AF that goes from point A through some point F that lies between sides AB and AC and is equidistant from both these sides. The constraint that F is the same distance from sides AB and AC is constructed as follows: First construct a circle centered on A and intersecting AB and AC—call the points of intersection D and E. Construct perpendiculars to the sides at these points. The perpendiculars necessarily meet between the sides—call the point of intersection F. Construct ray AF. AF bisects the angle at vertex A, as can be shown by congruent right triangles ADF and AEF. (Right triangles are congruent if any two sides are congruent because of the Pythagorean relationship, which guarantees that the third sides are also congruent.)

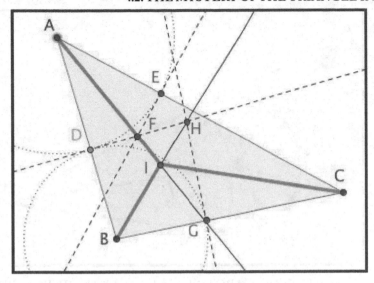

Figure 4.2: The construction of the incenter, I. The bisector of angle BAC, ray AF, is constructed so that any point on it lies between AB and AC and is equidistant from sides AB and AC.

As our second step, we similarly construct the bisector of the angle at vertex B. First construct a circle centered on B and intersecting side AB at point D—call the circle's point of intersection with side BC point G. Construct perpendiculars to the sides at these points. The perpendiculars necessarily meet between the sides—call the point of intersection H. Construct ray BH. BH bisects the angle at vertex B, as can be shown by congruent right triangles BDH and BGH.

Now mark the intersection of the two angle-bisector rays AF and BH as point I, the incenter of triangle ABC. Construct segment CI. We can see that CI is the angle bisector of the angle at the third vertex, C, in Figure 4.3. We construct perpendiculars IJ, IK, IL from the incenter to the three sides. We know that I is on the bisector of angles A and B, so IJ=IK and IJ=IL. From those two equations (and Euclid's favorite transactivity), we know that IK=IL, which means that I is also on the bisector of angle C.

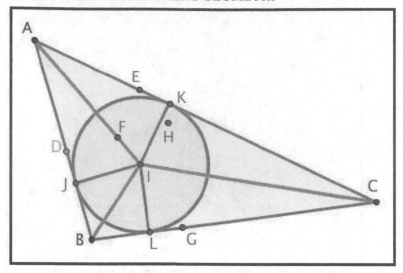

Figure 4.3: The incenter, I, of triangle ABC, with equal perpendiculars IJ, IK, and IL, which are radii of the inscribed circle.

We have now shown that point I is common to the three angle bisectors of an arbitrary triangle ABC. We can also construct a circle centered on the incircle, with radii IJ, IK, and IL. The circle is inscribed in the triangle because it is tangent to each of the sides. It is not shown here, but the vertex points of the triangle were dragged to show that all the discussed relationships are retained dynamically. Therefore, the fact that the bisectors of the three angles of a triangle are all concurrent is not a mysterious surprise, but a direct consequence of the dependencies we imposed when constructing the bisectors.

> The incenter of a triangle is not some mysterious property of the triangle, but a consequence of the dependencies constructed into the figure.

The incenter of a triangle is not some mysterious property of the triangle, to be discovered by deductive proof from a given figure like Figure 4.1, but a consequence of the dependencies constructed into the figure, such as the constraints imposed by constructing the bisector of the angle in Figure 4.2.

If we had "constructed" ray AF as the bisector of angle A in GeoGebra by simply using the built-in angle-bisector tool, we would not have noticed that we were thereby imposing the constraint that DF=EF. It was only by going step-by-step that we could see what dependencies were being designed into the figure by construction. The packaging of the detailed construction process in a new tool would have obscured the imposition of dependencies. This is the useful process of "abstraction" in mathematics: While it allows one to build quickly upon past accomplishments, it has the consequence of hiding what is taking place in terms of imposing dependencies. The abstraction of the construction experience into a fixed process and then into a "black box" tool is an example of reification.

While dragging figures that have already been constructed and even constructing with a large palette of construction tools can be extremely helpful to students for exploring geometric relationships and coming up with conjectures to investigate, such an approach can give the misimpression that the relationships are abstract truths to be accepted on authority and validated through routinized deduction. It is also important for students—at least for those students who want a deeper understanding of what is going on—to be able to construct figures for themselves, using the basic tools of straightedge (line) and compass (circle). They should understand how other tools are built up from the elementary construction methods and should know how to create their own custom tools, for which they understand the incorporated procedures.

Of course, simply constructing figures is not enough. One must be able to reflect upon what is being accomplished in the construction and what one is trying to accomplish—and that involves discourse. Within a social setting of collaboration, students will want to share their ideas, questions, conjectures and discoveries with their friends, generating occasions for geometric discourse and collaborative learning. In order to work together on tasks and benefit from each other's perspectives, they will have to exchange constructions and custom tools, which incorporate and preserve their creative insights. In a multi-user environment, small groups of students can explore dynamic drawings together and discuss the construction process as they work on it as a team.

4.3   TOPICS TO EXPLORE TRIANGLES AND THEIR INCENTERS

In later chapters (see Chapter 10), we will describe the VMT Project's approach to collaborative learning of dynamic geometry and curricular topics designed for virtual math teams. Here we see some simple sample activities for exploring the kinds of triangles and quadrilaterals that are possible in terms of the constraints used to construct them.

The topic in Figure 4.4 encourages groups of students to explore a number of triangles that were constructed with different constraints. The students can drag the vertices of the triangles to see which sides and angles are dependent upon other sides and angles. The students are prompted to consider what different constraints and combinations of constraints are possible. Poly1, which is a scalene triangle with no constraints on the sizes of its sides and angles, can be dragged on top of other triangles and be dragged to match them by exactly covering them. This can provide a highly visual and literally graspable sense of the otherwise abstract sense of congruence.

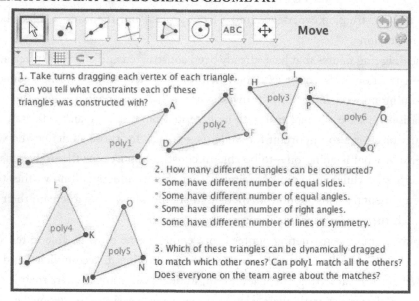

Figure 4.4: A topic about constraints for different kinds of triangles.

The situation with quadrilaterals is more complicated than with triangles. There are a lot more possibilities, as shown in Figure 4.5. This topic is similar to the previous one in supporting the interactive and collaborative exploration of possible constraints and the variety of forms that the constraints can impose on polygons.

Figure 4.6 allows students to construct the incenter of a triangle using the built-in tool for bisecting angles at the triangle's vertices. The students can then drag the vertices of the triangle to observe the behavior of the incenter point. They can create their own custom incenter tool, for quickly locating the incenter of any given triangle. While this gives the students a sense of the incenter by being able to drag triangles and observe their incenters, it does not provide the insight into the constraints that cause the incenter's properties as described in the previous section. This illustrates the limitations of certain approaches to dynamic geometry, particularly those that emphasize dragging. Of course, this topic just provides a first acquaintance with incenters. The students have not yet even seen how the incenter functions as the center of an inscribed circle. Future topics can come back to explore and expose the mystery of the incenter.

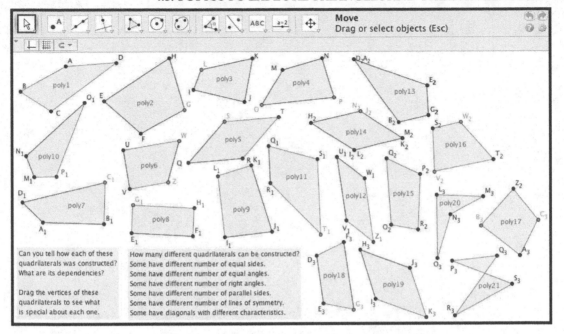

Figure 4.5: A topic about constraints for different kinds of quadrilaterals.

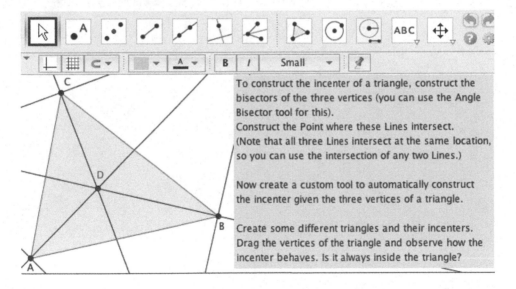

Figure 4.6: A topic for constructing the incenters of triangles, including creating a custom tool.

CHAPTER 5

Technology: Deconstructing Geometry

Chapter Summary

Dynamic-geometry software applications such as Geometer's Sketchpad, Cabri, and GeoGebra are described in this chapter as computer-supported environments for exploring an innovative approach to geometry. This approach is characterized in terms of dynamic dragging, dynamic construction, and dynamic dependencies. These characteristics distinguish it from traditional paper-and-pencil geometry in ways that can make visible the human-centered nature of geometry.

5.1 THE ORIGIN OF DYNAMIC GEOMETRY

Dynamic geometry emerged from the potential of personal computers to provide interactive diagramming tools with embedded computational support. The core technology actually considerably predates personal computers with Sutherland's (1963) SketchPad software, which provided a graphical user interface with an object-oriented draw program before there really were graphical user interfaces, object-oriented programming, or draw programs. Video games developed the technology further—and largely drove the personal computer market from its start.

In the late 1980s, Nicholas Jackiw, the designer and programmer of Geometer's Sketchpad, began working with Eugene Klotz on one of the first instances of a dynamic-geometry program at the Visual Geometry Project, a forerunner of the Math Forum (Scher, 2000). At about the same time, Jean-Marie Laborde began Cabri, in France. The developers of Geometer's Sketchpad and Cabri shared ideas in the mid 1990s. In 2002, Markus Hohenwarter launched GeoGebra as an open-source dynamic-mathematics environment.

These programs have subsequently become popular around the world. Although each of the programs has subtle differences in their geometric-construction paradigms and somewhat different functionality, they are fundamentally similar in their affordances for students of geometry. They make geometry dynamic by allowing a person using the system to construct a geometric diagram with labels and then to move the interconnected geometric objects by dragging their points around. As objects are moved, they maintain dependencies that were part of the construction process. This should be clear in the following example.

5.2   AN EXAMPLE OF DYNAMIC-GEOMETRY CONSTRUCTION

In Figure 5.1, we see a construction in which equilateral triangle DEF has been inscribed in equilateral triangle ABC[1]. Figure 5.2 shows the same construction after point D has been dragged upwards. A user can move Point D by placing the cursor on point D and dragging the point in the construction. However, the movement of point D is constrained by the construction to always remain on line segment AC and to not go past its endpoints. This is characteristic of dynamic geometry.

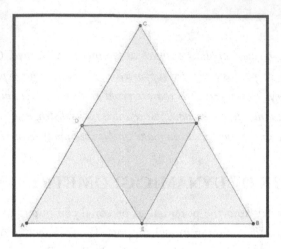

Figure 5.1: Inscribed equilateral triangles.

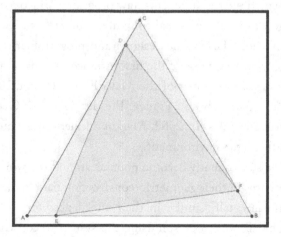

Figure 5.2: Inscribed equilateral triangles after dragging point D.

---

[1] This construction was suggested by (Öner, 2013).

Notice that in addition to point D moving, points E and F also moved when point D was moved. The line segments connecting these points and forming triangle DEF have moved with their endpoints, effectively rotating triangle DEF. This is because of how the inscribed triangles were constructed. They were constructed in a special way in order to preserve the equilateral characteristic of triangle DEF. The larger triangle ABC can also be rotated by dragging one of its vertex points, such as point A or B. No matter how any of the points in the construction are dragged, the other points will move in ways that maintain the equilateral character and inscribed relationship of the triangles.

By studying Figure 5.1 and Figure 5.2, it may be possible to figure out how to construct the triangles so that they will maintain their equilateral character dynamically. We can construct triangle ABC to be equilateral by following Euclid's first proposition. Starting from an arbitrary line segment AB, we construct a circle centered on point A and going through point B. Then we construct a second circle centered on point B and going through point A. These two circles intersect above and below AB and we mark one of the intersections as point C (see large arcs in Figure 5.3). We then construct triangle ABC, connecting the points. We know that triangle ABC is equilateral because (as Euclid argued) its three sides are equal in length to line segment AB because they are radii of the same circles. If one subsequently drags point A or B, changing the length of AB, then the circles with radius AB will both change, moving point C in precisely the right way to keep ABC always equilateral. We can say that the lengths of AC and BC—and thus the position of point C—are "dependent" upon the length of AB. Consequently, triangle ABC is defined by this dependency. Constructing dependencies is fundamental to dynamic geometry. As in the example we just went through, these dependencies are *implicit* in Euclidean geometry, but become *visible* in the construction and manipulation of dynamic geometry.

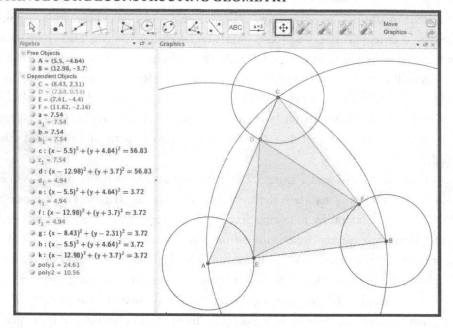

Figure 5.3: Constructing the dependencies for inscribed equilateral triangles.

Note that sides AC and BC are dynamically dependent upon side AB in the sense that if the length of AB changes, then the lengths of AC and BC will change correspondingly, maintaining the constraint of equality no matter how points are dragged or other changes are made. This goes significantly beyond the static constructions of Euclid, in which AC and BC are only guaranteed to be the same length as AB when AB is the specific length that it has in the drawing. Of course, Euclid's drawings were intended to be understood as general. Thus, AC and BC were understood to be the same length as AB—no matter what length AB was given to start with. In Euclid, one could only imagine different lengths for AB, but in dynamic geometry, one can actually change the length of AB dynamically and watch how built-in constraints are maintained.

Having constructed a dynamically equilateral triangle ABC, how do we construct an inscribed dynamically equilateral triangle DEF? That is the challenge of the given problem. We can place points D, E, and F on the three sides of ABC, but they will not be constrained to stay at equal distances from each other. If we try to use Euclid's Proposition 1, again we run into problems. Say we construct line segment DE (connecting a point D on side AC and a point E on side AB) and then construct circles of radius DE around D and E. The intersection will not fall along line BC. Even if it did happen to fall there, we could not locate point F at the intersection of three lines because that would be over-constrained. (According to Euclid, a point is defined by the intersection of two lines, not by the intersection of three lines.) Also, if the intersection just happened to fall on side BC, it would not stay on there when the figure was dragged.

We need a different approach. By dragging the triangles in Figure 5.2, we might notice that the distance of the vertices of the smaller triangle are always at equal distances from the corresponding vertices of the larger triangle. In other words (or symbols): AE=BF=CD (see Figure 5.3). In fact, if you specify that these three line segments are equal, it is easy to prove by Euclidean methods that the three triangles formed between the two equilateral triangles are all congruent. This ensures that the sides of the inner triangle are equal if the sides of the outer triangle are equal. Thus, if we can impose the constraint that AE=BF=CD, then we can construct a dynamically equilateral triangle DEF inscribed inside of an equilateral triangle ABC.

Figure 5.3 shows how the inscribed triangles are constructed within GeoGebra. Point D is placed on line AC. A circle is constructed with GeoGebra's compass tool, with center at C and going through D. The circle is moved to be re-centered on point A and point E is constructed where this circle intersects side AB of triangle ABC. The radius of the circle centered on point C and going through point D is the distance CD, so that when it is moved to point A it constrains the distance AE to be equal to CD. The same thing is done to construct point F. This establishes the dependency in the construction that AE=BF=CD. Triangle DEF is then constructed as a dynamically equilateral triangle.

In this example, we see how visualization (drawing) and conceptualization (proof) are so intermingled in dynamic geometry. By dragging the construction, you discover how to construct it—and you can then prove why that works. GeoGebra provides tools to explore, construct, and impose dependencies on the construction.

5.3 DEFINING CUSTOM TOOLS

The toolkit of GeoGebra reflects some of the refinements (reinterpretations) of Euclidean geometry in recent math pedagogy. For instance, it distinguishes as different kinds of objects: "lines" (infinite straight lines passing through two defining points), "segments" (finite line segments terminated at the two endpoints that define them) and "rays" (infinite lines starting at one endpoint and passing through a second defining point). Euclid called these all "straight lines." GeoGebra also provides a "compass" tool (used in Figure 5.3). This is based on the idea that Euclid used a straightedge and compass for his drawing and that one can fix the opening of a compass and draw circles with the same radius by locating the compass at different centers. However, Euclid does not do this in his proofs. After showing how to make equal-length line segments using a circle to construct an equilateral triangle in his first proposition, Euclid dedicates his second proposition to demonstrating how to copy a length from one line to another given point. Figure 5.4 (left) shows how to do this using GeoGebra, following Euclid's procedure. In this way, all of Euclid's constructions are built up from the basic principle that all radii of a circle are equal.

In Figure 5.4, the length of segment AB is copied to ray CD using the dozen steps of Euclid's Proposition 2 (detailed below). Then a custom tool is created to automate this process, much as the compass tool does. In addition, a custom tool is created to automate the construction of an equilateral triangle (Figure 5.4 upper right). The construction in Figure 5.3 is then recreated using the new custom tools: the base of the larger triangle is defined by two points, L and M, to which the new custom triangle tool adds point N. An arbitrary point O is next provided on LN as a vertex of the inner triangle. Using the new custom copy tool, the length of NO is copied onto LM, defining P, and the length of LP is copied onto MN, defining Q (Figure 5.4 lower right). Triangle OPQ, inscribed in LMN, is equilateral and can be dragged without losing its equilateral character.

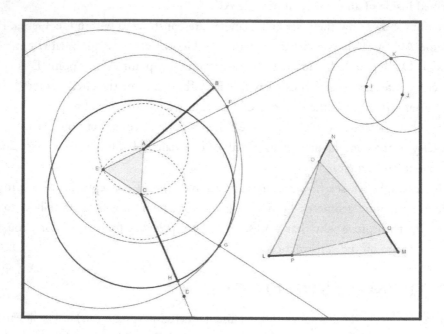

Figure 5.4: (Left) Copying a length, AB, from segment AB to segment CH on ray CD. (Upper right) Identifying the third vertex for an equilateral triangle IJK. (Lower right) Duplicating Figure 5.2 with the use of custom tools.

This illustrates how the tools of construction in dynamic geometry are intimately related to the procedures in Euclid's proofs. Once a valid construction procedure has been proven, one can define a tool to encompass that procedure, such as GeoGebra's compass tool for copying a line length in accordance with Proposition 2. Gradually, one can expand the construction toolkit with new custom tools—paralleling the way propositions build on one another systematically in Euclid's *Elements*. GeoGebra provides a toolkit of dozens of tools, which can be derived from straightedge and compass constructions in accordance with Euclid's propositions. Users can define their own versions of these or build further upon them. Once a student understands how a construction guarantees the relevant dependencies (such as that the length of CH is dependent on the length of AB), it is practical for the student to use a tool that conveniently automates that construction (copying a line segment).

Copying a segment length

Here is how segment AB was originally copied onto ray CD, using the procedure in Euclid's second proposition plus an extra circle to align the length along the ray.

The goal is to place at a given point along a given line a straight line equal to a given straight line.

Let C be the given point on ray CD, and AB the given straight line (Figure 5.4 left). Thus, it is required to place on ray CD starting at C a segment equal in length to segment AB. Let the equilateral triangle ACE be constructed on AC (using the construction procedure of Proposition 1). Let ray EA and ray EC be produced, extending out from the triangle. Let a circle centered on A and through B be produced, with point F at the intersection with ray EA. Again, let a circle centered on E and through F be produced, with point G at the intersection with ray EC. As Proposition 2 argues, EF=EG and EA=EC, so CG=AF; but AB=AF, so CG=AB and the length AB has been copied to point C. Now let a circle be produced with center C going through G and let point H be at the intersection of this circle and ray CD.

Then, CH=CG, so also CH=AB and the length AB had been copied to segment CH along ray CD.

5.4 DYNAMIC DRAGGING

Dynamic geometry differs from previous presentations of geometry in at least three significant features: dynamic dragging, dynamic construction, and dynamic dependencies.

The ability to drag points is the most immediately striking characteristic of dynamic geometry. Most academic research on dynamic geometry has focused on this feature. Most classroom usage of dynamic geometry also centers on this feature, providing students with pre-constructed dynamic diagrams and encouraging them to explore the diagrams by dragging points.

Previous media for diagrams have not allowed one to vary the figures except in imagination. Papyrus, clay tablets, parchment, books, pencil on paper and chalk-on-blackboard were not interactive media. The most one could do was to stare at the fixed diagram and imagine moving points or lines to vary the configuration. This meant that one rough graphical representation might have to illustrate infinite possible variations. For instance, a proof concerning equilateral triangles might apply to equilateral triangles of all sizes, rotated at all possible angles, while the illustrative diagram itself had a fixed size and inclination.

Dynamic dragging changes the nature of geometry. In Euclid, a point is a fixed location. In dynamic geometry, a point is at a location, but can always be dragged to an infinity of different locations, depending upon whether it is constrained or dependent. This creates three classes of points: those that are completely free to move, those constrained to stay on a line (segment, circle, etc.), and those dependent on an intersection and not able to be dragged directly (but moved in response to the movement of other geometric objects based on dependency relations). The ability to drag points dynamically has fundamental implications throughout the mathematical system of dynamic geometry. Dragging shows its relevance to construction in the importance of the "drag test." It affects the methods of proof by emphasizing the use of superposition and spatial transformations. Even the definitions of geometric objects have to be defined differently since, for instance, a scalene triangle can be dragged into appearing like an isosceles or equilateral triangle.

In the preceding example (Figure 5.1), for instance, it would have been hard to know important features of the diagram without being able to drag the vertices of the two triangles. Through dragging point A, one can easily and naturally discover that the two triangles remain equilateral and inscribed as the size and orientation of the larger triangle is varied over arbitrary ranges (but DF is not necessarily parallel to AB and D is not a midpoint of AC). Through dragging point D, one discovers as well that the inner triangle can remain equilateral and inscribed with point D anywhere along AC, including at the endpoints. One may also notice that the area of triangle DEF varies continuously from a minimum when point D is centered on side AC to an area equal to that of triangle ABC when point D is at an endpoint of AC. Significantly for the example, one may notice while dragging point D that AE=BF=CD remains true.

With fixed diagrams, it took a certain "professional vision" (Goodwin, 1994) of mathematicians to see important mathematical relationships in diagrams. Certain features of geometric configurations are visible even in fixed diagrams. For instance, it is visibly apparent in the drawing of ABC in Figure 5.3 that the circles centered on A and B of radius AB actually do intersect (at some point C). Whether this remains true for any configuration of A and B may be ascertained by staring at the diagram and imagining different locations for A and B. Dragging makes relationships easier to see—providing a way to train students to see like mathematicians.

> Dragging makes relationships easier to see—providing a way to train students to see like mathematicians.

Another traditional skill of mathematicians is to design a diagram to be effective for a given proof. For instance, Figure 5.1 illustrates a proposition: that an equilateral triangle can be inscribed in another equilateral triangle. However, it illustrates a special case, which might not generalize: the base AB is roughly horizontal and the point D is roughly at the midpoint of AC. Figure 5.2

may represent the general case better. It also makes more salient the fact that AE=BF=CD. An experienced mathematician might decide to use the later diagram. However, in dynamic geometry, one can start with either and then drag it into the other. The ability to drag offsets the need for the traditional skill of carefully designing illustrative diagrams. It makes it easy for students to drag a figure to explore what special cases exist and what relationships seem to persist in general as specifics change. It is no longer crucial to select a "representative" case since an arbitrary view can be dragged through whole ranges of possible variations.

Of course, it is possible that students will not drag a construction into every possible case or even that a given dynamic construction cannot be dragged into every case covered by a specific proposition. However, dragging can provide the mediated experience of apprenticeship in geometry that can lead to the ability to conduct what Husserl (1929/1960) called "eidetic variation" in one's imagination to reveal constants under change. Having engaged in dynamic-geometry experiences of variation through dragging, students may subsequently internalize this visualization into variation in their imagination.

Dragging also gives students a hands-on, visceral sense of the constraints and characteristics of a geometric diagram. It enhances the bodily involvement of the interaction between person and diagram in which "creative discovery" can take place (Merleau-Ponty, 1955). Perhaps this will be even further heightened when tablet computers fill the role that clay tablets originally played. Exploration through dragging is intertwined with the possibilities of construction. As a student learns to initiate various kinds of constructions, she starts to see new possibilities for dragging, for seeing constraints and patterns and possibilities. As her body is extended by the computer interface into the digital world, she gains a sense of how to move within that world, to live and perceive in a dynamic-geometry world (Merleau-Ponty, 1961/1964). Then, as the student starts to look at the dynamic environment through the eyes of a designer of structural dependencies, she can see constraining relationships at work, as well as interesting potential transformations of them. Such embodied, skilled vision produces targets or hunches (informal conjectures) to explore through purposeful dragging.

5.5 DYNAMIC CONSTRUCTION

Previous media for diagrams not only limited variation, they required the diagrams to be completely constructed prior to the presentation of the proof. Thus, where Euclid's Proposition 2 begins in the English translation, "Let A be the given point" (Euclid, 300 BCE/2002, p. 3), this is actually stated in the original Greek in the perfect imperative (as already having been done): "Let the point A have been taken" (Netz, 1999, p. 25). The proof then proceeds to point to the already existing diagram and to describe the relationships within it. The text often relies on the pre-existence of the diagram for its sense. As an example, after Euclid specifies line AB in Proposition 1, he says, "With center A and distance AB let the circle BCD be described" (Euclid, 300 BCE/2002, p. 3). Point B has been defined as an endpoint of line AB and point D is simply an unspecified point anywhere on the new circle. But point C cannot be defined in the text until another circle is described, which intersects the first circle at point C, thereby specifying point C. It is only because the whole diagram already exists and includes point C that the text of the proof can use the label C as part of the designation of the first circle.

As Netz (1999) documents with numerous examples, Euclid's texts often rely upon the pre-existing diagrams for their sense. On the other hand, the diagrams rely on the texts for their interpretation. Text and diagram are mutually determinative, with the labels of points relating the two. Dynamic geometry overcomes the necessity of completing one before the other. The diagram can be constructed in parallel with the unfolding of the textual argument—at least in a live presentation. (In this printed document, we are limited to viewing static screenshots interspersed in the text.)

Livingston (1999) analyzes in detail the significant difference between how a conjecture is explored and how its proof is presented. One must first discover an interesting relationship and then piece together an argument. This usually proceeds through exploration, with its trials, deadends, and backtracking. The final presentation is then orchestrated as a logical deduction, straight from givens to conclusion with the minimum necessary steps. The conclusion is presented as though it necessarily always existed—rather like the refined diagram that pre-existed the proof.

The past perfect tense has always characterized mathematics. Even as new objects were created in history—conics, irrational numbers, logarithms, infinitesimals, imaginary numbers, hyper-spheres—they were always taken as having always already existed. They were not treated as newly *created* human artifacts, designed for their interesting properties, but as *discovered* ideal objects in an otherworldly realm of mathematical objects (Lakoff & Núñez, 2000). Whether or not this view motivated Plato's theory of Forms, subsequent mathematics generally adopted a Neo-Platonic attitude, obscuring the important role of exploration and invention in the practice of mathematics.

Dynamic geometry can reverse this obfuscation. Students can now construct diagrams as an integral part of their exploration of geometric relationships. Using the construction tools of dynamic geometry, students can explore mathematical conjectures through trial constructions. The bureaucratic format that Euclidean proofs have evolved into can be replaced with active exploration, which does not assume the diagram is complete beforehand, treats mathematical objects as human artifacts designed to have interesting features, leads to moments of *aporia* and breakthroughs of insight as deduction unfolds as a creative form of discovery.

The ability to construct dynamic diagrams that present intriguing puzzles—which support exploring conjectures and which illustrate proofs—is itself a subtle skill, a skill that must be learned through instruction, apprenticeship and practice. This skill can be developed as part of the process of learning geometry content. For instance, the geometric objects like points, lines, circles and triangles are also graphical objects in dynamic-geometry environments; students can learn the characteristics of the objects by constructing and dragging the graphics. In fact, much of Euclid's *Elements* can be read as instruction in construction:

- Proposition 1, how to construct an equilateral triangle;

- Proposition 2, how to copy a line segment of a given length to another position;

- Proposition 3, to measure off the length of a shorter segment along a longer one;

- Proposition 9, to bisect an angle;

- Proposition 10, to bisect a line segment;

- Proposition 11, to construct a perpendicular to a line at a point on it;

- Proposition 12, to construct a perpendicular to a line from a point not on it; etc.

The art of construction has always been central to geometry, although it has not always been stressed as a creative skill.

5.6   DYNAMIC DEPENDENCIES

The key to constructing for exploration is the construction of dependencies. This is another potential implicit in Euclid, but not adequately recognized, acknowledged, or researched.

As we have seen, the construction in Proposition 1 demonstrates how to build in the dependency that defines an equilateral triangle: that its three sides must be of equal length. Given an initial side AB, Euclid adds circles centered on points A and B, each of radius AB. He then labels an intersection of the two circles as point C, the third vertex of the constructed equilateral triangle, ABC. The lengths of the new sides AC and BC are dependent upon the length of side AB because they are radii of circles of which AB is a radius—and all radii of a given circle are the same length by definition of a circle. In a fixed drawing, we might just say that AC and BC have been constructed to be the same numeric length as AB. However, in a dynamic construction, one can drag point A or point B and change the length of AB. If the dependency has been properly constructed, then point C will move in response to the movement of point A or point B precisely the right way to maintain the equality of all three sides. The lengths of AC and BC are dependent upon the length of AB—however that may change under dragging—and not just on its current numeric value.

This role of dragging in dynamic geometry leads to the important "drag test." When someone constructs part of a drawing incorporating a constraint, they should then drag the involved parts of the drawing to make sure that the intended constraint is maintained. For instance, in constructing the equilateral triangle, they may find out that point C fails to stay on both circles when point A or B is dragged, thus revealing a fault in the construction. The drag test unites dragging, construction and dependencies by putting dragging at the service of checking a construction to make sure that the intended dependencies are maintained dynamically.

The dynamic diagram in Figure 5.1 was constructed in such a way that it remained a diagram of two inscribed equilateral triangles no matter how any of its points were dragged. The dependencies included that AB=AC=BC; that points D, E, and F remain on segments AC, AB, and BC, respectively; as well as that AE=BF=CD. The defined dependencies ensure that the two triangles remain inscribed and both equilateral under any change in size or rotation of either triangle or the dragging of any point. Note that there is no direct specification that DE=DF=EF, although the fact that the interior triangle remains equilateral is an indirect dependency of the construction

It is possible to have a computer whiteboard similar to Sutherland's (1963) original Sketch-Pad in which lines and points can be drawn as movable objects. One can draw an equilateral triangle on such a whiteboard by placing three lines of equal length meeting at their endpoints. However, if one then drags a vertex, the triangle falls apart entirely, loses its equilateral characteristic, or fails to re-size.

A dynamic-geometry environment must implement computational mechanisms behind the scenes to both maintain the desired dependencies and at the same time to allow permitted manipulations. In fact, the first thing the environment does is to keep track of:

- which objects are independent and can be dragged freely (like A and B);

- which are constrained and can only be dragged in limited ways (like D); and

- which are dependent, cannot be dragged directly at all, but just move in response to the other points on which they are dependent (like C, E, and F).

It requires very special software to support dynamic geometry. The dynamic-geometry applications we have today—such as Geometer's Sketchpad, Cabri, or GeoGebra—were carefully designed to maintain arbitrarily complex geometric dependencies while making the user experience seem extremely natural. This is the hidden power of dynamic geometry. Once one gets used to the paradigm of dynamic geometry and thinks in terms of constructing dependencies, everything automatically works the way that one would expect it to. The user does not have to worry about the hidden software mechanisms.

Dependencies lie at the heart of Euclid's geometry, but they have been largely buried in the traditional understanding of geometry. This is a philosophic issue. Heidegger might say that the being of the geometric objects was concealed through the Greek and then the Roman and then the German and then the English and then the American way of caring for and speaking about the objects and their dependencies.

The traditional understanding of geometry that has been passed down from the Greeks through its subsequent translations, reinterpretations, and refinements over the centuries confuses the causality of dependency and proof. Consider the diagram of inscribed equilateral triangles (Figure 5.2). One could start with equilateral triangle ABC in the completed diagram and specify that AE=BF=CD. Then one could prove that triangle DEF must be equilateral through a logical deduction, perhaps including an argument about the three small triangles outside of DEF being congruent. This would establish the truth of the equilateral nature of DEF. That is the traditional perspective. Euclid's proofs are commonly conceived of as such discoveries of existing truths in the realm of Platonic ideas. Euclid's *Elements* are now read as building up an axiomatic system for proving these truths.

However, this reverses the causality. For, if we have constructed DEF by using the constraint that AE=BF=CD, then we already know that we imposed this constraint in order to construct an inscribed triangle that would be equilateral. It is not a matter of discovering some mysterious otherworldly truth; it is a matter of having intentionally built in the character of equal side lengths into our construction of DEF. It is not a matter of a formal logical deduction, which unfolds with necessary truth. The drawing of equal circles at A, B, and C is not originally a means for proving that the sides of an equilateral triangle have "always already been" equal; the circles are *part of the construction of the dependency* that itself ensures that the sides will be and will remain equal.

The truth of the proof was built in by the construction. It was hard to see this the way that geometry has been conceptualized throughout history, but easy to see in dynamic geometry if one focuses on the construction of the dependencies as an active, creative, inquiry process. We built in the dependency as we constructed the diagram: that is why the triangles are equilateral! Taking the diagram as already given before the proof is presented, combined with the traditional assumptions about the nature of geometric objects as divorced from human activity, hides what has transpired. Experience with dynamic geometry—including dragging, constructing, and designing dependencies—exposes the *creation* of objects, diagrams and relationships by people.

> Few research publications discuss the role of dependencies in dynamic geometry… especially the relationship of dependencies to proof. This is a symptom of the extent to which the nature of geometry has been obscured.

Shockingly, the mathematics and education literature on dynamic math has scarcely mentioned this central role of designed dependencies—and of the ability to construct dependencies in dynamic geometry. Although dependencies lie at the heart of proof and although dynamic-geometry software is explicitly built on the maintenance of dependencies, very few research publications discuss the role of dependencies in dynamic geometry, none in depth. In particular, they do not discuss the relationship of dependencies to proof. This is a symptom of the extent to which the nature of geometry has been obscured.

In a typical geometry proof, recognition of the central underlying dependency is the key potential insight into why the proof works—the door to the "aha moment." The diagram illustrates some relationship not because of a mysterious otherworldly truth, but because the diagram was constructed with dependencies that built in that relationship. If students learn to think in terms of dependencies, to construct diagrams around dependencies and to search for dependencies, then geometry might be a lot more exciting and meaningful. The students might consider themselves more successful as mathematical thinkers.

While most classroom use of dynamic geometry today merely uses it as a visualization tool, to allow students to drag existing diagrams around, the technology has a greater power: to empower students to construct their own diagrams, to build their own dependencies into the objects and even to fashion their own dynamic construction tools. Then they can read Euclid's *Elements* as a guide to designing and constructing interesting objects and tools, rather than as an old-fashioned compendium of irrelevant truths to be memorized. Geometry can become an exciting design challenge, in which one creates innovative mathematical objects and imposes interesting dependencies through thoughtful construction.

CHAPTER 6

Collaboration: Group Geometry

Chapter Summary

The collaborative usage of dynamic geometry by teams of students can make more visible its human-centered nature. To support collaboration, the software must be adapted, raising a number of issues in the design of a multi-user environment. The GeoGebra dynamic-mathematics software was incorporated into the VMT collaboration environment. The process of turning single-user GeoGebra into a collaborative version is described here and a number of multi-user design issues are discussed. The chapter reviews the major technical issues that were addressed and discusses the benefits for collaborative learning of integrating the GeoGebra software into the VMT environment.[2]

6.1 SUPPORTING COLLABORATIVE DISCOURSE AND ACTION

The effort to support collaborative dynamic geometry among students who may not be co-located involved embedding a dynamic-geometry software system within an online collaboration environment. The Virtual Math Teams (VMT) system—including the history of its development—has already been described in (Stahl, 2009). The VMT system includes a Lobby for users to create chat rooms, to invite other people to them and to browse through existing rooms by project community, math subject, activity topic and student team (see Figure 6.1). It supports learning by individuals, small groups and communities (e.g., the students in a course) with the incorporation of text-chat, shared-whiteboard, wiki-sharing, and web-browsing media, which can be configured in tabs when chat rooms are created (see Figure 6.2). Thus, it is designed to support collaborative learning conceived as operating through processes, practices and resources that traverse levels of analysis, as will be discussed in Chapter 8.

Research on early VMT usage suggested that the addition of a dynamic-mathematics system would significantly enhance the ability of the VMT software to support collaborative mathematical discourse in virtual math teams. GeoGebra was selected because its source code was available as open source and it had an extensive API (application programmer's interface). The first task was to embed the GeoGebra application in a VMT chat-room tab (see Figure 6.3). Because both VMT and GeoGebra are programmed in Java, this was conceptually straightforward. Math Forum programmers developed a proof-of-concept integration in 2009 and 2010. In 2011 and 2012, the

---

[2]   Anthony Mantoan contributed to an earlier draft of this chapter

integration was re-implemented, using the GeoGebra API. Use of the API kept most of the new software separated from the GeoGebra source code so that frequent updates of GeoGebra could be incorporated easily, allowing the VMT system to take advantage of on-going open-source development of GeoGebra. This development work was done in coordination with the GeoGebra lead developers, so that they extended the API to meet the needs of VMT. In the longer term, this will facilitate the GeoGebra developer community in developing its own multi-user version, possibly for use on tablets and mobile devices.

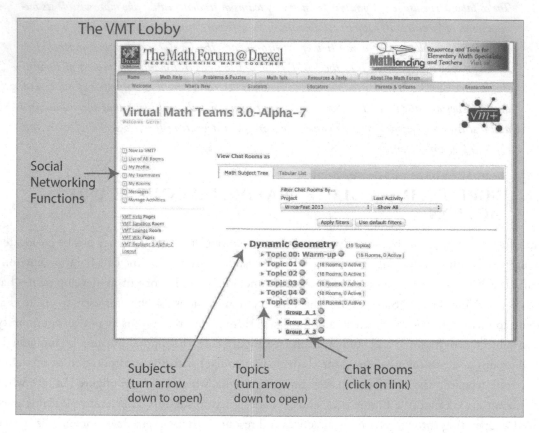

Figure 6.1: The VMT Lobby interface.

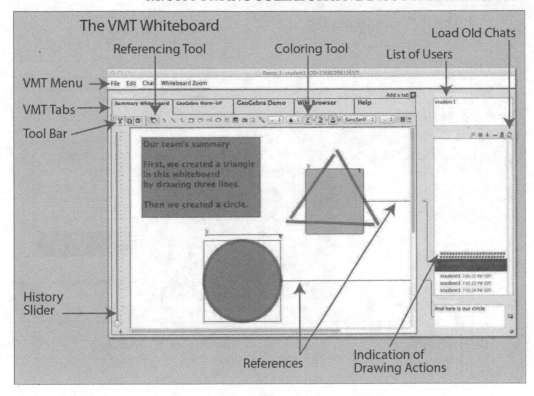

Figure 6.2: A VMT chat room with a shared whiteboard tab.

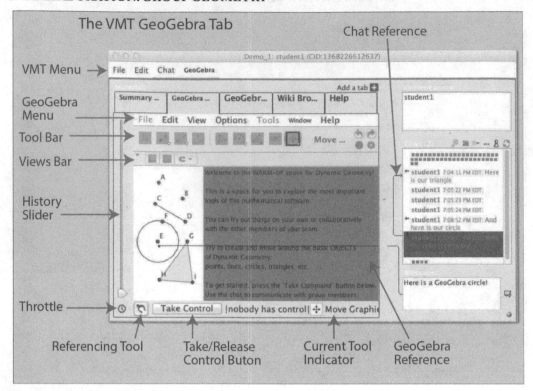

Figure 6.3: A VMT chat room with a GeoGebra tab.

Although embedding GeoGebra in a VMT tab was relatively easy, the real problem was much deeper. GeoGebra was designed from the ground up to be used by a single user on a single computer. For online collaboration, we wanted multiple users to be able to view the same figure and to observe each other dragging its points and constructing new objects. We wanted this to happen in real time and to appear natural so people could experience co-presence at the figure while they chatted about it. In order to support what were described in Chapter 5 as the core dimensions of dynamic geometry—dynamic dragging, dynamic construction, and dynamic dependencies—we needed to support co-presence, intersubjective shared understanding, and group cognition, as will be discussed in Chapter 8.

The first technical hurdle was to design a suitable software architecture for multi-user engagement with GeoGebra. VMT implements a standard client-server model, where software clients on the computers of students send messages to the VMT server, which then distributes the messages to all the clients (computers of students in the same chat room). No client—not even the one that sent the message—takes any action until it gets the message from the server.

This presented an immediate problem for embedding GeoGebra, which is strictly single user. In contrast to the client-server model of VMT, each instance of GeoGebra on each client builds and maintains its own independent dynamic-geometry construction, which is not dependent on the server. However, the construction on each client must be kept in sync with the other clients, so that every student in the same chat room sees the same thing and can discuss it and manipulate it. Furthermore, we want all action to appear seamlessly instantaneous to a user dragging an object, so we cannot make GeoGebra wait until a message goes to and comes back from the server before the action is shown on the screen of the student who is taking the action.

This forced us to implement multi-user GeoGebra essentially as a peer-to-peer architecture, using the VMT server as the communication channel between the clients. When a user takes some action on a GeoGebra tab, the GeoGebra action is implemented in that client's GeoGebra tab. At the same time, the VMT client sends a message to the server with a GeoGebra command equivalent to the action that took place. The VMT server sends the action to all clients (including the initiator). The initiator must ignore the return message from the server since it has already performed the action. The other clients then execute the command, which results in updating their construction so that it matches the sender's. In this way, all the clients are kept in sync. Because the action of the original sender is performed immediately without waiting for the message to go to the server and then come back, the sender's action appears immediately and seamlessly. As long as the delay between one student taking an action and the other students seeing the results is a fraction of a second, the illusion of simultaneity and co-presence is maintained for the whole team.

This solution allowed the display of GeoGebra figures and actions to be handled primarily by the GeoGebra software on the student computers, and the communication of actions to be handled by the VMT software on the central server computer, which also communicated the chat and changes in other VMT chat-room tabs. On the one hand, this kept the two software modules relatively independent to facilitate software upgrades and maintenance. On the other hand, the separation complicated the programming of features that had to span the two areas. For instance, there are VMT features like awareness messages, activity logging, the history slider, and the pointing tool, which affect both the GeoGebra tab and the VMT wrapper. In addition, the requirement of maintaining speedy communication among the clients introduced mechanisms that spanned the two independent program code bases.

6.2   SUPPORTING DYNAMIC DRAGGING AND CO-PRESENCE

To support the fluid use of dynamic dragging and the observation of points and other geometric objects being smoothly dragged, the software system has to respond quickly to user actions and has to display the results of actions without noticeable or disruptive lags. As one drags a point in GeoGebra, a number of messages are sent describing its new position many times a second. This allows the drag to be duplicated on other clients quite accurately. At first, we had tried just broadcasting the original start position of an object and then its final position after a drag. Unfortunately, that gave too little sense of co-presence and too little information about how the object was dragged to clients observing another client's actions.

However, the approach of broadcasting hundreds of intermediate locations of a dragged point every second created too much messaging traffic across the Internet. Imagine a student in Singapore dragging a 10-sided polygon with interior line segments. Each point and line, along with all the dependencies in the figure would have to have its description and location information broadcast to Philadelphia and then that information would all have to be broadcast back to each of the other students' computers. Even if the school in Singapore had considerable Internet bandwidth and the Math Forum server were powerful, this volume of update traffic would soon result in response delays that would interfere with effective collaboration. Even chat messages would be delayed, so that students would not know if others were paying attention.

In addition, all of the events that are broadcast are also saved as part of the history of the chat room. When a student enters a room in which some activity has already taken place, the history has to be loaded and all of the GeoGebra construction and display mechanisms have to process and replay that history in order to display its end state to the student. The same thing takes place when a researcher or anyone else opens the VMT Replayer for that room. This results in long delays in opening an existing room or viewing it in the Replayer.

The first thing we did to address this was to make sure to only send necessary updates. GeoGebra has independent objects and dependent objects. The position and other characteristics of dependent objects can be calculated based on the independent objects. Therefore, we only send out updates for independent objects, and let each client recalculate the dependent ones, essentially shifting much (and often most) of the work of updating to the client's local machine. For instance, if a 10-sided polygon is regular (equilateral), then 8 of its vertices and all of its sides are dependent upon two vertices. We can send the location of the two points and have the client build the whole polygon from them.

The next thing we did was to implement "update throttling" in our clients. By watching the mouse status the software can determine when updates are due to objects being dragged. In that case, it skips a certain number of updates, only broadcasting periodically. It also watches the mouse for a "button release" event, so it can be sure to always broadcast the final position of the objects. However, GeoGebra sends out updates for every single object that is being moved. So we could not simply skip a fixed number of updates, since that would result in certain objects in a construction being updated during a drag event, and others not being updated. The effect is that the construction is distorted until the user releases the mouse button, and the final update is sent out to put everything in its final place. To solve that problem, the VMT software gets a list of selected independent objects from the GeoGebra software. It skips a number of updates for the entire group of objects, and then sends out one combined update for the whole selection.

A challenge here is finding the right number of updates to skip. If too few are skipped, the system will still become bogged down. If too many are skipped, the movements of objects will look choppy and other users may not be able to tell what the mover did. We have been experimenting with a variety of numbers for this to try to find the right balance. One consideration is that the right balance for one task may not be the right balance for a different task. We have set the default threshold for 10, so that only about one intermediate position in 10 is broadcast. While dragging is not completely smooth at this setting, it provides a good sense of the drag. Since in most rooms the majority of actions are dragging, this setting reduces the number of broadcasts by almost 90%.

In addition, we have provided a threshold button so that users can adjust the setting. If they want to see more accurate dragging, they can decrease the number skipped. If they are concerned about delays when dragging complex figures, they can increase it. Along with several other measures to speed up display of the GeoGebra tab, loading of used rooms, scrolling of history and display of the Replayer, this threshold mechanism has solved the major network-load problem and start-up delays.

Since GeoGebra maintains relationships between objects in the construction, it must recalculate the construction when changes are made. For complex constructions, these calculations can be time consuming, even for a modern computer. The normal way VMT reloads chat rooms is to replay every event that occurred, recreating the whole history. We found that rooms that had been used extensively—say, for two hours or so—and had multiple GeoGebra tabs could take many minutes to load. This was mostly due to GeoGebra having to recalculate all those historical changes to the construction. Our solution here is to save snapshots of the construction every time a user finishes a turn in control of constructing in the GeoGebra tab. Now, when the room is loaded, each event is loaded into the history, but it is not replayed in GeoGebra. When all the events have been loaded the snapshot is selected from the last "Release Control" event, and that is loaded in the GeoGebra tab. That cuts the load times for extensively used rooms to less than a minute.

Similar mechanisms were introduced in the history slider and the Replayer. In addition, for the history slider and the Replayer, a threshold tool is provided. It allows the user to move through the history at different speeds, either in the history slider of the GeoGebra tab or in the Replayer. For quick browsing the user can set the threshold to "minimum," for a detailed study to "complete," or somewhere in between.

The controls for some of these mechanisms are shown in the accompanying figures. In Figure 6.4, you can see the "Take Control" button. This gives one user the ability to engage in construction in the GeoGebra tab. All users who are in the same chat room with the same GeoGebra tab open will be able to see the GeoGebra actions taken by this user. A user who is not in control of construction in the tab can scroll back through the history of GeoGebra actions in that tab—notice the tick marks along the left of the tab lining the history scrollbar. Also, notice in the chat pane the presence of small colored squares. These each signal a GeoGebra action; they are color coded to correspond with the user whose chat postings are the same color.

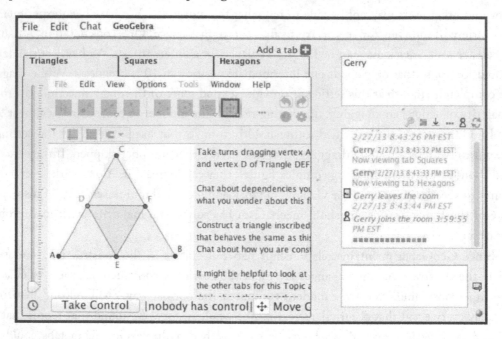

Figure 6.4: A VMT chat room with the "Take Control" button, the history slider, and action squares.

In Figure 6.5, the "Take Control" button has been pressed and the user sees the message "you have control"; if someone else had control, then that user's login name would be shown. To the right is an indication of which construction tool is currently active in the tab. Notice that the chat includes messages when users change the tab they are displaying. In this way, everyone in a team—i.e., in the same chat room—can tell where their team members are looking, who currently has control of the construction and what construction tool is active. They will be able to see any change to the construction or dragging of objects practically as they are done. They can also adjust the "Event Throttle" to avoid annoying delays in display updates and they can "Share Your View" to adjust everyone in the team to the same level of zoom and focus. Through these tools, displays and mechanisms, a sense of co-presence at a shared geometric figure can be created and maintained.

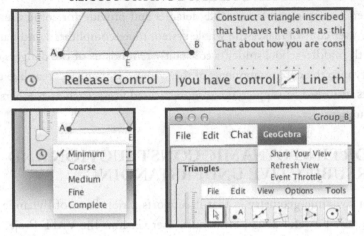

Figure 6.5: The "Release Control" button, the history threshold menu, and the "Event Throttle."

The "Share Your View" option was introduced because users would get confused when they did not see the same thing on their screen as other users in the room. This was because GeoGebra does not distribute user actions that are not related to the construction, but are just viewing adjustments. A user can zoom in or out, scroll around the view, or turn the axis and grid on or off without affecting what other users see. Consequently, one user may be constructing or dragging an object in an area that is off the screen for another user. To help with this we implemented a "Share Your View" menu option. Even if a user does not have control, they can select this option to "push" their view settings out to the other users' clients. Currently, this only matches up the zoom level and the view center point, but that is usually enough to avoid misalignments of view, which cause some users to not see important objects that others see and chat about.

A final tool for supporting co-presence is the VMT pointing tool. That was always part of VMT, even before GeoGebra was introduced. This tool allowed a user to reference from a chat posting to an object or area in the shared whiteboard. When one typed a chat message, one could select an object in the whiteboard or a rectangular area in the whiteboard. Then, when the message was posted, everyone could see an arrow going from the posting to the whiteboard object or area. This supported deixis, which is considered important for co-attending to an object, a critical component of co-presence (see Chapter 8).

There are many ways in which we have tried to foster awareness of what people are doing in a VMT chat room with GeoGebra tabs. Some of these mechanisms already existed in VMT in the past, others have been added. Many have been changed to seem more natural or to avoid interfering with the main interactions. It is hard to design awareness features so that they work well in a wide range of different use cases yet do not become invasive under other scenarios. Features that are effective for a dyad working on a simple problem in one tab may not work well for a larger group of collaborators engaged in a complex task involving jumping around between different kinds of tabs. We have tried to implement reasonable defaults and provide for some user control as well. Of course, adding user control makes the whole system more complicated and harder to learn and to use. Testing with middle-school students constantly reminds us of the dangers of designing too much functionality into the core components of the system, although in areas like the Replayer and assessment reports, we need to support more sophisticated users, such as teachers, system administrators and researchers.

6.3   SUPPORTING DYNAMIC CONSTRUCTION AND INTERSUBJECTIVE UNDERSTANDING

A major aspect of dynamic geometry is that it supports a rich form of dynamic construction by users. This area required careful design for a multi-user version. The VMT Project is the first sustained effort to produce a truly collaborative form of dynamic geometry. Although it has not been widely publicized, there were fleeting attempts by the creators of Geometer's Sketchpad, Cinderella, and GeoGebra to make their products multi-user (personal communications, July 2012). However, none of these efforts reached the point of actually having users try out the collaboration. This is not surprising, given the complex issues that arise. There have also been attempts to skirt the issues by embedding single-user systems inside of learning management environments like Blackboard, Elluminate, or Moodle; these were screen-sharing approaches, which turned out to be awkward at best.

> The VMT Project is the first sustained effort to produce a truly collaborative form of dynamic geometry.

A central problem with having multiple users working on a construction is to make sure that two clients do not change the same part of the construction at the same time. For example, if one user is creating points for a polygon and then another user moves one of the points or uses it to construct a different object, the intended construction is destroyed. GeoGebra assigns labels to new points in alphabetical order. If two users simultaneously create Point C, then there is a conflict. This can easily happen because two clients can each create a new point C before either receives notification of the other one. Suppose that two points already exist and one user defines a line with them while another defines a circle. Then the line and circle will be dependent upon each other in a way that no one intended. Aside from users stepping on each other's toes, GeoGebra can become confused and end up in an error state if multiple users are adding to or deleting from the construction at the same time.

To prevent such conflicts, we implemented a "Take Control" button. Only one user can take control at a time, and for all the other users, all creation tools in GeoGebra are disabled. While this might seem to restrict users too much, given that we want them to engage in construction, it actually has a positive effect on collaboration. It prevents people from going off on their own and ignoring the work of others. It forces them to communicate about taking turns. This leads to the group paying attention to one person's construction activities at a time. Of course, everyone can engage in chat, asking why the person in control is doing certain things, make suggestions or point out interesting things that occur. This promotes intersubjective shared understanding (see Chapter 8), because the group is acting as a single agent.

One thing that a user can do when someone else has control of construction is to review past actions to recall what the group did in the recent past, other things they tried and how they got to where they are now. This is supported by the history slider (shown in Figure 6.4). The history slider was a useful function in the shared whiteboard of the original VMT system and we wanted to extend it to GeoGebra tabs. However, maintaining the history for each GeoGebra instance requires some care. Since objects in GeoGebra have relationships and a history that is maintained separately in each client, a client cannot accept changes to the current construction from other clients, while browsing through the history. The latest changes would not correspond to the historical state of the construction being displayed. Our solution here is to simply buffer updates until the user returns to the current state. Then all the buffered events are processed in the order they were received.

In order to support dynamic construction by a team, we implemented the control mechanism along with awareness displays indicating who has construction control in a given tab, what tool they are using and who else is viewing that tab. We also implemented a history slider to allow users to browse past actions in the team construction without interfering with the current construction.

6.4 SUPPORTING DYNAMIC DEPENDENCIES AND GROUP COGNITION

According to Chapter 5, a major goal of having students experience dynamic geometry is for them to gain an understanding of dynamic dependencies. Dynamic dragging can be used to provide a visual acquaintance with behaviors resulting from hidden dependencies. Following that, dynamic construction should incorporate into geometric figures specific dependencies among their elements. An understanding of dependencies in geometry can provide a basis for deep understanding of important relationships, enabling students to explain reasons for their noticings and even proofs for their conjectures.

One way to guide students to insightful experiences of dynamic dependencies is to provide them with problems in which one can see relationships that are maintained during variation through dragging and in which success in constructing successful solutions is achieved through strategic building in of dynamic dependencies. This can be approached through providing a set of individually interesting problems.

Perhaps a more effective approach—and this hypothesis is still being tested in schools— would be to provide a systematic curriculum. Here, one activity in dynamic geometry would build on the previous ones, much like Euclid's propositions relied for their proofs on earlier propositions, often in strategic sequences. Furthermore, the activities and accompanying resources (images, sample constructions, instructions, background materials) would be systematically designed to empha-size and make visible and accessible the dynamic dependencies involved. In a collaborative setting, groups of students would have a scaffolded opportunity to discuss the dependencies involved and to reflect on the role of these dependencies in the solution of problems, in the formulation of explanations and as a basis for understanding generalizable principles. The following chapters will explore this approach in various ways.

One way of supporting the use of a systematic curriculum of dynamic-geometry activities is to provide mechanisms for seeding chat rooms with resources to guide the students. Different groups of students will enact these resources in diverse ways, pursuing a variety of interpretations of the "problem" and "goal," as well as adapting experiences from prior sessions in distinctive ways. Our curriculum (see Chapter 10) consists of a series of topics, each presented in its own chat room. For instance, a student group named "Group_3" would have their own chat room for each topic in their curriculum. Each room might have several GeoGebra tabs. When the students meet in a room, they will see the several tabs already containing some materials for the topic. There might be textual instructions; there might be geometric figures to drag; or there might be images of figures to construct.

The VMT environment includes tools for teachers or curriculum developers to set up rooms with resources in GeoGebra tabs. In Figure 6.6, the interface for "Create New Room" has been filled out to create nine chat rooms for nine groups. The rooms will be named "Group_1" to "Group_9." They will all be part of the "WinterFest 2013" project, for topic "Topic 05" in the "Dy-namic Geometry" subject. Three GeoGebra tabs will be in each room, along with the standard chat pane. GeoGebra files containing constructions have been specified to be pre-loaded into each tab.

Another support for dependencies is custom tools. When a student group comes to an un-derstanding of a dynamic dependency that they want to be able to use easily in the future, they can create a custom tool that embodies that dynamic dependency. For instance, once a group under-stands how to construct an equilateral triangle where the side lengths are dynamically dependent upon the length of the first side, then they can save this construction as a custom tool and add that tool to the tool bar. Similarly, when they understand how to construct a line perpendicular to another line and passing through a given point, they can create a custom tool for quickly generating perpendiculars. Some of these tools already exist among GeoGebra's hundred tools. However, by creating a custom tool, a group learns how the tool works and what dependencies the tool enforces. In addition, the process of creating a custom tool collaboratively and testing it out can enrich the group's understanding of design decisions made in the details of the creation. There are many func-tions for which no tool exists in GeoGebra. For example, there is no tool for a simple function like copying an angle so that the new angle is dependent on the original dynamically. There are also no tools for creating the various centers of a triangle, like an incenter.

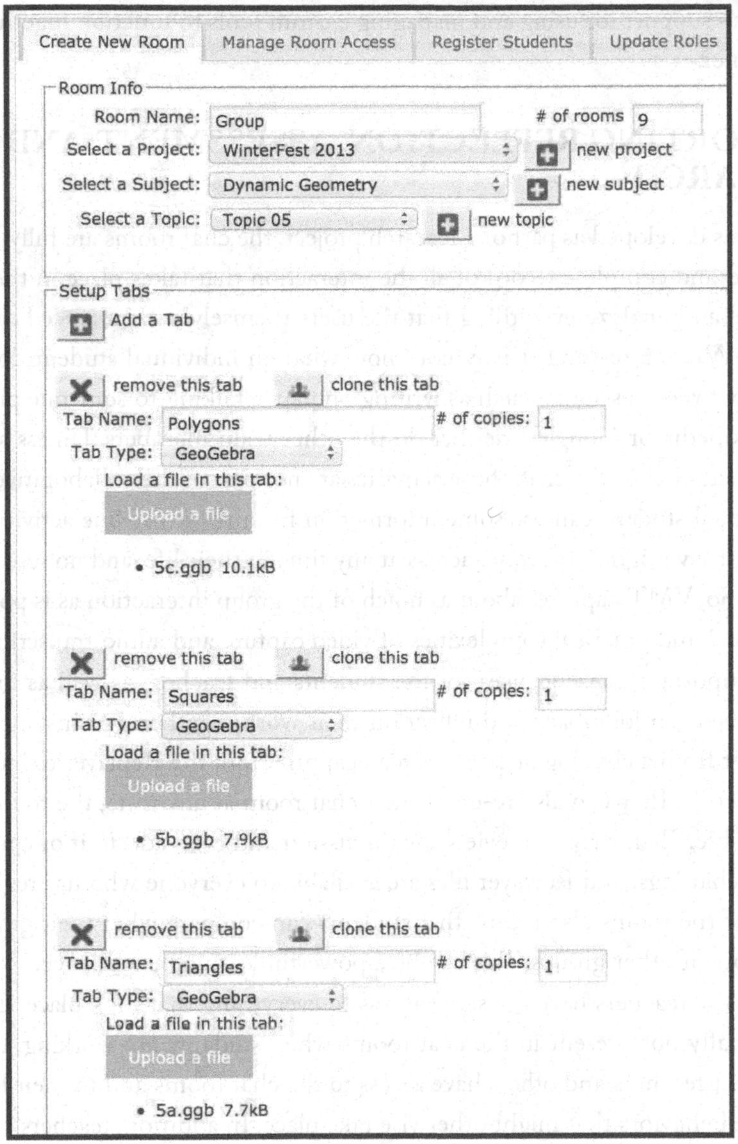

Figure 6.6: Interface for creating rooms with loaded figures in tabs.

While GeoGebra already supports custom tools, there were issues to be worked out for implementing custom tools in a collaborative online environment. The standard single-user GeoGebra saves a user's custom tools on the local hard disk. That means that a user who works on different computers (e.g., in a school computer lab) has to save files with the custom tools and transport the files around to retain use of the custom tools. In a group context, we wanted the whole group to have access to a custom tool that any one person created. In fact, that was necessary in order to have constructions that use the custom tool be properly displayed in everyone's client. So we had to adjust GeoGebra's support for using and managing custom tools to function together in a workable and natural manner.

6.5   SUPPORTING REFLECTION, ASSESSMENT, AND RESEARCH

Because VMT was developed as part of a research project, the chat rooms are fully instrumented to capture a detailed and complete record of all the interaction that takes place in them and to allow researchers to see and analyze everything that the users themselves experienced of the interaction with each other. While a researcher may not know what an individual student does off the computer during or between sessions—such as writing on paper, talking to someone physically present or browsing Wikipedia or Google—neither do the other team members. Unless someone reports on their off-line activities in the chat, those activities are not part of the collaborative interaction. Of course, an individual student can use some information from those off-line activities, but they can also use anything they might have come across at any time in their life, and no researcher can know about all of that. So, VMT captures about as much of the group interaction as is possible—without the methodological and practical complexities of video capture and audio transcription.

This has important consequences for the students and teachers as well as for researchers. It means that students can look back and reflect on their work together. For instance, a student can capture an excerpt from a chat log or even a screen capture from the Replayer to include in a report on their group's work. They can also re-enter their chat room at any time; the rooms are persistent and remain available. Then they can review the discussion and even add to it or continue the work. The chat rooms, chat logs, and Replayer files are available to everyone who has registered in VMT. The availability of the rooms also means that students can compare what their group did with results and behaviors of other groups. This can be a powerful learning experience.

Of course, the teachers have the same access to everything that took place. Even though the teachers are typically not present in the chat rooms when students are working, the fact that the students know that teachers and others have access to the chat rooms and to their logs may temper some undesirable behaviors that might otherwise take place. In addition, teachers can keep track of how much each student participated in sessions and gather a sense of how the class did on different topics. They can use these views to perform formative assessments. This can lead to discussions that are more effective, if the students are part of a face-to-face classroom. The teacher can decide what aspects of the curriculum need more discussion and perhaps which students can present accomplishments—either successes or failures—that warrant class discussion (Stein et al., 2008). Teacher reviews of how the sessions went can also lead to revisions of the curriculum.

Building an environment for collaborative dynamic geometry includes designing tools for reviewing and analyzing what took place in group sessions. These display and visualization tools can serve students, teachers, and researchers. We have some displays that have been part of VMT for years and others that have been recently developed. Clearly, a lot more are possible; learning analytics and visualizations are continuously under development and testing. Experienced math teachers—who are taking professional development courses as part of the project—are conducting student assessments using the data saved in the VMT system and the tools and displays available.

Because the multi-user system is a client-server system, all activity by people anywhere in the world using the system passes through the central server computer. All the interaction messages that are passed around the clients are stored in the server. That allows researchers access to all of the history. The down side of this is that it is hard to get a handle on who has done what and where the interesting data lies. We are currently tying to compile this information automatically in ways that can guide research. Our means of displaying and reporting what has taken place include: a dashboard, logs in different formats, Replayer files, pivot tables, visualizations, and case profiles.

The dashboard shown in Figure 6.7 is particularly useful for teachers to track what is going on in student groups while the groups are active in chat rooms. It can be displayed for any chat room and immediately gives a summary of the activity in that room. A teacher can see which students are present and how active they have been—without the teacher having to enter the room and intervene in the student collaboration. A teacher can open several of these dashboards and refresh the display periodically to know who is currently active. At the bottom of the dashboard are buttons to produce reports. The reports are immediately downloaded to the teacher's desktop and reflect all activity up to the moment the report was generated.

The downloaded reports include spreadsheet logs in different formats and the Replayer file for the room. In addition, there is a pop-up chat log. The pop-up chat log is particularly handy for quickly browsing the on-going chat. As shown in Figure 6.8, it displays the activity spread across a column for each student. This provides a good visual overview of how the work is shared and how the discussion goes from student to student. Of course, one can also read the comments that students post and see what GeoGebra actions they are taking.

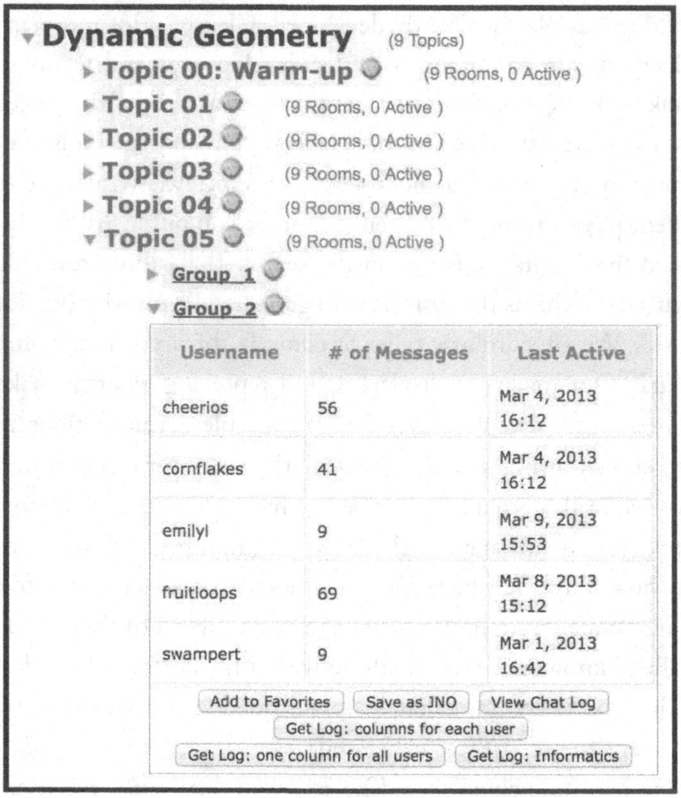

▼ Dynamic Geometry   (9 Topics)
  ▶ Topic 00: Warm-up ◉   (9 Rooms, 0 Active)
  ▶ Topic 01 ◉   (9 Rooms, 0 Active)
  ▶ Topic 02 ◉   (9 Rooms, 0 Active)
  ▶ Topic 03 ◉   (9 Rooms, 0 Active)
  ▶ Topic 04 ◉   (9 Rooms, 0 Active)
  ▼ Topic 05 ◉   (9 Rooms, 0 Active)
      ▶ Group_1 ◉
      ▼ Group_2 ◉

Username	# of Messages	Last Active
cheerios	56	Mar 4, 2013 16:12
cornflakes	41	Mar 4, 2013 16:12
emilyl	9	Mar 9, 2013 15:53
fruitloops	69	Mar 8, 2013 15:12
swampert	9	Mar 1, 2013 16:42

[Add to Favorites] [Save as JNO] [View Chat Log]
[Get Log: columns for each user]
[Get Log: one column for all users] [Get Log: Informatics]

Figure 6.7: The dashboard of reports on a chat room listed in the VMT Lobby.

Chat transcript for the

Chat Index	Date	Time Start Typing	Time of Posting	cheerios	fruitloops	cornflakes	
1	03/01/2013		15:11:09		joins the room		
2	03/01/2013		15:11:50			joins the room	
3	03/01/2013	15:11:52	15:11:53		heyyyyyyyyyyyyyy		
4	03/01/2013	15:13:04	15:13:05			hi	
	03/01/2013		15:13:26			[Taking control on tab Triangles]	
	03/01/2013		15:13:26			[changed Geogebra tool to Move]	
5	03/01/2013	15:13:28	15:13:30			i will go first	
	03/01/2013		15:14:09			[moved item A on tab Triangles]	
	03/01/2013		15:14:20			[moved item D on tab Triangles]	
	03/01/2013		15:14:22			[changed Geogebra tool to Move Graphics View]	
	03/01/2013		15:14:22			[Releasing control on tab Triangles]	
	03/01/2013		15:17:03		[Taking control on tab Triangles]		
	03/01/2013		15:17:03		[changed Geogebra tool to Move]		
	03/01/2013		15:17:22		[moved item A on tab Triangles]		
	03/01/2013		15:17:22		[moved item A on tab Triangles]		
6	03/01/2013		15:17:25	joins the room			

Figure 6.8: A pop-up chat log accessible from the dashboard.

An alternative display of the chat is shown in Figure 6.9. Here, the log is consolidated in one column. This is useful for publication in reports (like Log 7.12 in this book). The "Event Type" column can be filtered to just include specific categories of events, such as chat messages posted by students, GeoGebra actions taken by the students or awareness and system messages generated by the software. For chat postings, start and post times are both given, to help discover to what previous post someone is responding.

	A	B	C	D	E	F	G	H
1	Line	Date	Start Time	Post Time	Duration	Event Type	User	
2	1	3/1/13		15:11:09	0:00:00	system	fruitloops	joins the room
3	2	3/1/13		15:11:50	0:00:41	system	cornflakes	joins the room
4	3	3/1/13	15:11:52	15:11:53	0:00:01	chat	fruitloops	heyyyyyyyyyyyyyy
5	4	3/1/13	15:13:04	15:13:05	0:00:01	chat	cornflakes	hi
6		3/1/13		15:13:26	0:00:21	Geogebra: Triangles	cornflakes	tool changed to Move
7	5	3/1/13	15:13:28	15:13:30	0:00:02	chat	cornflakes	i will go first
8		3/1/13		15:14:09	0:00:39	Geogebra: Triangles	cornflakes	updated Point A
9		3/1/13		15:14:20	0:00:11	Geogebra: Triangles	cornflakes	updated Point D
10		3/1/13		15:14:22	0:00:02	Geogebra: Triangles	cornflakes	tool changed to Move Graphics View
11		3/1/13		15:17:03	0:02:41	Geogebra: Triangles	fruitloops	tool changed to Move
12		3/1/13	15:17:22	15:17:22	0:00:00	Geogebra: Triangles	fruitloops	updated Point A
13	6	3/1/13		15:17:25	0:00:03	system	cheerios	joins the room
14		3/1/13		15:17:40	0:00:15	Geogebra: Triangles	fruitloops	updated Point D
15		3/1/13		15:17:43	0:00:03	Geogebra: Triangles	fruitloops	updated Point D
16		3/1/13		15:17:46	0:00:03	Geogebra: Triangles	fruitloops	tool changed to Move Graphics View
17	7	3/1/13	15:17:50	15:18:09	0:00:19	chat	fruitloops	when i move vertex a the whole triangle of abc moves
18	8	3/1/13	15:17:58	15:18:43	0:00:45	chat	cornflakes	when i moved point c the triangle stayed the same and either increased or decreased in size, butit was equivalent to the original triangle
19		3/1/13		15:18:09	0:0:-34	Geogebra: Triangles	cheerios	tool changed to Move
20	9	3/1/13	15:18:14	15:18:52	0:00:38	chat	fruitloops	but when i tryed to move vertex d, it couldnt go behind triangle abc
		3/1/13		15:18:15	0:0:-37	Geogebra:	cheerios	tool changed to Move Graphics View

Figure 6.9: A spreadsheet with one column of chat log, which can be filtered by event type.

A good report for browsing among rooms for activity is the pivot table shown in Figure 6.10. Using this spreadsheet, one can "drill down" from the project community level (Spring, 2013) to math subject (Dynamic Geometry), curricular topic (Topic 05), small group (Group 2), event type (chat), individual student (Cornflakes), and posted data (detailed chat postings). Information at the different levels can be sorted, filtered, and counted. Simple statistics can be computed. This is a useful report for comparing the activity of different groups and the students within the groups. For instance, in the displayed view, one can see how much each student contributed to the chat, how much each worked in the "Triangles" and the "Squares" GeoGebra tabs in Topic 02 and who was the most active overall in this topic. Group 3 seems to have been much less active than Group 2, but Group 1 was even more active. One could now drill down to get a sense of what all the activity in Group 1 was about.

Spring 2013 Lalor & Riccobono	27206
▼ Dynamic Geometry	27206
▶ Topic 00: Warm-up	68
▶ Topic 01	5933
▶ Topic 02	3675
▶ Topic 03	3006
▶ Topic 04	2650
▼ Topic 05	6972
▶ Group_1	1402
▼ Group_2	843
▼ cheerios	357
▶ awareness	7
▶ chat	43
▶ Geogebra:Squares	113
▶ Geogebra:Triangles	181
▶ system	13
▼ cornflakes	146
▶ awareness	6
▶ chat	27
▶ Geogebra:Squares	48
▶ Geogebra:Triangles	53
▶ system	12
▶ emilyL	15
▼ fruitloops	316
▶ awareness	10
▶ chat	55
▶ Geogebra:Squares	98
▶ Geogebra:Triangles	142
▶ system	11
▶ swampert	9
▶ Group_3	354
▶ Group_4	1182

Spring 2013 Lalor & Riccobono	27206
▼ Dynamic Geometry	27206
▶ Topic 00: Warm-up	68
▶ Topic 01	5933
▶ Topic 02	3675
▶ Topic 03	3006
▶ Topic 04	2650
▼ Topic 05	6972
▶ Group_1	1402
▼ Group_2	843
▶ cheerios	357
▼ cornflakes	146
▶ awareness	6
▼ chat	27
2013-03-01 15:13:05 - cornflakes -> hi	1
2013-03-01 15:13:30 - cornflakes -> i will go first	1
2013-03-01 15:18:43 - cornflakes -> when i moved point c the triangle stayed the	1
2013-03-01 15:22:54 - cornflakes -> yes	1
2013-03-01 15:23:53 - cornflakes -> sure	1
2013-03-01 15:24:23 - cornflakes -> yes	1
2013-03-01 15:26:41 - cornflakes -> ecf arent moving	1
2013-03-01 15:27:52 - cornflakes -> because they are sconstrained or restricted	1
2013-03-01 15:28:29 - cornflakes -> yea	1
2013-03-01 15:29:07 - cornflakes -> sure	1
2013-03-01 15:48:15 - cornflakes -> right	1
2013-03-01 16:20:06 - cornflakes -> agrreeed	1
2013-03-04 15:20:41 - cornflakes -> right	1
2013-03-04 15:23:48 - cornflakes -> yes you had to make the point between the c	1
2013-03-04 15:25:27 - cornflakes -> yea same thing	1

Figure 6.10: A pivot table of chat postings, for students in Topic 05.

The pivot table is a flexible spreadsheet for exploring quantitative relationships among groups and individuals. To get quick visual impressions of comparisons among groups, we can use bubble graphs, like that in Figure 6.11. This image represents the activity of a group working for two hours. It represents their activity in chat, the whiteboard, GeoGebra tabs and other actions during 5-min time slices.

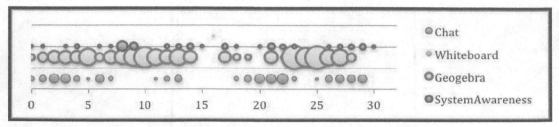

Figure 6.11: Bubble graph of Group 2 working on Topic 5.

Many other configurations of this data are possible. In the set of bubble charts in Figure 6.12, each of the six groups that worked on Topic 5 for two hours in the same classroom are compared. In these charts, the height of the bubble represents how many of a certain kind of action (chat, whiteboard, GeoGebra, or other) took place during the 5-min time slice. The size of the bubble represents how many people were involved in the chat or other kind of activity (usually 1, 2, or 3 people).

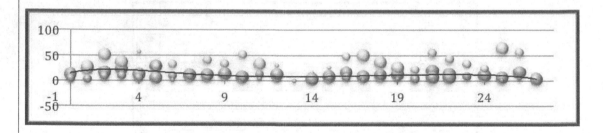

Group 1

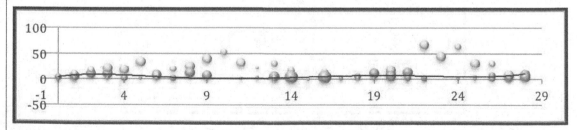

Group 2

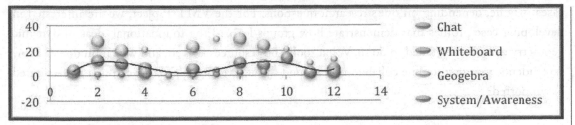

Group 3

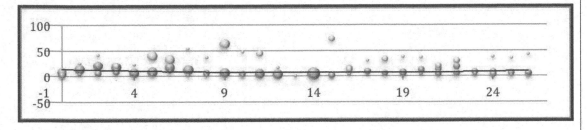

Group 4

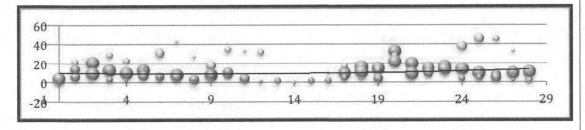

Group 5

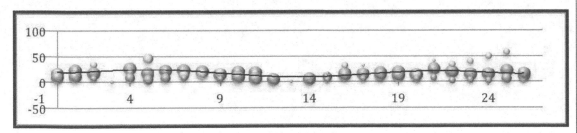

Group 6

Figure 6.12: Bubble graphs comparing six groups working on Topic 5, with trend lines for chat.

Certainly, many other visualizations and displays are possible. For researchers, these help to deal with a mass of data—to get useful overviews and some indications of where interesting cases may lie, depending on one's research questions. For the VMT Project, we are interested in developing case profiles that demonstrate how groups learned the foundational ideas of dynamic geometry or how they failed to do so. What tools and resources helped, and which hindered? How do students engage in online collaboration around dynamic geometry? How can this be facilitated or supported?

CHAPTER 7

Research: Analyzing Geometry

Chapter Summary

Chat logs of several small groups who worked on a challenging geometry problem online are analyzed in this chapter. Frequent analysis of usage of an innovative educational system is necessary to drive cycles of design. The VMT Project's design-based research into multi-user GeoGebra involved feedback from many pilot studies of teams working on sequences of activities. This included teams of researchers on the VMT Project, teams of teachers involved in professional development to prepare them to use the software with their students, as well as teams of students using various versions of software and topics. This chapter looks at how these teams interacted in exploring a dynamic-geometry activity involving inscribed equilateral triangles. In addition to seeing how groups enacted the affordances of the collaborative dynamic-geometry environment, the analyses illustrate group cognition—the accomplishment of challenging problem-solving tasks through collaborative interaction at the group level.

The educational research field of computer-supported collaborative learning (CSCL) arose in the late 1990s to explore the opportunities for collaborative learning introduced by the growing access to networked computational devices, like personal computers linked by the Internet (Stahl, Koschmann & Suthers, 2006). The seminal theory influencing CSCL was the cognitive psychology of Vygotsky (1930/1978). He had argued several decades earlier that most cognitive skills of humans originated in collaborative-learning episodes within small groups, such as in the family, mentoring relationships, apprenticeships or interactions with peers. Skills might originate in inter-personal interactions and later evolve into self-talk mimicking of such interactions—often ultimately being conducted as silent rehearsal (thinking) or even automatized non-reflective practices (habits). In most cases of mathematics learning, the foundational inter-personal interactions are mediated by language (including various forms of bodily gesture) (Sfard, 2008; Stahl, 2008). Frequently, the early experiences leading to new math skills are also mediated by physical artifacts or systems of symbols—more recently including computer interfaces.

Based on a Vygotskian perspective, a CSCL approach to the teaching of geometry would involve collaborative learning mediated by dynamic-geometry software and student discourse. In the past decade, we have developed the VMT collaborative-learning environment and have integrated a multi-user version of GeoGebra into it. In developing this hybrid system, we have tested our prototypes with various small groups of users.

Recently, we have used the figure discussed in Section 5.2—of an equilateral triangle inscribed inside of another equilateral triangle—as the basis of an activity for virtual math teams exploring dynamic geometry. This problem was suggested by Öner (2013) because it lends itself nicely to a combination of dynamic dragging and dynamic construction. For us, it is also attractive because of its central concern with dynamic dependencies. Thus, it combines in a deep and tangible way what we characterized in Chapter 5 as the three primary dimensions of dynamic geometry.

Later, in Section 8.9, we will see how this problem was solved by two students working face-to-face using Geometer's Sketchpad in the original experiment conducted by Öner. First, in this chapter, we review how the same problem was approached by three kinds of teams within the VMT Project: by members of our research project, by teachers in our professional development course and by students of one of those teachers in a middle school.

We initially tried out the problem of constructing inscribed equilateral triangles in two teams composed of members of the VMT Project team. The problem was given to the groups in the form seen in Figure 7.1. We will call the two teams Group A (Jan, Sam, and Abe) and Group B (Lauren, Cat, and Stew). The group members are adults already familiar to varying degrees with VMT and GeoGebra.

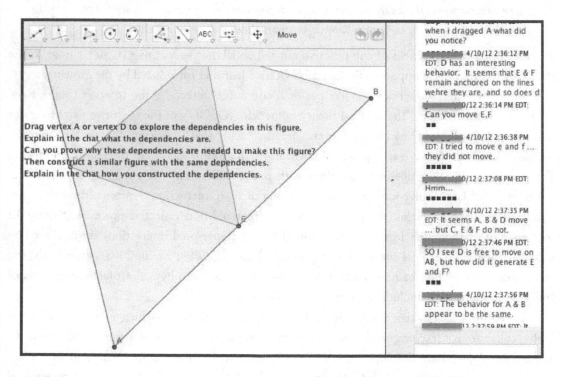

Figure 7.1: The dragged construction with the problem statement and some chat.

7.1   RESEARCHERS DESIGN DEPENDENCIES

Group A starts by coordinating their online activity. They decide who will have initial control of the GeoGebra manipulation and they discuss in the text-chat panel the behavior they see as points of the construction are dragged (Log 7.1). They begin by dragging each of the points in the diagram (Figure 7.1).

6	14:33:56	Sam	I am good with somebody taking a stab at the dragging ...
7	14:34:10	Sam	I think maybe tell us what you intend to drag and we can discuss what we observe?
8	14:34:18	Jan	Go ahead Abe. Why don't you move the points in alphabetical order
9	14:34:36	Abe	Ok
10	14:34:43	Abe	I will try to drag point A
11	14:35:08	Jan	So the whole triangle moves... it both rotates around point B and it can dilate
12	14:35:14	Sam	So, A seems to move all the other points and scalle the whole drawing.
13	14:35:14	Jan	Which are you moving now
14	14:35:20	Sam	What are you moving now?
15	14:35:35	Abe	I first moved 1 and then D.
16	14:35:45	Sam	A, then D.
17	14:35:46	Sam	ok
18	14:36:05	Jan	so D was stuck on segment AC
19	14:36:12	Abe	when i dragged A what did you notice?
20	14:36:12	Sam	D has an interesting behavior. It seems that E & F remain anchored on the lines wehre they are, and so does d
21	14:36:14	Jan	Can you move E,F
22	14:36:38	Sam	I tried to move e and f ... they did not move.
23	14:37:08	Jan	Hmm...
24	14:37:35	Sam	It seems A, B & D move ... but C, E & F do not.
25	14:37:46	Jan	SO I see D is free to move on AB, but how did it generate E and F?
26	14:37:56	Sam	The behavior for A & B appear to be the same.
27	14:37:59	Abe	It appears that the triangles remain equilateral.

Log 7.1: The researchers drag points in the diagram.

Note that the problem statement in Figure 7.1 does not say that the triangles are equilateral or inscribed. By having Abe drag points A and D, the group quickly sees that the vertices of the inner triangle always stay on the sides of the outer triangle (e.g., log lines 18 and 20), indicating that the smaller triangle is inscribed in the larger one.

As Abe drags each of the vertex points, the group notices that points A, B, and D are free to move, but that C, E, and F are dependent points, somehow determined by A, B, and/or D. Jan asks Sam to drag E and F, but Sam finds that they cannot be dragged. This sparks Jan to express wonder about how the position of point D (as it is dragged while A, B, and C remain stationary) generates the positions of E and F (line 25). This is a move to consider how the diagram must be constructed in order to display the behavior it does during dragging. Meanwhile, Abe notices in line 27 that the triangles both remain equilateral during the dragging of all their vertices.

Within about 3-min of collaborative observation, the group has systematically dragged all the available points and noted the results. They have noticed that the triangles are both inscribed and equilateral. They have also wondered about the dependencies that determine the position of E and F as D is dragged. Now they start to consider how one would construct the dynamic diagram (Log 7.2).

47	14:45:39	Jan	What are we thinking...
48	14:46:07	Abe	okay,we have two equilateral triangles, with the inner one constrained to the sides of the outer triangle.
49	14:46:12	Sam	I think Abe summarized what is happening nicely - that both triangles remain equilateral when any of the 3 movable points are moved.
50	14:46:26	Jan	Agreed.
51	14:47:01	Jan	The thing I'm wondering about is how to generate the specific equilateral triang.e
52	14:47:02	Sam	Yes, another good bpoint - the one is contained in the other ... further, the three points of the inner triangle are constrained by the line segments that make up the outer triangle.
53	14:47:03	Abe	let's try to construct the figures?
54	14:47:20	Jan	For example, given a point on AB and a point on AC, there exists an equilateral triangle
55	14:47:38	Jan	But that's not this sketch b/c only one point is free. The rest are constrained
56	14:49:37	Jan	I'm wondering if all the three triangles that are outside the little equilateral triangle yet inside the big one are congruent.
57	14:50:39	Abe	When you say all three triangles, do you mean the three sides of the one of the triangles?

Log 7.2: The researchers wonder about the construction.

First, they all agree on the constraint that the triangles must remain inscribed and equilateral. Abe suggests that they actually try to construct the figure (line 53); through such a trial, they are likely to gain more insight into an effective construction procedure, which will reproduce the dragging behavior they have observed. Jan first notes that an equilateral triangle can be defined by the two points of its base. However, he also notes that in the given figure only one of the vertices is free and it determines the other two (line 55). This leads him to wonder, "if all the three triangles that are outside the little equilateral triangle yet inside the big one are congruent" (line 56). If they are congruent, then corresponding sides will all be of equal length. Abe relates the sides of the three little congruent triangles to the three sides of the interior triangle and to the three segments on the sides of the exterior triangle. Following the excerpt in Log 7.2, Group A measures the three segments AE, BF, and CD, discovering that they are always equal to each other, even when their numeric length changes with the dragging of any of the free points (Log 7.3).

72	14:53:33	Jan	That means that CD, AE, and CF also have to be the same length, bc big triangle is equilateral
73	14:53:42	Abe	did you change what is being measured? or did you resize the figure?
74	14:53:58	Jan	I just moved point D along the side of the equilateral triangle
75	14:54:35	Abe	i c
76	14:56:16	Abe	So, shall we summarize the dependencies that we notice?
77	14:57:11	Jan	Sure who wants to start?
78	14:57:45	Sam	The inner triangle is contained by the outer triangle.
79	14:58:05	Sam	segment AC is the boundary of point D
80	14:58:14	Sam	Segment CB is the boundary of point F
81	14:58:24	Sam	Segmemt AB is the boundary of point E
82	14:58:55	Jan	So I think we may want to say F is on CB a bit differenlty.
83	14:59:10	Sam	Both triangles are equalateral no matter how the three movable points -- A, B & D -- are moved.
84	14:59:14	Jan	It is not free to move on CB. It is stuck in a particular location on CB defined by where D is on CA
85	15:00:09	Abe	The line segment CB cannot move.
86	15:00:10	Jan	So I think F is CD units away from B on BC. Its not constructed as an equilateral triangle, it happens to be an equilaterl triangle because of the construction
87	15:00:26	Jan	Agreed. I meant segment of length CB
88	15:00:38	Jan	Do you all buy that...
89	15:00:39	Jan	?

90	15:00:50	Sam	@Jan - I think that's covered by saying that both triangles are always equaleteral ... it implies both points move in conjunction with the third. (D) ... Of course, I don't teach the teachers who teach math (much), so you may have a better sense of the conventions. :D
91	15:00:59	Sam	I'll buy it.
92	15:01:04	Abe	yes, i agree!
93	15:02:28	Abe	The same can be said about E, it's constructed to be CD units from A.

Log 7.3: The researchers identify dependencies of the inscribed equilateral triangles.

After noting the key dependency that they discovered—segment lengths AE=BF=CD—they list the other dependencies involved in constructing the figure. Line 86 provides a conjecture on how to construct the inner triangle. Namely, it is not constructed using Euclid's method from Proposition 1 (the way the exterior equilateral triangle could have been). Rather, point F is located the same distance from B on side BC as D is from C on AC: a distance of CD. Jan asks the rest of his group if they agree (line 88). They do. Abe adds that the same goes for the third vertex: point E is located the same distance from A on side AB as D is from C on AC: a distance of CD. The work of the group on this problem is essentially done at this point. A few minutes later (line 110), Jan spells out how to assure that AE=BF=CD in GeoGebra: "Measure CD with compass. Then stick the compass at B and A."

We have seen here that Group A went through a collaborative process in which they explored the given figure by varying it visually through the procedure of *dragging* various points and noticing how the figure responded. Some points could move freely; they often caused the other points to readjust. Some points were constrained and could not be moved freely. The group then wondered about the constraints underlying the behavior. They conjectured that certain relationships were maintained by built-in dependencies. Finally, the group figured out how to accomplish the *construction* of the inscribed equilateral triangles by defining the *dependencies* in GeoGebra.

Group B went through a similar process, with differences in the details of their observations and conjectures. Interestingly, Group B made conjectures leading to at least three different construction approaches. First, Stew wondered if the lengths of the sides of the interior triangle were related to the lengths of a segment of the exterior triangle, like DE=DA (Log 7.4). The group then quickly shared with each other the set of basic constraints—inscribed and equilateral—similar to Group A's list of constraints.

15	14:37:00	Stew	and it appears that the side lengths of the inner triangle are related to the length of a portion of the orignal side
16	14:37:08	Cat	so also, there must be a constraint about the segments remaining equal, no?
17	14:37:31	Cat	@Stew, why can't they just be equal to each other?
18	14:37:47	Lauren	yes, visually it sure looks like equilateral triangles
19	14:37:53	Stew	yes, I think the triangles are equilateral or something like that.?
20	14:38:00	Lauren	D is free to move on AC, but E and F cant be dragged
21	14:38:58	Lauren	constructing the outer equilateral will be easy, but how do you think we should plan the construction of the inner triangle?
22	14:39:24	Stew	you can construct an equilateral but how do you make it so that its vertices are always on the outer triangle?
23	14:39:57	Lauren	Im thinking place D on AC, and construct an equilateral from there, with intersections on the sides of the outer triangle
24	14:40:12	Lauren	should we try and see what happens?
25	14:40:13	Cat	yeah, i'm not sure about making the other points stay on their respective segments
26	14:40:27	Cat	but we can maybe see the answer when we get closer
27	14:40:35	Stew	I think we'll get intpo trouble with the third side
28	14:40:38	Lauren	yeah, that will be the tricky part, but i think if we intersect they will be constrained
29	14:40:41	Stew	but, sure, let's try it
30	14:40:53	Lauren	may I start?
31	14:40:59	Cat	go for it!

Log 7.4: The researchers notice while dragging points in the diagram.

Group B sees that the inner triangle must remain both inscribed and equilateral. This raises difficulties because the usual method of constructing an equilateral triangle would not in general locate the dependent vertex on the side of the inscribing triangle (line 22). This group, like Group A, decides to start construction in order to learn more about the problem (line 24). They do not have a complete plan for the construction, but they decide to start constructing in order to explore how things turn out. They begin by constructing triangle ABC and placing point D on AC. They anticipate problems constructing triangle DEF and ensuring that both E and F remain on the sides of the inscribing triangle while also being equidistant from D. Note that the members of the team are careful to make sure that everyone is following what is going on and agrees with the approach.

45	14:44:53	Lauren	anyone have any ideas for the inner triangle?
46	14:45:37	Stew	One thing I noticed is that the sidelength of the inner triangle appears to be the distance of the longer segment on the original triangle
47	14:46:17	Cat	i wish i could copy the board :) i know that is not ideal, though
48	14:46:40	Cat	i forget what the tools do exactly, and want to just remind myself
49	14:46:57	Stew	If you made a circle that fit inside the original triangle, then its point of tangency or intersection might be useful
50	14:47:31	Stew	the trick might be to find the center of such a circle.
51	14:48:15	Stew	There are interesting centers made by things such as Cat was suggesting, the angle bisectors, or perpendicular bisectors
52	14:48:33	Lauren	yes - the center of each triagle probably is the same - do you think?
53	14:48:54	Lauren	angle bisecotrs would work
54	14:49:05	Stew	I don't think they have the same center
55	14:49:44	Lauren	maybe not....

Log 7.5: The researchers conjecture about the construction.

In line 46 (Log 7.5), Stew repeats his conjecture about side DE equaling the length of "the longer segment" of AC, i.e., either CD or AD depending on which is longer at the moment. This conjecture is visibly supported by the special cases when D is at an endpoint of AC or at its midpoint. When D is at an endpoint, DE=AC or DE=AB (and AB=AC); when D is at the midpoint of AC, DE=AD=DC because the three small triangles formed between the inscribed triangles are all equilateral and congruent.

Then the group switches to discussing a quite different conjecture that Lauren had brought up earlier and that Cat is trying to work on through GeoGebra constructions. That conjecture is that it would be helpful to locate the centers of the inscribed triangles, construct a circle around the center and observe where that circle is tangent to or intersects triangle ABC. In general, triangles have different kinds of centers, formed by constructing bisectors of the triangle's angles or by constructing perpendicular bisectors of the triangle's sides. The team discusses which to use and whether they might be the same center for both of the triangles.

Lauren does some construction (Figure 7.2). She locates a point, D, at which triangle ABC's angle bisectors meet. However, she then abandons this approach (Log 7.6).

80	15:01:40	Stew	that's we can come back to that if you want to explain what you did
81	15:02:26	Cat	Lauren, did you create A and B to have equal radii>
82	15:02:27	Cat	?
83	15:02:31	Lauren	I abandoned the center, and worked with the lengths of the sides
84	15:02:57	Lauren	used the compass tool to measure the distance from D to C
85	15:03:08	Lauren	and then found that distance from each of the other vertices
87	15:03:24	Lauren	using the fact that all equilateral triangles are similar
88	15:03:30	Lauren	questions?
89	15:04:05	Lauren	is everyone convinced the inner triangle is as it should be?

Log 7.6: The researchers construct the dependencies of the inscribed equilateral triangles.

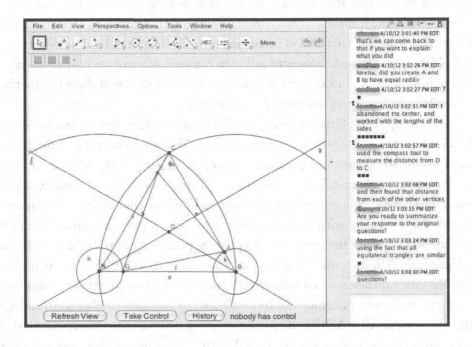

Figure 7.2: The researchers find the center and construct equal line segments.

Instead, she pursues a new conjecture, related to Stew's earlier observations: "we know by similar triangles, that each line of the inner is the same proportion of the outer" (Lauren, line 75). She uses the GeoGebra compass tool with a radius of CD to construct circles around the other vertices of triangle ABC (lines 84, 85), just like Group A had done. This locates points where the circles intersect the triangle sides for placing the other vertices of the inscribed triangle with the constraint that CD=AE=BF. She then concludes by asking if the other group members agree that this constructs the figure properly.

Like Group A, Group B initiated a collaborative process of exploring the given diagram visually with the help of dragging points. They developed conjectures about the constraints in the figure and about what dependencies would have to be built into a construction that replicated the inscribed equilateral triangles. They decided to explore trial constructions as a way of better understanding the problem and the issues that would arise in different approaches. Eventually, they pursued an approach involving line segments in the three congruent smaller triangles.

It is interesting to note the role of the three small triangles formed between the two inscribed triangles. These small triangles are not immediately salient in the original diagram. Triangles ABC and DEF are shaded; the smaller triangles are simply empty spaces in between. They become focal and visible to the groups due to their relationships with the sides of the salient triangles, and particularly with the segment CD. It is the fact that these three smaller triangles are congruent that supports the insight that the necessary constraint is to make CD=AE=BF. The smaller triangles become visible through the exploratory work of dragging, conjecturing, and constructing this dependency. This is precisely the kind of perception that can occur in the scaffolded inter-personal setting of collaborative dynamic geometry and then can gradually mature into increased professional vision (Goodwin, 1994) and mastery of practices of observation and discourse by the individual team members as developing students of mathematics.

Both Group A and Group B find a solution to the problem they address by taking advantage of the affordances of collaborative dynamic geometry. Their understanding of the problem (Zemel & Koschmann, 2013) develops gradually through dragging points, noticing how other points respond, wondering about effective constraints and conjecturing about possible dependencies to construct. Next, they begin exploratory construction. These are trial-and-error attempts in different directions. Some reach deadends or are simply put aside as more promising attempts catch the group's attention. Finally, the group agrees upon a key dependency to build into the construction. This dependency—in its connections to related geometric relationships—forms the basis for persuading the group members of a solution to the problem. This is implicitly a justification or proof of the solution. In the end, the group can construct a set of inscribed equilateral triangles, building in the dependency that CD=AE=BF. They can then prove that the triangles are inscribed and equilateral by referring to the dependency that CD=AE=BF, along with certain well-known characteristics of equilateral and congruent triangles.

Although both groups reached a similar conclusion, their paths were significantly different. First, they defined their problem differently. Group A focused on listing the constraints that they noticed from dragging points and then on proving that the given triangles were in fact equilateral. Group B, in contrast, quickly realized that it would be difficult to construct triangle DEF to be both inscribed and equilateral, since these characteristics required quite different constraints, which would be hard to impose simultaneously. Whereas Group A coordinated its work so that the members followed a single path of exploration and conjecture, Group B's members each came up with different conjectures and even engaged in some divergent explorative construction on their own before sharing their findings. Despite these differences, both groups collaborated effectively. They listened attentively and responded to each other's comments. They solicited questions and agreement. They followed a shared group approach. Together, they reached an accepted conclusion to a difficult problem, which they would not all likely have been able to solve on their own, illustrating effective group cognition (Stahl, 2006).

The analysis of Groups A and B illustrates the approach of collaborative dynamic geometry. The groups took advantage of the three central dimensions of dynamic geometry—dragging, construction, and dependencies—to explore the intricacies of a geometric configuration and to reach—as a group—a deep understanding of the relationships within the configuration. They figured out how to construct the diagram and they understood why the construction would work as a result of dependencies that they designed into it.

7.2 TEACHERS DESIGN DEPENDENCIES

During a teacher-professional-development course offered as part of the VMT Project, middle-school and high-school teachers met online for ten weeks. They read and discussed—both in the VMT synchronous chat rooms and in Blackboard asynchronous discussion forums—readings about dynamic-geometry teaching, collaborative learning, academically productive (or accountable) talk (Michaels, O'Connor & Resnick, 2008; Resnick, O'Connor & Michaels, 2007), and mathematical practices (CCSSI, 2011). They also participated within small groups in several hour-long synchronous sessions using multi-user GeoGebra in VMT. In one of those sessions, they were presented with the inscribed-triangles problem. In this section, we analyze the work of one of the groups, consisting of four teachers.

Before this group session, the teachers were given an individual assignment to hone their GeoGebra skills. This consisted of a two-page set of instructions. It stepped them through an exercise using the compass tool to create new line segments whose lengths would be dependent upon given segments (similar to Euclid's second proposition and to the student topic in Figure 10.7). Then it stepped them through the construction of an equilateral triangle using circles (similar to Euclid's first proposition and to the student topic in Figure 10.8).

The teachers begin their group session by setting up their collaboration in response to a page of instructions, which states:

> *In the tab "Original figure," you will see a diagram consisting of two triangles. Decide on roles and proceed to explore the figure as a group. Discover what dynamic relationships hold for the two triangles.*

This figure was selected because it lends itself to group exploration of dependencies. If you dis-cover the dependencies through dragging the figure, that will help you to construct your own figure like this. Record your observations and hypotheses about the figure in the Summary tab.

After about 15 min, move to the "Our group's construction" tab. Try to re-create the figure from the first tab. What constraints or dependencies can you use for your construction to make sure that your figure has the same dynamic relationships as the original figure? Discuss this in the chat and summarize your discussion in the Summary tab. As you construct, make sure that everyone in the group understands how the construction is being done and why this approach will ensure the proper dependencies.

The group allocates time for the initial exploration of the given figure of the triangles, decides how they will maintain a running summary of their work and determines who will take control in GeoGebra first. The "Original figure" tab is shown in Figure 7.3.

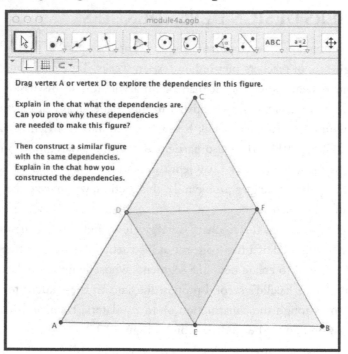

Figure 7.3: The original figure tab for the teachers.

The group begins their work by exploring the dependencies. Within the allotted 15 min, each member contributes to summarizing the group's findings (see Log 7.7).

Line	Post Time	User	Message
61	19:12:55	emilyL	I think we are supposed to focus on the dependencies
62	19:12:57	sholland	Use the 5th from the right
63	19:14:15	michele_colon	one of the dependencies could be that the triangles are equilateral
64	19:14:42	emilyL	ok
65	19:16:04	sholland	Could D be a "point on line" AC
66	19:15:59	emilyL	did someone show the lengths yet?
67	19:16:39	JL123	I took control for a breif second I wanted to see about the equilateral by the view it looks like one side may be longer but moving it gave me a better view I agree eqilateral
68	19:16:54	sholland	Also maybe line segment then the a regular polygon tab
69	19:16:29	michele_colon	I think so, and E on AB and F on BC

Log 7.7: The teachers determine dependencies.

They agree that the two triangles are constrained to be equilateral and that the vertices of the interior triangle are constrained to stay on the sides of the exterior triangle. The group then turns to discuss how they can construct triangles that exhibit the same dependencies as the original figure:

85	19:20:46	JL123	can any other points move the figure? this may help to know when we construct ours
86	19:20:48	michele_colon	Sheila, I think so too, big triangle first
87	19:21:13	JL123	So we are thinking Big triangle with polygon tool and small with compass?
88	19:21:50	sholland	CEF are all grayed out so probably not
89	19:22:27	michele_colon	I'm not sure about the polygon tool, but I think the big needs to be constructed first so that D, E, and F can be constructed on their correct sides
90	19:22:01	sholland	yes

Log 7.8: The teachers plan their construction.

As shown in Log 7.8, they argue that they must construct the exterior triangle first so that the vertices of the interior triangle can be located on its sides. They are especially interested in which points on the triangles are free to move and which are constrained to be at fixed positions (determined by the other points). In particular, Sholland notes that points C, E, and F are colored black ("grayed out") in the figure. The teachers have previously noted that GeoGebra colors dependent points black and free points blue. This is an indication that points C, E, and F will have to be constructed in a way that makes them dependent on previously constructed objects.

EmilyL draws the conclusion from this that, "Since AB are blue but that was the original segment and then using the two circles and radii to create original large triangle?" (line 107). In other words, they should start with a line segment AB since points A and B have to be free. Then they can use the procedure they practiced in their individual assignments to construct the exterior equilateral triangle using circles of equal radii around points A and B. The group follows EmilyL's proposal and constructs triangle ABC. They then display the lengths of the sides, showing they are all equal. This confirms that they have constructed an equilateral triangle. In Log 7.9 they all celebrate this accomplishment.

117	19:26:09	JL123	so what do we construct first? lets have some sort of a gmae plan
118	19:26:40	emilyL	I think large first with the two circles the way we did on individual. what do you guys think?
119	19:26:40	michele_colon	I agree with what Emily said here for our first part
120	19:27:05	michele_colon	yay, they are equilateral
121	19:27:10	emilyL	nice showing the lengths!
122	19:27:07	sholland	Definately equilateral triangles

Log 7.9: The teachers confirm that the triangles are equilateral.

The group does some more exploration and learns about the GeoGebra tools. They wonder if using the regular-polygon tool on segment AB will also produce a point C that is black. They learn how to shade in the interior of a triangle with the polygon tool and to hide the construction circles. They place point D on a side of their triangle and notice that it can be dragged around all sides of the triangle because they located the point on the polygon rather than on one of the side segments. They wonder if the point tool can produce the same effect as the intersection tool and are surprised to find that it can.

As the rest of the group is discussing these side issues in their "Our Construction" tab, EmilyL makes a key discovery in the "Original Figure" tab, as seen in Log 7.10.

204	19:41:15	emilyL	I HAVE AN IDEA!!
208	19:42:01	emilyL	can everyone go to Original fig for a second
209	19:42:15	JL123	yes I was just checking it out for idea
210	19:42:16	michele_colon	sure Emily
211	19:42:21	sholland	original
212	19:42:45	emilyL	watch as I move D, AD will stay congruent to CF and BE
213	19:43:20	JL123	yes
215	19:43:33	emilyL	I think I know what to do with that compass tool we did in the individual
216	19:44:30	JL123	What if we form 2 more circles to intersect the large triangle and make intersecting points where they meet?
217	19:43:35	michele_colon	good observation, maybe use the compass tool on those segments?
218	19:43:25	sholland	okay
224	19:44:39	emilyL	Can I share my idea?
226	19:44:47	JL123	yes of course
227	19:44:53	michele_colon	please!
228	19:45:28	emilyL	I think if we use the compass tool and make it the same measure as AD and then move it to where the center is C then B, this will work
229	19:45:51	emilyL	and then use points and polygon tool to connect
230	19:46:01	JL123	I was thinking that too make two more circles
231	19:46:06	emilyL	Jena, kind of like forming two circles
232	19:46:13	emilyL	but using the compass tool!
233	19:46:15	sholland	Try it emily. It's a good idea
234	19:46:11	JL123	see I like it Emily
235	19:46:14	michele_colon	i think that will work too
236	19:46:32	JL123	Yes the compass tool so there is more control
237	19:46:27	emilyL	ok first getting rid of E
238	19:46:55	emilyL	choosing the compass tool to get the measure of AD
239	19:47:23	emilyL	selecting A then D and making C the new center point
242	19:47:45	emilyL	does everyone see the new circle?

244	19:47:50	michele_ colon	yes
245	19:47:49	sholland	yes
247	19:48:11	JL123	Yes emily good work

Log 7.10: The teachers have a key idea.

As she states in line 212 of Log 7.10, EmilyL has the idea that under dragging, segment lengths AD=CF=BE. She invites everyone into the "Original Figure" tab and she then drags point D around and around, showing that the three vertices of the inner triangle always maintain equal distances from the corresponding vertices of the exterior triangle. She then associates this central dependency of the figure with the use of the compass tool, as practiced in the individual activity. Namely, she knows that the compass tool can be used to copy segment lengths (e.g., to construct CD and BE) so that they will remain dependent upon the original length (e.g., segment AD).

The other group members all respond with agreement to EmilyL's observation and to her suggestion to use the compass tool. In fact, the others indicate that they already understand how to use the compass tool here (lines 216–218). After a distraction caused by an instructor entering the chat room with an announcement (lines 219–223, not shown), EmilyL brings the group back to her proposal. She describes explicitly what she plans to do. The others agree. She emphasizes the use of the compass tool and the others agree again. Then she narrates as she uses the compass tool. The compass tool is tricky to use because you must set the radius of a circle first (e.g., using points A and D), and then move the circle to a new center (e.g., point B or C). Unfortunately, the movement of the circle is not visible to other participants, so it is important to narrate what is being done.

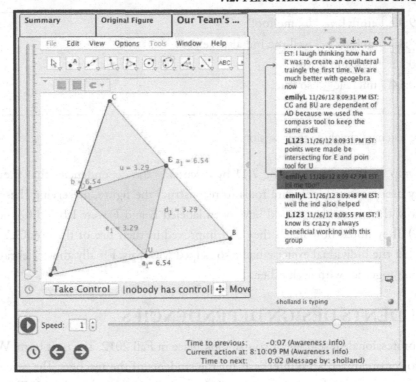

Figure 7.4: The teachers' solution with lengths marked.

The team continues by having other group members construct the figure to make sure that everyone is able to do it. They discuss aspects of the GeoGebra tools that they find interesting. They also reveal the lengths of all the triangle sides in order to confirm visually that the triangles remain equilateral when dragged (see Figure 7.4).

351	20:08:24	sholland	So did we use the compass tool for all 3 points or just 2?
352	20:08:49	JL123	yes lets just discuss dependencies further and I think our work is done here
353	20:08:45	emilyL	only 2
354	20:08:52	emilyL	in ours G and U
355	20:09:04	JL123	compass for 2
356	20:09:30	sholland	I laugh thinking how hard it was to create an equilateral traingle the first time. We are much better with geogebra now
357	20:09:31	emilyL	CG and BU are dependent of AD because we used the compass tool to keep the same radii
358	20:09:31	JL123	points were made be intersecting for E and poin tool for U
359	20:09:55	JL123	I know its crazy n always beneficial working with this group

360	20:09:42	emilyL	lol me too!!
361	20:09:48	emilyL	well the ind also helped
362	20:10:11	sholland	yes
363	20:10:14	michele_colon	so true!

Log 7.11: The teachers conclude their session.

They wrap up the session in Log 7.11 by discussing the dependencies that they discovered and how they used various GeoGebra tools to reconstruct the figure, preserving these dependencies. (Somehow, the points that should have been labeled E and F were labeled G and U in their construction.) They noted how much they had improved in their use of the GeoGebra tools and pointed out that the individual exercise had also helped with this. Finally, they celebrated the benefits of working together with each other.

7.3   STUDENTS DESIGN DEPENDENCIES

The teacher-professional-development course took place in Fall 2012. The next term, Winter 2013, the VMT Project organized a "WinterFest" for the students of the teachers. The teachers selected collaborative online GeoGebra activities for their students. Most started with Topics 1–4 (see Chapter 10). One of the teachers who participated in the chat analyzed in the previous section then had the seven groups of her students work on Topic 5, the problem of inscribed equilateral triangles. In this section, we shall analyze the chat log of one of those student groups in some detail. They spent two hour-long sessions on Topic 5. In the first session, they worked on the inscribed triangles and in the second session on the inscribed squares. Although they looked at the inscribed hexagons tab, they never had time to work on it. The three tabs of Topic 5 are shown in Figure 7.5. Figure

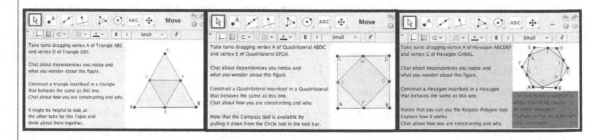

7.5: The tabs of Topic 5: triangles, squares and hexagons.

Starting in Log 7.12, all of the chat postings of three students are listed. The students have login names: Fruitloops, Cornflakes and Cheerios. They are middle-school students in 8th grade (about 14 years old). They are in the teacher's honors algebra course and are engaged in the WinterFest in a computer lab after school. They have had very little previous exposure to geometry—only about a week during the previous year's pre-algebra math course. They begin by following the instructions in the opening tab: "Take turns dragging vertex A of Triangle ABC and vertex D of Triangle DEF."

Line	Post Time	User	Message
3	15:11:53	fruitloops	heyyyyyyyyyyyyyy
4	15:13:05	corn-flakes	hi
5	15:13:30	corn-flakes	i will go first
7	15:18:09	fruitloops	when i move vertex a the whole triangle of abc moves
8	15:18:43	corn-flakes	when i moved point c the triangle stayed the same and either increased or decreased in size, butit was equivalent to the original triangle
9	15:18:52	fruitloops	but when i tryed to move vertex d, it couldnt go behond triangle abc
10	15:18:54	cheerios	does the inner triangle change its shape when u move vertex a
11	15:19:34	fruitloops	try moving it...
12	15:20:38	cheerios	nvm it doesnt
13	15:22:43	fruitloops	yeah when you move vertex a, the inner triangles changes size but never shape
14	15:22:54	corn-flakes	yes
15	15:23:35	fruitloops	can i try to make the circle equilateral triangle fist?
16	15:23:38	cheerios	yes
17	15:23:53	corn-flakes	sure
18	15:24:11	fruitloops	wait, fist we should talk about the other vertexes
19	15:24:23	corn-flakes	yes
20	15:24:28	cheerios	agreed

21	15:24:48	fruitloops	so cheerios since you have control what happens when you move the different vertexes?
22	15:25:26	cheerios	when you move vertex a triangle dfe dont move at all it just becomes smaller when you shrinnk the big triangle and vice versa
23	15:25:56	fruitloops	what about point e? c? F?

Log 7.12: The students explore the triangles.

The students drag points A and D. They quickly see that the interior triangle is confined to stay inside triangle ABC and that both triangles retain their shape when dragged. Fruitloops is eager to start constructing an equilateral triangle using circles. They have just watched a video of that construction in class, and had learned it in Topic 2. However, Fruitloops reconsiders and suggests that they explore further by dragging the other points. In Log 7.13, they start to discuss the dependencies in more detail.

24	15:26:41	corn-flakes	ecf arent moving
25	15:27:00	fruitloops	point c e and f cant move
26	15:27:52	corn-flakes	because they are sconstrained or restricted
27	15:27:53	fruitloops	point d can only make point f and g move but nothing else
28	15:28:29	corn-flakes	yea
29	15:28:50	fruitloops	okay want to try to conssrtuct it?
30	15:29:01	cheerios	yup
31	15:29:07	corn-flakes	sure

Log 7.13: The students discuss dependencies.

The students note that points C, E, and F are "constrained or restricted," so they are not free to be dragged. They also note that dragging point D will move points E and F. This will turn out to be a key dependency, although the students do not discuss it as such. They are now ready to begin the construction task. Fruitloops begins the construction with a segment GH and two circles of radius GH centered on points G and H, respectively. Fruitloops gets stuck at line 32 of Log 7.14 and Cheerios takes over, drawing the triangle connecting point I at the intersection of the circles with points G and H. Fruitloops wants to remove the circles, but seems to understand in line 34 that they cannot erase the circles without destroying the equilateral triangle. Cornflakes hides the circles by changing their properties.

32	15:30:26	fruitloops	what should i do next?
33	15:32:22	fruitloops	so how do we get rid of the circles then?
34	15:32:54	fruitloops	if we cant delete them, what do we do?
35	15:34:37	fruitloops	so i think triangle igh is like triangle abc
36	15:36:30	fruitloops	now that the first triangle is good, what should we do?

Log 7.14: The students construct the first triangle.

In line 35, Fruitloops suggests that they have succeeded in replicating the outer triangle. In Log 7.15, Fruitloops makes explicit that their previous observation about movement of point D affecting points E and F implies a dependency that may be relevant to their construction task. Cheerios and Cornflakes express interest in this line of argument. They all agree to proceed with trying constructions in order to figure out just what needs to be done. As with designing the exterior triangle, the results of dragging provide an impetus for construction, but not a blueprint. The participants launch into a trial-and-error process, guided by some vague ideas of things to try.

37	15:47:48	fruitloops	d moves but f and e dont
38	15:48:04	fruitloops	so both f and e are dependent on d
39	15:48:18	cheerios	so what does that mean
40	15:48:37	fruitloops	so if we make a line and use the circle thing, maybe we can make it somehow
41	15:48:15	corn-flakes	right
42	15:49:09	cheerios	lets try
43	15:49:29	cheerios	and we will jsut figure it out .. by making the line thing
44	15:49:14	fruitloops	how?
45	15:50:18	cheerios	f and e are restricted
46	15:51:19	fruitloops	we can make their d point by just using a point tool on our triangle to make point j
65	16:11:35	fruitloops	so what ere you dong now?

Log 7.15: The students experiment.

They begin their trial with the knowledge that point D is freer than points E and F, which are dependent on D. Therefore, they decide to start by constructing their equivalent of point D on a side of their exterior triangle. Note the gap of about 12 min from line 46 to the next chat posting.

For the three students, this was a period of intense experimentation in using GeoGebra. Unfortunately, they did not chat about what they were doing during this period. We have to look at a more detailed log and step through the VMT Replayer slowly to observe what they were doing.

The logs shown so far have all been filtered to show only text-chat postings. Log 7.16 is a more detailed view of the log including GeoGebra actions, such as selecting a new GeoGebra tool from the tool bar or using the selected tool to create or change a GeoGebra object. It also includes system messages, such as announcing that a user has changed to view a different tab. (The GeoGebra actions are not assigned line numbers. The system messages are assigned line numbers; they account for the line numbers missing in the chat logs in this section.)

	15:57:10	Geogebra:-Triangles	cheerios	tool changed to Move
	15:57:27	Geogebra:-Triangles	cheerios	updated Point A
	15:57:28	Geogebra:-Triangles	cheerios	tool changed to Move Graphics View
	15:58:35	Geogebra:-Triangles	cornflakes	tool changed to Move
	15:58:39	Geogebra:-Triangles	cornflakes	updated group of objects G,H
	15:58:42	Geogebra:-Triangles	cornflakes	tool changed to Move Graphics View
47	15:59:08	system	cornflakes	Now viewing tab Squares
48	15:59:13	system	cornflakes	Now viewing tab Triangles
49	15:59:17	system	cornflakes	Now viewing tab Hexagons
50	15:59:21	system	fruitloops	Now viewing tab Squares

Log 7.16: The students view other tabs.

In this excerpt from the detailed log, we can see that Cornflakes used certain GeoGebra tools to change specific objects in the construction. We also see that Cornflakes—like Fruitloops and Cheerios—looked at the other tabs. This is just a sample of what took place during the 12 minutes. There were actually 170 lines in the detailed chat for that period. During all this activity, the students made very little direct progress on their construction. They constructed some lines, circles, and points. They engaged in considerable dragging: of the original figure, of their new triangle, and of their experimental objects. They also each looked at the other tabs.

Finally, Cheerios provided the key analysis of the dependency: AD=BE=CF. The others immediately and simultaneously agreed with the analysis. In Log 7.17, Cheerios went on to project this dependency onto their construction.

66	16:18:30	cheerios	as i was movign d segment da is the same distance as segment be
67	16:18:52	cheerios	and also cf
68	16:19:41	cheerios	our kg is the same as ad
69	16:20:06	corn-flakes	agrreeed
70	16:20:06	fruitloops	i agree
71	16:21:21	cheerios	there should be a point on segment gh which is the same distance as kg and also between segment uh
72	16:22:00	cheerios	it should be ih not uh
73	16:23:39	cheerios	so i used the compass tool and measured kg and used point i as the center and created a circle

Log 7.17: The students make a key observation.

Cheerios narrated line 73 while she used the compass tool to measure the length from their point on the side of the exterior triangle to one of its vertices and to transfer that length to another side from another vertex. Then Cornflakes took control of the construction, placed a point where the compass intersected the side and then repeated the process with the compass to construct another point on the third side. Fruitloops then took control and used the polygon tool to construct a shaded interior triangle connecting the three points on the sides of the exterior triangle. She then conducted the drag test, dragging points on each of the new triangles to confirm that they remained equilateral and inscribed dynamically. Thus, all three not only agreed with the plan, but they also all participated in the construction. The team as a unit thereby accomplished the solution of the problem in tab A.

At that point, they had been working in the room for over an hour and had to leave quickly. Three days later, the team reassembled in the same chat room to continue work on Topic 5. They had hurriedly completed the construction of the inscribed triangles, but had not had a chance to discuss their accomplishment. Furthermore, they had not had any time to work on the other tabs.

Cheerios resumes the discussion by announcing that they have to explain what they did (see Log 7.18). This directive may have come from the teacher before the session started. Cheerios begins to explain what they had done at the end of the previous session. Cornflakes joins in. When Cornflakes says, "you had to make the point between the two circles," Cheerios clarifies (line 96): "not between the circles (but) where the segment intersect(s) with the circle." Cornflakes may have been confusing the construction of the first triangle (with intersecting circles) with that of the interior triangle (with the compass circle intersecting the triangle side). At any rate, Cheerios uses the formal mathematical terms, "segment" and "intersect," and Cornflakes indicates that they are in agreement on what took place in the construction.

90	15:16:18	cheerios	we have to explain what we did
91	15:19:48	cheerios	so first u have to plot a random point on the triangle we used k . then i realised the distance from kg is the same as im and rh
92	15:22:51	cheerios	then you have to use the compass tool in are case are the length of are radius is kg so then we clicked those 2 points and used vertex i as the center the way to plot are second point of are triangle is where the circle and segment ih intersect
93	15:20:41	corn-flakes	right
94	15:23:53	cheerios	and then we repeated that step with the other side and h was the center
95	15:23:48	corn-flakes	yes you had to make the point between the circles
96	15:24:21	cheerios	not between the circles where the segment intersect with the circle
97	15:25:27	corn-flakes	yea same thing

Log 7.18: The students explain their construction.

Fruitloops then raises a question about the dependencies among the points forming the vertices of the interior triangle in Log 7.19. She notes that the two points constructed with the compass tool are colored black (or shaded dark), an indication of dependent points.

98	15:26:04	fruitloops	so then why are point m and r shaded dark and don tact the same as k
99	15:25:52	cheerios	its differnt
100	15:25:58	cheerios	different*
101	15:26:00	corn-flakes	yes i know
102	15:26:14	cheerios	they are restricted
103	15:26:35	fruitloops	but whyy???????
104	15:26:45	corn-flakes	yeah if its a darker its restricted i think

105	15:26:52	cheerios	yes
106	15:26:56	cheerios	correct
107	15:28:30	fruitloops	but why are m and r restricted but k isnt?
108	15:30:33	corn-flakes	because the invisible cirlcels are still there
109	15:31:35	fruitloops	okay so its because we made k by just using the point tool and putting it on the line but with m and r we maade it through using circles so technicaly, the circle is still there but its hidden but we just dont see it.
110	15:31:56	fruitloops	and i think we can move on because i understand it well. do you guys get it?
111	15:31:44	corn-flakes	right
112	15:31:49	cheerios	yup
113	15:32:04	cheerios	yes
114	15:32:10	corn-flakes	sure

Log 7.19: The students explain the dependencies.

The students all agree that the two points are different from the first one in terms of being more restricted. However, Fruitloops requests more of an explanation about why this is. Corn-flakes—who had originally hidden the circles formed by the compass tool by changing the properties of the circles to not show themselves—explains that the circles are still in effect. Fruitloops then explicates that the difference is that the first point was just placed on a side of the larger triangle (so it can be dragged, as long as it stays on the side), but the more completely restricted two points were constructed with the circles (so they must stay at the intersections of the circles with their sides, so they cannot be dragged at all). Although the compass circles have been hidden from view, the dependencies that they helped to define (the intersections) are still in effect. One could go on to discuss how moving the first point will alter the lengths that define those circles and therefore will move the other points, but the students state that they all understand the reason why the different points are colored differently and have different dependencies. They are ready to move on and all change to the tab with inscribed squares.

118	15:32:52	fruitloops	can i try dragging it?
119	15:32:56	cheerios	yea
120	15:33:44	cheerios	u can try now fruitloops
121	15:35:03	fruitloops	so b and a move and points c,h,d,g, and f dont move
122	15:35:28	fruitloops	and e is restrricted
123	15:35:34	corn-flakes	E IS RESTRICTED
124	15:35:58	fruitloops	do how do we create a square like the outer square?
125	15:36:54	cheerios	we have to talk about the dependencies and stuff
126	15:37:01	cheerios	read the instructions

Log 7.20: The students explore the square.

The students start again by dragging to explore dependencies. In Log 7.20, Fruitloops does the dragging and reports three classifications of points. Two points of the outer square can move (freely), one point of the inner square is "restricted" and the other points don't move (are dependent). Cornflakes echoes the "E IS RESTRICTED" as though she would like to discuss this special status. Cheerios also tries to insist on more discussion of the dependencies. However, Fruitloops repeatedly asks how they can construct a square. They have constructed many triangles in previous sessions, but never a square.

127	15:38:45	fruitloops	how but how do we make the square?
128	15:39:11	fruitloops	like i know how to make the triangle but now the square
129	15:39:11	cheerios	a grid
130	15:39:20	corn-flakes	olets start by cinstructing a regular square
131	15:39:16	cheerios	a grid
132	15:39:47	fruitloops	i think we should make perpendicular lines somehow
133	15:39:58	cheerios	use the perpindicular line tool
134	15:43:21	fruitloops	the first line segment would be like ab
135	15:43:27	corn-flakes	yes
138	15:51:24	cheerios	how do u know ji is straight
139	15:55:40	fruitloops	i dont know what to do because the points arent the same color
140	15:56:38	fruitloops	now after you make the perpendicular lines try to make the circles\

| 141 | 15:57:48 | fruitloops | i think you need to know use the polygon tool and make the square |
| 142 | 15:58:50 | cheerios | i made a line segment which was if than i used the perpendicular line tool and made 2 lines on each side then used the compass tool and clicked on each point and then the center vertex was i and then made a another circle except the center vertex is j and connected all the points |

Log 7.21: The students construct the first square.

There is again considerable experimentation taking place in GeoGebra during Log 7.21. Note that this log spans 20 min. The three students took turns trying various approaches using the tools they were familiar with and gradually adding the perpendicular line tool. They were considering the definition of a square as having all right angles, so they first talked about using a grid and then constructing perpendiculars. In line 139, Fruitloops questions how to construct the square in such a way that the points are the same colors as in the original inscribed squares figure. While this could provide a clue to the construction, it seems to introduce more confusion than anything else. Eventually, Cheerios succeeds in constructing a dynamic square (see Figure 7.6), and describes the procedure in line 142.

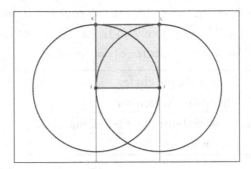

Figure 7.6: The students construct a square.

The student construction of the square is quite nice. It closely mirrors or builds upon the construction of an equilateral triangle, which the students have mastered: it has a base side (segment IJ) and two circles of radius IJ centered on I and J. For the right-angle vertices at I and J, perpendiculars are constructed at I and J. Because segments JK and IL are radii of the same circles as IJ, all three segments are constrained to be equal length. This determines the four corners of a quadrilateral, IJKL, which is dynamically constrained to be a square.

As soon as the outer square is constructed, Fruitloops proposes to inscribe the squares by following a procedure analogous to the procedure they used for inscribing the triangles (see Log 7.22). While she narrates, the team actually constructs the inscribed square and conducts the drag test on it.

143	15:59:10	fruitloops	now we need to use the compass tool lilke we did in the triangles tab
144	15:59:57	fruitloops	because af is equal to ec and dh and bc
145	16:01:15	cheerios	then used to polygon tool and then hid the circles and lines
146	16:01:07	fruitloops	correct
147	16:01:36	fruitloops	and we used the circles to make the sides equal because the sides are their radius
148	16:02:39	fruitloops	point m is like point e because it moves around
149	16:02:48	fruitloops	and its the same color
150	16:04:14	fruitloops	good!!

Log 7.22: The students make another key observation.

Fruitloops notes (line 147) that the segments between the outer and inner square along the sides of the outer square (IP, JM, KO, LN) are constrained to be equal in length because they are dependent on circles that were constructed with the compass tool to have radii that will always be equal to the length of JM. Point M moves freely on JK just like point E on AC, and M is the same color as E, indicating that it has the same degree of constraint.

151	16:04:40	fruitloops	now hide the circles
152	16:05:25	fruitloops	the points match up
153	16:06:00	fruitloops	it works! just like the original circl;e
154	16:05:47	cheerios	yay it works

Log 7.23: The students test their construction.

In Log 7.23, the team hides the construction circles that impose the necessary dependencies. They use the drag test and conclude that their construction works the same as the original inscribed-squares construction that they were supposed to duplicate (see Figure 7.7).

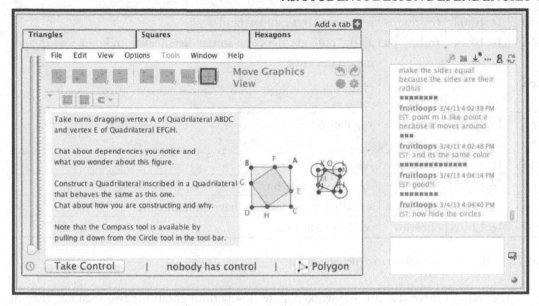

Figure 7.7: The students construct an inscribed square.

Cheerios summarizes the procedure they followed, in Log 7.24. Fruitloops notes that the points N, O, and P are colored dark because they are completely dependent upon where the compass circles intersect the sides of the exterior square. Cheerios reiterates that it is the distance along the sides up to these points that is constrained to be equal and Fruitloops agrees, clarifying that the distances are constrained because they are all dependent on the same radii. Cornflakes agrees. They have completed the assignment in the second tab and are out of time before they can start on the third tab.

155	16:09:42	cheerios	so just plotted a random point on line segment jk and then used the compass tool and clicked on point m and j (radius) and then clicked k to be the center and then plotted the point where line segment kl intersect with the circle and repeated these steps on the other sides
156	16:09:18	fruitloops	i think points o, n, and p are dark because they weere made using the original circles
157	16:08:23	corn-flakes	yess
158	16:09:32	corn-flakes	yea i agreeee
159	16:10:27	cheerios	the distance between m and j is the same between ok and ln and pi

160	16:10:02	fruitloops	yeah i saw and i understand
161	16:10:44	fruitloops	all the radii are the same so the distances from ko,ln, and ip and jm are the same
162	16:10:18	corn-flakes	same
163	16:10:57	corn-flakes	yup i agrree
164	16:11:01	cheerios	yes
165	16:11:03	fruitloops	should we move on?
166	16:11:33	fruitloops	actually i dont think we have enough time
167	16:12:02	cheerios	yeah so next time

Log 7.24: The students summarize dependencies.

The team of three students has worked quite closely throughout the two sessions. They have collaborated on all the work, taking turns to engage in the dragging and construction. They have discussed the dependencies both in the original figures and in their re-constructions. They have tried to ensure that everyone on the team understood the findings from the dragging, the procedures in the constructions and the significance of the dependencies.

In both tabs, the team began with exploratory dragging to get a sense of dependencies in the original figure. Then they experimented with constructions, guided by some sense of what to look for and things to try, but without a clear plan. Eventually, they discovered a good solution, described it explicitly, tested it with the drag test and discussed the underlying dependencies that made it work.

7.4   WORKING WITH DEPENDENCIES

In each session reviewed in this chapter—the teams of researchers, the group of teachers, and the triad of students—the work on the problem of inscribed polygons involved an integration of dragging, constructing and designing dependencies. The different teams brought contrasting backgrounds to the task. The researchers had been involved in various ways in developing the computer system and the teacher-professional-development training. The teachers were all experienced classroom math teachers, some of whom often taught geometry. The students had not yet taken a course on geometry and had previously only been briefly exposed to some basic geometry concepts. Yet, all the sessions followed a similar pattern.

The work in each case began with investigative dragging of points to determine what relationships among the geometric objects (points and line segments) were maintained dynamically—i.e., under change of relative position, or dragging. Once the team had a sense of what relationships had to be maintained, they started to experiment with constructing new objects and building in relationships among them through construction techniques. The construction furthered the team's understanding of the needed dependencies, which they had begun to gather from their dragging. Often, they would return to drag the original figure more as they deepened their understanding from construction trials. They did not work according to a clear and explicitly articulated plan; they experimented. Solving the problem was not a matter of following a rational plan with goals and sub-goals, but a process of creative actions aimed at discovering how dynamic-geometric reality responds.

> Solving the problem was not a matter of following a rational plan with goals and sub-goals, but a process of creative actions aimed at discovering how dynamic-geometric reality responds.

In the end, when a group felt it had succeeded at re-creating the original inscribed figure, they reflected on the dependencies involved. In doing so, they deepened their understanding of how dependencies work in dynamic geometry and how one can effectively construct dependencies in the dynamic-geometry environment.

Particularly, the logs of the student work suggest that the promise of dynamic geometry is starting to be realized.

Perhaps the paper most focused on the notion of dependency in the early research on dynamic geometry was a conference paper entitled, "Coming to know about 'dependency' within a dynamic-geometry environment" (Jones, 1996). Written almost two decades ago when Geometer's Sketchpad and Cabri existed in their original versions, the paper emphasized the difficult but central aim of having students gain an understanding of dependency relationships:

> As Hölzl et al. (1994) discovered when they observed pupils attempting to construct a rectangle, the students had to come to terms with "the very essence of Cabri; that a figure consists of relationships *and that there is* a hierarchy of dependencies" (emphasis in original). An example of this hierarchy of dependencies is the difference (in Cabri 1 for the PC) between basic point, point on object and point of intersection. While all three types of point look identical on the screen, basic points and points on objects are moveable (with obvious restrictions on the latter). Yet a point of intersection cannot be dragged. This is because a point of intersection depends on the position of the basic objects which intersect. In their study, Hölzl et al. found that students need to develop an awareness of such functional dependency if they are to be successful with non-trivial geometrical construction tasks using Cabri. The experience of Hölzl et al. is that "Not surprisingly, the idea of functional dependency has proved difficult [for students] to grasp." (pp. 145-146)

In the preceding analysis of the student sessions, we saw that the three students became quite aware of the different dependency status of certain free points (points A and B), constrained points on lines (point D) and dependent points at intersections (points C, E, and F). They learned that these different statuses are indicated by different coloring of the points in GeoGebra, and they were concerned to make the points in their re-created figure correspond in color to the respective points in the original figure. They explicitly discussed points placed on a line being constrained to that line during dragging and points defined by intersections (of two circles, of two lines or of a circle and a line) being dependent on the intersecting lines and therefore not able to be dragged independently. As they worked on the tasks in this session and discussed their findings, the group developed a more refined sense of dependencies. One can see this especially in the way that one student would restate another student's articulation of dependencies and how everyone in the group would agree to the restatement.

Although there are various indications that one student could express more clearly than another an action to be taken—such as a construction step—or a statement of a finding or an accomplishment, the three students worked very closely together. They built on each other's actions and statements to accomplish more than it seemed any one of the students could on her own. They all agreed in the chat on each step and each conclusion. Each phase of the session—the explorative dragging, the experimental constructing and the determination of dependencies—was an accomplishment of the group.

Of course, the task instructions provided some guidance in pursuing these steps. However, once the teams started in the direction prompted by the instructions, they did not simply follow the instructions. They became engrossed in team-work that continued in a natural and self-motivated way. The relatively minimal instructions served as a successful catalyst. They were necessary to guide the participants during an early collaborative-learning experience. In the future, the groups should be able to proceed when such "scaffolds" have been removed—as the students did in successfully constructing a square on their own. Furthermore, in the future the individual group members should be able to do similar work by themselves (even in their heads) as a residual effect of their group work. It is unlikely that the lessons would be learned as well if the participants just read a textbook description of the procedures that they practiced hands-on and collaboratively in these sessions.

In each case, the design-based research project got feedback—both from the participants directly and from the analysis of their logs—to refine the instructions. This helped us to develop resources to guide student groups to experience dynamic geometry in terms of the underlying dependencies. In Chapter 8, we will consider the nature and role of resources in supporting math discourse and group interaction. Then in Chapter 9, we will discuss the need to provide a curricular context incorporating specific kinds of designed resources, which can be enacted by student groups to guide them to experiences of human-centered mathematics. Finally, in Chapter 10, we will present the set of curricular resources that have been designed for WinterFest 2013.

CHAPTER 8

Theory: Resources for Geometry

Chapter Summary

Experience with virtual math teams provides insight into the nature of collaborative learning as involving the co-creation of co-presence, intersubjective shared understanding, and group cognition. Early trials with the collaborative dynamic-geometry environment also emphasize the need for providing teachers and students with a variety of resources to support their mathematical work. This chapter discusses the implications of these findings for the theory of how learning takes place on multiple levels of analysis—individual, small-group, and community—and how learning can be supported with resources for collaborative interaction.

Studies of computer-supported collaborative learning (CSCL) have begun to explore processes of online group cognition—such as small-group methods of problem solving—and how various technological and interactional resources and media can be provided to promote productive mathematical discourse.

This chapter first presents:

1. an analysis of *co-presence* as a foundational aspect of online interaction in an excerpt of mathematical chat discourse;

2. based on how the students in this excerpt actually interact, it develops a notion of *intersubjective shared understanding* as necessary for the possibility of collaborative knowledge-building dialog; and, finally,

3. this is followed by a discussion of consequences for the design of computer support for academically productive online *group cognition*.

Then the chapter explores the analytic levels of:

1. individual interpretation and learning;

2. group collaborative knowledge building; and

3. community practices or cultural values.

It considers how connections across these analytic levels can be mediated by a variety of *interactional resources*. Such resources may be emergent from previous interaction, enacted in current interaction and evolved for future interactions. Resources contribute to the inherited shared world, to the current joint problem space and to future-oriented goals of the group. They are both discovered and created in the interactional work of the group; both adopted from individual and social knowledge and contributing to personal and institutional changes. They can take many forms.

8.1 AN EXCERPT OF COMPUTER-SUPPORTED DISCOURSE

The studies of digital interaction by virtual math teams presented in (Stahl, 2009) adopt an ethnomethodological interest in how interaction is actually carried out in particular online contexts. They assume that the "member methods" (Garfinkel & Sacks, 1970) or "group practices" (Stahl, 2011b) of computer-mediated interaction developed by small groups of students may differ significantly from commonsense assumptions of researchers based on experience with face-to-face interaction. If this is true, then it is important to explore actual instances of digital interaction before—or as part of—designing interventions in such settings.

This section reviews how a team of three students collaboratively achieved a cognitive accomplishment as a distributed online group. The log of their interaction makes visible mechanisms by which academically productive discourse can—and did—arise naturally in settings of computer-supported collaborative learning. The data analysis presented here is not intended as an illustration of pre-existing theories; rather, theory emerged from this and similar data.

Figure 8.1 (left) shows a screenshot of the Virtual Math Teams (VMT) software environment, being used by three middle-school students. They volunteered to participate in this online,

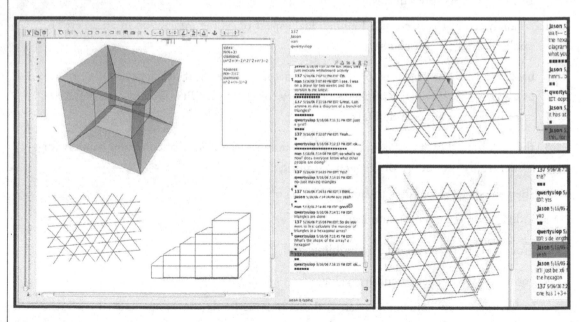

Figure 8.1: The VMT interface near the beginning (left), middle (upper right) and end (lower right) of the excerpt.

synchronous math activity with other students from around the world. The students are collaboratively investigating mathematical patterns (combinatorics) related to sequences of geometric figures. We analyze this chat rather than a WinterFest 2013 chat because in this chat the students were not co-located and did not know each other outside of the chat, so the phenomena involved in establishing co-presence, shared understanding and group cohesion are more clearly visible. In the WinterFest chats, the students often had existing interpersonal relationships and may have been seated in the same computer lab during the sessions.

When this chat took place, VMT did not include a GeoGebra tab, but just a generic shared whiteboard. Seen in the lower right of the whiteboard is a stair-step pattern of blocks remaining on the board from the students' previous day's session. Currently, the students are considering a pattern of regular hexagons, which they will visualize in a grid of triangles they construct in the lower left.

Log 8.1 shows a chat excerpt from the session. Three students—whose online names are 137, Qwertyuiop, and Jason—are chatting.

line	time	student	chat post
705	19:15:08	137	So do you want to first calculate the number of triangles in a hexagonal array?
706	19:15:45	qwertyuiop	What's the shape of the array? a hexagon?
707	19:16:02	137	Ya.
708	19:16:15	qwertyuiop	ok...
709	19:16:41	Jason	wait-- can someone highlight the hexagonal array on the diagram? i don't really see what you mean...
710	19:17:30	Jason	hmm.. okay
711	19:17:43	qwertyuiop	oops
712	19:17:44	Jason	so it has at least 6 triangles?
713	19:17:58	Jason	in this, for instance
714	19:18:53	137	How do you color lines?
715	19:19:06	Jason	there's a little paintbrush icon up at the top
716	19:19:12	Jason	it's the fifth one from the right
717	19:19:20	137	Thanks.
718	19:19:21	Jason	there ya go :-)
719	19:19:48	137	Er... That hexagon.

Log 8.1: "Wait…. I don't really see"—establishing co-presence.

In line 705, student 137 poses a math question of potential interest to the small group. Then Qwertyuiop seeks to understand the mathematical shape that 137 proposed. Qwertyuiop next draws the grid of triangles to see if he understands what 137 means by "hexagonal array."

Jason effectively halts the discussion (line 709) to seek help in seeing the hexagonal form that 137 and Qwertyuiop see. Jason's posting is designed to bring the group work to a halt because he does not see what 137 and Qwertyuiop are talking about. This is an important collaboration move, asking the others to clarify what they are talking about. Jason is referring to the group meaning-making process, and halting it so he can fully participate.

Jason phrases his request in terms of "seeing" what the others "mean." This seeing should be taken literally, in terms of vision and graphics. Jason asks the others to "highlight the hexagonal array on the diagram" so he can see it in the graphics.

Creating several extra lines, 137 outlines a large hexagon, as shown in the upper right of Figure 8.1. This provides what Jason needs to be part of the group problem-solving effort. Jason not only says, "Okay" but he contributes a next step (line 712) by proposing a math result and giving a visible demonstration of it with a highlighted small hexagon. Giving a next step shows understanding and takes the idea further. Jason points from his chat posting. Note the green rectangle highlighting a small hexagon and the line connecting Jason's current chat posting (line 713) to this highlighted area (Figure 8.1 upper right); this is an important feature of the VMT system supporting online pointing or deixis. Pointing is a critical function for shared understanding—and must be supported explicitly (by a function like this or more commonly by an explicit textual description) in a digital environment, where bodily gestures are not visible to others.

After Jason draws the visual attention of the other participants to a particular example of a smallest hexagon, consisting of 6 triangles, 137 asks Jason how to change the color of lines in the whiteboard. In line 715, Jason responds and 137 changes the color of the lines outlining the larger hexagon. Color becomes an effective method for orienting the team to a shared object. This use of colored lines to help each other see focal things in the whiteboard will become an important established group practice in the team's continuing work. In line 719, 137 outlines a larger hexagon, with edge of 3 units (Figure 8.1 lower right).

At this point, the group has established an effective *co-presence* at a mathematical object of interest. Through a variety of interactional practices—which the group members have adapted from past experiences or constructed on the spot—the group has regulated its interaction and focused its common vision into a "being-there-together" (Stahl et al., 2011) with the object that they have constituted as an hexagonal array. The group is now in a position to explore this object mathematically.

line	time	student	chat post
720	19:20:02	Jason	so... should we try to find a formula i guess
721	19:20:22	Jason	input: side length; output: # triangles

722	19:20:39	qwertyuiop	It might be easier to see it as the 6 smaller triangles.
723	19:20:48	137	Like this?
724	19:21:02	qwertyuiop	yes
725	19:21:03	Jason	yup

Log 8.2: "Like this…."—building intersubjective shared understanding.

In line 720 (see Log 8.2), Jason explicitly proposes finding a formula for the number of elemental triangles in a hexagonal array with side-length of N. Qwertyuiop suggests a way of seeing the hexagonal array as consisting of six identical sectors, which he ambiguously refers to as "the 6 smaller triangles." 137 checks what Qwertyuiop means by asking him "Like this?" and then dividing up the large hexagon with three red lines, forming six triangular forms inside of the blue outline (see Figure 8.1, lower right).

This is a move by Qwertyuiop to see the representation of their problem as a much simpler problem. As Jason notes (in Log 8.3), now they only have to compute the number of elemental triangles in each of the six identical triangular sectors and then multiply that result by 6 to get the total. Furthermore, the simpler problem can be solved immediately by just looking. As Jason says, each sector has 1+3+5 triangles. The human eye can recognize this at a glance ("subitize"), once it is properly focused on a relevant sector (Lakoff & Núñez, 2000, p. 19).

The important mathematical problem-solving move here is to see the problem in a new way. Qwertyuiop sees the hexagon *as* a set of six symmetrical sectors. The important discourse move is to share this new view with the team. This is accomplished collaboratively in lines 722–725: Qwertyuiop proposes a new way of seeing the array; 137 outlines it, using their new technique of colored lines; and Jason aligns with them. They each participate in seeing the same thing (seeing the hexagon as composed of six triangles), in demonstrating to each other that they see this new way, and then in building on each other to count the small triangles visually. They thereby collectively go beyond the co-presence of seeing the same thing to actually build knowledge together about the shared object. This group knowledge constitutes an *intersubjective shared understanding* of the mathematical structure of the object. Through the sequence of steps outlined above, the members of the group have articulated an understanding that they share as a result of their co-presence and of their shared textual and graphical actions.

726	19:21:29	qwertyuiop	side length is the same…
727	19:22:06	Jason	yeah
728	19:22:13	Jason	so it'll just be x6 for # triangles in the hexagon
729	19:22:19	137	Each one has 1+3+5 triangles.
730	19:22:23	Jason	but then we're assuming just regular hexagons

731	19:22:29	qwertyuiop	the "each polygon corrisponds to 2 sides" thing we did last time doesn't work for triangles
732	19:23:17	137	It equals 1+3+...+(n+n-1) because of the "rows"?
733	19:24:00	qwertyuiop	yes- 1st row is 1, 2nd row is 3...
734	19:24:49	137	And there are n terms so... n(2n/2)
735	19:25:07	137	or n^2
736	19:25:17	Jason	yeah
737	19:25:21	Jason	then multiply by 6
738	19:25:31	137	To get 6n^2

Log 8.3: "To get 6n^2"—accomplishing group cognition.

Note in the chat in Log 8.3 how the three students build on each other's postings to construct the general formula for any size array: $6n^2$. Having collaboratively de-constructed the complicated problem into visually simple units, they now take turns in re-constructing the problem symbolically and for any size hexagon. They are able to work on this together because of their co-presence, which allows them to orient to the same objects, with a shared understanding of the terms (e.g., "hexagonal array," "side length"), graphics (colored border lines), procedures (divide into 6, then multiply by 6), and goals ("find a formula"). Note that they have articulated each of these in the chat text, so that they can share the experience of each. The words evoke the phenomena, making them co-present for the students.

Having counted the number of triangles in the array during this excerpt, the students will next want to count the number of line segments. This is more complicated, but the group will extend the methods we have just observed to accomplish their task. Taking advantage of multiple symmetries, they will use colored lines to break the pattern down into visually simple patterns, outline specific focal areas and attend to shared objects, where their optical systems can do the counting. Some of the smaller units are harder to visualize and there are issues of possible overlap among the sectors. But using the skills we observed and developing those skills incrementally, the group will succeed in achieving a sequence of group-cognitive accomplishments (for a detailed analysis, see Çakir & Stahl, 2013).

8.2   CO-PRESENCE IN COMPUTER-SUPPORTED DISCOURSE

Co-presence—through co-attending as a basis for shared understanding—by a small group includes many of the basic features of an individual attending to and interpreting an object of interest. Attending to something involves focusing on it as the foreground object, assigning everything else to its background context (Polanyi, 1966). For instance, the students in the excerpt above foreground a specific hexagon against the background of the larger array of lines by coloring its outline or highlighting it with the pointing tool. Attending to an object involves seeing it "as" something or some way (Goodwin, 1994; Heidegger, 1927/1996; Wittgenstein, 1953). Co-attending supports a shared interpretation, viewing or understanding by creating the co-presence of attending in a shared way to a shared object in a shared world. For instance, the students view the larger hexagon "as" a set of six triangular sectors by visually dividing the hexagon with red lines that outline the sectors and by texting, "it might be easier to see it as the 6 smaller triangles." (Note that the terminology Qwertyuiop naturally uses here explicitly involves "to see it as….")

> Co-attending supports a shared interpretation, viewing or understanding by creating the co-presence of attending in a shared way to a shared object in a shared world.

8.3 INTERSUBJECTIVE SHARED UNDERSTANDING

The establishment of shared understanding in a small group through co-attending to shared objects is essential for collaboration (Evans et al., 2011; Mercer & Wegerif, 1999). However, in an online context the usual techniques of body positioning, gaze, and gestural pointing with fingers are not available for creating and maintaining shared attention. Virtual teams must invent new methods to coordinate attention or make use of special tools in the software that may be provided to support this.

Previous VMT studies have analyzed cases in which small groups of online students have developed methods for creating, maintaining and repairing shared understanding—similar to what was discussed in the previous section. For instance, small groups working in the VMT environment have:

- co-experienced a shared world (Stahl et al., 2011) by developing shared group practices (Medina, Suthers, & Vatrapu, 2009; Stahl, 2011b);

- used the posing of questions to elicit details needed to establish and confirm the sharing of understandings (Zhou, Zemel & Stahl, 2008);

- built a "joint problem space" (Teasley & Roschelle, 1993)—i.e., a shared understanding about a set of topics—with ways of referencing them—an "indexical ground" (Hanks, 1992)—that is shared and supports co-attending (Sarmiento & Stahl, 2008);

- developed group methods for bridging across temporal breaks in interaction to reestablish a group memory or shared understanding of past events (Sarmiento & Stahl, 2007);

- repaired their shared understanding in the face of breakdowns (Stahl, Zemel & Koschmann, 2009);

- integrated text chat and sequences of whiteboard actions to communicate complex mathematical relationships (Çakir, Zemel & Stahl, 2009); and

- solved math problems by proceeding through logical sequences of steps collaboratively (Stahl, 2011a).

The analysis of the excerpt of interaction presented above and these other studies of VMT have identified the following features of the mediation of digital interaction: co-presence, intersubjective shared understanding and group cognition.

One can distinguish two paradigms of shared understanding.

1. A rationalist paradigm assumes that individuals each have a stock of propositions in their minds that represent their current beliefs or opinions. The corresponding conception of shared understanding starts from the individual understandings of two people and tries to establish equivalence of one or more propositions they hold. This is sometimes called "cognitive convergence," where the goal is to converge the separate mental models, internal representations or propositional contents of the two people: sharing as mutual exchange.

2. The alternative paradigm of shared understanding—exemplified by the analysis in this chapter—starts from the shared world and a view of intentionality as consciousness of an object, rather than as a mental construct by an ego. This is the view of situated and distributed cognition, where individuals are situated in and active with a shared, intersubjective world consisting of meaningful objects for which they care: sharing as acting together.

20th century philosophy from Hegel (1807/1967) and Husserl (1936/1989) through Marx (1858/1939), Heidegger (1927/1996), Sartre (1968), Merleau-Ponty (1945/2002), and Wittgenstein (1953) has rejected the starting point of a transcendental ego in favor of consciousness as a social and fundamentally shared phenomenon. Now, even at the neuron level, the discovery of mirror neurons points to a physiological, specifically human, basis for shared cognition (Gallese & Lakoff, 2005). We can immediately experience the world through the eyes and body of other people. We can feel their pain if we see another person's body hurt and their face grimaced. As Wittgenstein (1953) argued in other ways, there is no such thing as private feelings of pain or of private meanings of language: we are co-present in an intersubjectively shared and commonly understood world.

8.4   GROUP COGNITION

Vygotsky (1930/1978) claimed that intersubjective (group) cognition precedes intra-subjective (individual) cognition. He conducted controlled experiments to show that children were able to accomplish cognitive tasks in collaboration with others at an earlier developmental age than they were able to accomplish the same tasks on their own. Individual-cognitive acts are often preceded by and derivative from group-cognitive acts. For instance, individual reasoning or action (dividing a figure, coloring a border) by a student in the VMT data may be based upon earlier group practices. According to Vygotsky, individual mental thinking is fundamentally silent self-talk. Thus, individual-student reasoning can often be seen as reflective self-talk about previous group accomplishments. In such cases, self-reports about individual cognition—through think-aloud protocols, survey answers, or interview responses—are what Suchman (2007) refers to as post-hoc rationalizations. They are reinterpretations of group cognitions by the individual (responsive to the interview situation and relying on commonsensical conceptions of individual cognition). In this reading of Vygotsky, group cognition has a theoretical priority over individual cognition. If one accepts this, then the theoretical analysis of shared understanding and the practical promotion of it become priorities. The emerging technologies of networked digital interaction provide promising opportunities for observing and supporting the establishment of shared understanding in online educational environments.

Based on experiments in computer support of small-group knowledge building from 1995–2005, the construct of *group cognition* was proposed in (Stahl, 2006) to begin to define the relevant focus on group-level cognitive achievements. Analyses of studies from 2006–2009 in (Stahl, 2009) continued to explore the practicalities of supporting group-level cognition. The present book extends this line of research, reporting on work from 2010–2013.

Group cognition is not a physical thing, a mental state or a characteristic of all groups. It is a unit of analysis. What it recommends is that analysts who are studying digital interaction should look at the small-group unit of analysis (Stahl, 2010a). Too often, collaborative learning researchers reduce group-level phenomena either to individual psychological constructs or to societal institutions and practices (Stahl, 2013). But, as we have seen in the preceding excerpt, there are group methods and processes taking place at the small-group unit of analysis that are not reducible to the mental behaviors of an individual or to the institutions of a community.

For instance, the three students above collaboratively solved their problem through a sequence of postings that elicit and respond to each other. Qwertyuiop proposed the view of the hexagon as 6 sectors; 137 summed the series of triangles in one sector to n^2; Jason provided the answer by multiplying the value for one sector by the number of sectors. The result was a group product of the group interaction.

If one student had derived this result, we would call it a cognitive achievement of that student. Since the group derived it, it can be called an achievement of group cognition. This does not mean there is some kind of "group mind" at work or anything other than the interaction of the three students. Rather, it means that the analysis of that cognitive achievement is most appropriately conducted at the group unit of analysis, in terms of the interplay of the posting and drawing actions shared by the group.

The absolute centrality of public discourse and shared understanding to the success of group cognition—successful knowledge building at the group level—in the context of digital interaction implies the need for productive forms of talk within the group. Digital environments to support collaborative knowledge building must be carefully designed to foster co-presence, intersubjective shared understanding, and group cognition.

8.5   RESOURCES FOR CONNECTING LEVELS OF ANALYSIS

As we have seen in this chapter and in the philosophy chapter (Chapter 3), it is possible to analyze interactions in VMT by focusing on different units of analysis—typically on the individual (personal), small-group (interactional) and community (social) units. In the following, we will explore the idea that the levels of personal learning, group cognition and community knowledge building may be connected by emergent *interactional resources*, which can mediate between the levels. A preliminary theory of the connection of the levels will be sketched. This will have implication for later chapters in which curriculum for gradually providing math teachers and math students with a complex of resources relevant to dynamic geometry is described as an example of how to support the connection of small-group interaction with individual understanding and with cultural practices in the study of collaborative dynamic geometry.

Analysis of learning, cognition, and knowledge building in CSCL are often conducted on one of the three levels of individual learning, small-group cognition, or community knowledge building. This tri-partite distinction is grounded in the nature of CSCL. With its focus on collaborative learning, CSCL naturally emphasizes providing support for dyads and small groups working together. In practice, CSCL small-group activities are often orchestrated within a physical classroom or virtual community context by providing some initial time for individual activities (such as background reading or homework practice) followed by the small-group work and then culminating in whole-class sharing of group findings. Thus, the typical classroom practices tend to create three distinguishable levels of activity. Often, the teacher sees the group work as a warm-up or stimulation and preparation for the whole-class discussion, which is then facilitated directly by the teacher. Conversely, the importance of testing individual performance and valuing individual learning posits the group work as a training ground for the individual participants, who are then assessed on their own, outside of the collaborative context. In both of these ways, group cognition is treated as secondary to either individual or community goals. By contrast, the role of intersubjective learning is foundational in Vygotsky (1930/1978), the seminal theoretical source for CSCL. Regardless of which is taken as primary, the three levels are actualized in CSCL practice, and the matter of their relative roles and connections becomes subsequently problematic (Dillenbourg et al., 1996; Rogoff, 1995; Stahl, 2006).

While these different units, levels, dimensions, or planes are intimately intertwined, research efforts generally focus on only one of them, and current analytic methodologies are designed for only one (Stahl, 2013; Suthers et al., 2013). Furthermore, there is little theoretical understanding of how the different levels are connected. To the extent that CSCL researchers discuss the connections among levels, they often rely upon commonsensical notions of socialization and enculturation, popularizations of traditional social science, based on face-to-face interactions. There are no explicit empirical analyses of the connections for online groups, and it is even hard to imagine where one would find data that would lend itself to conducting such analyses (Stahl et al., 2012).

The individual unit of analysis is the traditional default in the learning sciences and in cognitive psychology. It is supported by widespread training of researchers in the methods of education and psychology. In the era of cognitive science, analysis made heavy usage of mental models and representations (Gardner, 1985). With the "turn to practice" (Lave & Wenger, 1991; Schatzki, Knorr Cetina & Savigny, 2001), the focus shifted to communities-of-practice. Group cognition lies in the less-well-charted middle ground (Stahl, 2006). It involves the semantics, syntactics, and pragmatics of natural language, gestures, inscriptions, etc. These meaning-making processes involve inputs from individuals, based on their interpretation of the on-going context (Stahl, 2006, esp. Ch. 16). They also take into account the larger social, historical, cultural, linguistic context, which they can reproduce and modify (Stahl, 2013).

This chapter argues that the connections between the individual, group, and community planes can be analyzed as taking place through the mediation of *interactional resources*. Applying this approach to the learning of mathematics, the chapter adopts a discourse-centered view of mathematical understanding as the ability to engage in *significant mathematical discourse* (Sfard, 2008; Stahl, 2008). Here, "discourse" includes gesture, inscription, drawing, computer representation, and symbol, as well as speech and text; these multiple modes are often closely interwoven in effective interaction in VMT (Çakir & Stahl, 2013; Çakir, Zemel & Stahl, 2009).

> The connections between the individual, group and community planes can be analyzed as taking place through the mediation of interactional resources.

Computer technologies play a central role in mediating the multi-level, intertwined problem-solving, learning, and knowledge-building processes that take place in CSCL settings. From a CSCL perspective, innovative technologies should be carefully designed to support this mediation. This involves considering within the socio-technical design process of collaboration environments how to prepare groups, individuals, and communities to take advantage of the designed functionality and to promote mathematical thinking at all levels. The following discussion suggests that it is important to supply appropriate *resources*, to allow groups to understand, enact, and adapt those resources to their needs and to facilitate the emergence of new resources from the group interactions. This can permit processes at different units of analysis to connect and support each other.

8.6   INTERCONNECTED PLANES

How are the major planes of learning connected; how can we connect investigations at different units of analysis? In Figure 8.2, we see highway ramps or bridges used as resources for connecting road levels or landmasses. While we are interested in linguistic interactional resources in this chapter, it may be helpful to first consider the more intuitive case of a physical resource. A ramp or bridge often creates a possibility that did not otherwise exist for going from one level to another at a given point. To go from a local road to a limited-access superhighway, one must first find an available on-ramp. To cross a river from one side to the other, one may need a bridge. This is the individual driver's view. From a different vantage point—the perspective of the resource itself—the creation of a ramp or the building of a bridge "affords" connecting the levels (Dohn, 2009).

Figure 8.2: Connecting ramps for the I-90 bridge across the Hudson River. Photo: G. Stahl, Albany, NY, 2012.

By "affords," we do not simply mean that the connecting is a happy characteristic or accidental attribute of the bridge, but that the bridge, by its very nature and design, "opens up" a connection, which connects the banks of the river it spans. This view of artifacts was largely introduced in the philosophy of Heidegger; it later became influential in CSCL through various theories derived from his approach. In his early work, Heidegger (1927/1996) analyzed how the meaning of a tool was determined by the utility of the tool to the human user, within the network of meaning associated with that person's life and world. In his later writings, Heidegger (1935/2003) shifted perspective to focus on things like bridges (see Figure 8.3), paintings, sculptures, pitchers, and temples in terms of how they themselves opened up new worlds, in which people could then dwell. In considering the intersubjective world in which collaboration takes place on multiple connected levels, we might say that the work of resources like bridges is to contribute the spanning of shores within the way that the world through which we travel together is opened up as a shared landscape of resources for discourse and action.

This transformation of perspective away from a human-centric or individual-mind-centered approach became characteristic for pioneering theories in the second half of the 20th century, including various theories of situated and distributed cognition. It is a shift away from the individualistic, psychological view to a concern with how language, tools and other resources of our social life work. It is a post-cognitive move since it rejects the central role of mental models, representations and computations in traditional cognitive science. The things themselves have effective affordances; it is not just a matter of how humans manipulate models in which the things are re-presented to the mind.

> The work of resources like bridges is to contribute the spanning of shores within the way that the world through which we travel together is opened up as a shared landscape of resources for discourse and action.

Figure 8.3: The bridge across the Neckar River, discussed by Heidegger (1950/1967). Photo: G. Stahl, Heidelberg, Germany, 2012.

The analytic focus and even the locus of agency are shifted from the individual mind to tools, artifacts, instruments, discourse, and inscriptions. In phenomenology, Husserl (1929/1960) called for a return to "the things themselves" (*die Sache selbst*) and Heidegger (1950/1967) analyzed "the thing" (*das Ding*) separate from our representation of it. In ethnomethodology, Garfinkel and Sacks (1970) followed Wittgenstein's (1953) linguistic turn to focus on the language games of words and the use of member methods as conversational resources (Koschmann, Stahl & Zemel, 2004). In distributed cognition, Hutchins (1996) analyzed the encapsulation of historical cognition in cultural artifacts like navigational instruments. In actor-network theory, Latour (1990; 1992; 2007) uncovered the agency of various kinds of objects in how they move across levels in enacting social transformations. Recently, Rabardel (see Lonchamp, 2012; Overdijk et al., 2012; Ritella & Hakkarainen, 2012) analyzed the genesis of socio-technical instruments, which only gradually become useful as they are adapted and enacted in practice.

Our proposal to use the term "resources" is intended to carry forward into the 21st century these groundbreaking approaches to the study of how the various planes of human interaction are connected. The phrase "interactional resource" is proposed as an inclusive expression for all the kinds of things that can be brought into discourse. Vygotsky (1930/1978) used the term "artifact" to refer to both tools and language as mediators of human cognition; we prefer to use the broader term "resource" as it has more recently been used in sociocultural analysis (Ackerman et al., 2008; Arvaja, 2012; Cekaite, 2009; Furberg, Kluge & Ludvigsen, 2013; Karlsson, 2010; Linell, 2001; Medina, Suthers, & Vatrapu, 2009; Suchman, 1987) for entities referenced in discourse. Like artifacts, resources are often identifiable units of the physical world (including speech and gesture) that are involved in meaning-making practices—spanning the classical mind/body divide of the physical vs. the mental.

It is important to avoid assuming that just because a noun like "resource" is used that it refers to a certain kind of object.

1. Interactional resources can take on many forms—as will be discussed here—including physical and verbal artifacts, but also social practices, group methods, gestures, syntactic markers, etc. They can be anything that enters into the interaction and helps to enable it.

2. Interactional resources are created, developed, adapted, situated, evolved and made meaningful within the process of interaction. They are not something previously fully formed, simply taken as is and used within the interaction.

Rather than starting out from some preconceived ontology of interactional resources—even one as broad as Vygotsky's inclusion of tools and language—we start from the *question* of interactional resources. In looking for actors—to use Latour's generic term—that play a role in mediating interactions within small online teams of math students, we are open to all sorts of things that effect, are useful for, influence, or make possible the interaction in the way that it concretely takes place. It is obvious that a broad range of linguistic elements, such as technical terms, symbols, methods of repair, forms of questioning, etc. must be included. Also, to be included are tools or artifacts, such as hardware and software communication media, specific interface functions, training materials, established construction procedures, etc. Moreover, as we conduct specific analyses of collaboration and fine-grained investigations of interaction, we discover additional forms of interactional resources, as do relevant theories, such as theories of representation, reference, semantics, linguistics, interaction, collaborative learning, discourse, dialog, and technology.

A central research issue for CSCL is how collaborative knowledge building takes place. The main problem seems to be to understand the role of both individual cognition and societal institutions in the small-group meaning-making processes. Figure 8.4 shows a diagram in which "Cultural Artifacts" serve to connect the three planes of meaning-making processes. The diagram was originally based on an eclectic combination of major theories influential in CSCL. Some of those approaches—collaborative knowledge building, group and personal perspectives, mediation by artifacts, and interaction analysis—were further described in (Stahl, 2002). Work on the theory illustrated there led to a need for new case studies to explore collaborative knowledge building.

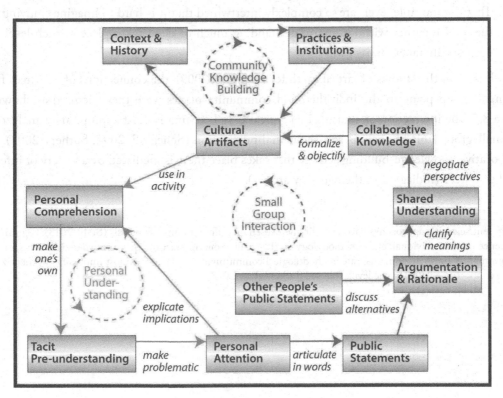

Figure 8.4: A diagram of factors involved in knowledge building. Adapted from (Stahl, 2000).

In recent years, the VMT Project has conducted case studies of small-group problem solving. In doing so, it has tried to focus exclusively on the small-group unit of analysis. This approach is based upon three observations.

1. That most CSCL studies in the past have focused either on the individual (cognitive) plane or on the community (practices) plane. For instance, studies either code utter-

ances of individuals (Strijbos & Stahl, 2007) and reduce interaction to contributions of individuals or else they view interaction as participation in community processes and institutions. In terms of strict methodology, the small-group unit of analysis has been under-researched in CSCL.

2. That the small-group unit is fundamental to learning. As Vygotsky (1930/1978) said, one learns most human skills in social interaction first, only then being able to develop those skills individually. Furthermore, processes of meaning making and knowledge building are more visible in small-group interaction than in individual cogitation, making them easier to study.

3. That the multiple levels are so complexly intertwined that it is hard to imagine studying them all together without first understanding much of what takes place at each level, temporarily taken on its own.[3]

Based on the studies of virtual math teams (Stahl, 2009), the connections of resources from the small-group plane to the individual and community planes were then pictured as shown in Figure 8.5. The interaction of students in a typical CSCL setting is most appropriately analyzed at the small-group unit of analysis as a sequential progression (Schegloff, 2007; Suthers, 2007). The collaborative knowledge-building activity that takes place there is mediated by a variety of interactional resources (indicated in the figure by arrows).

---

[3] Different scientific approaches have accordingly focused on different units of analysis (Stahl, 2013): cognitive science on the individual; ethnomethodology on the small-group interaction; quantitative social science on the community. These incommensurate methodological commitments rendered it almost impossible to theorize the connections between the levels (but see Suthers et al., 2013).

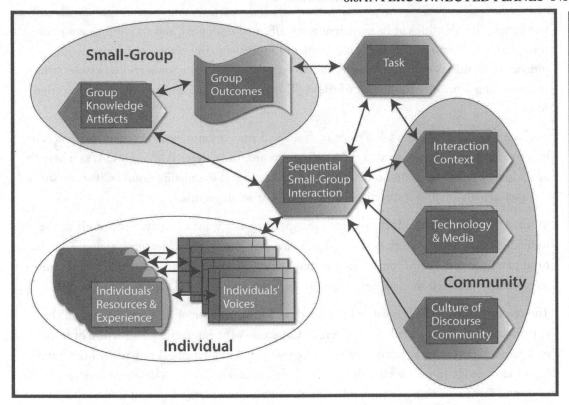

Figure 8.5: A diagram of sources of interactional resources and the connections they mediate. Adapted from (Stahl, 2013).

Figure 8.4 and Figure 8.5 are not meant to reify different levels or processes as necessarily having some kind of independent existence outside of our analyses, but to suggest some constraints between different phenomena to hypothesize, and flows of influence to measure. The distinctions and resource-mediated connections represented by boxes and arrows in the chart are intended to help operationalize an infinitely complex and subtle matter of collaborative knowledge building for purposes of concrete analytic work by CSCL researchers.

Levels in Conversation Analysis?

Some researchers, such as ethnomethodologists, argue against distinguishing levels. However, the view of levels of analysis in this chapter may actually be consistent with ethnomethodology. For instance, in their introduction to ethnomethodologically inspired Conversation Analysis (CA), Goodwin and Heritage (**1990**, p. 283)—two of the writers most explicit about the theory underlying ethnomethodological studies—open with the following claim. "Social interaction is the primordial means through which the business of the social world is transacted, the identities of its participants are affirmed or denied, and its cultures are transmitted, renewed and modified." This statement implicitly distinguishes social interaction, individual identities and community cultures—asserting the tight connections between them, and invoking a priority to the first of these. (This is exactly what the preceding section tried to do.)

Social interaction typically takes place in dyads and small groups, so interaction analysis can be considered to be conducted at the small-group unit of analysis. Although CA, as a branch of sociology, refers to community-level social practices and linguistic resources, its case-study analyses usually involve interactions within dyads or small groups.

While CSCL researchers focus on small groups, they also want to analyze the levels of the individual and of the culture as such—e.g., individual identities and learning changes, or cultural practices and institutional forces. In this chapter, we propose that interactional resources are centrally involved in mediating these connections within CSCL settings.

The resources that CSCL must analyze are different from those of interest to CA, and the approach to interaction analysis is different. CA studies the interactional structure of informal conversation (e.g., adjacency-pair typology and turn-taking rules) rather than the building of knowledge in online chat about school mathematics; CA has a different conception of resources for interaction as community practices ("member methods"); and CA is interested in the co-construction of social order rather than in inquiry about domain knowledge.

However, analysis of the ways in which interactional resources bridge from group phenomena to individual and community phenomena should be of similar concern to CA and CSCL.

CSCL sequential small-group discourse brings in—through interactional references, as described in the next section—resources from the individual, small-group and community planes and involves them in procedures of shared meaning making. This interaction requires co-attention to the resources—and thereby shares them among the participants. The process results in generating new or modified resources, which may then be retained at the various planes. The resources that are brought in and those that are modified or generated often take the form of designed physical artifacts and adopted elements of language. The resources tend to originate in group interaction, and then they are subsequently established as effective for individuals and communities. In words similar in intent to those of Goodwin and Heritage, "small groups are the engines of knowledge building. The knowing that groups build up in manifold forms is what becomes internalized by their members as individual learning and externalized in their communities as certifiable knowledge" (Stahl, 2006, p. 16).

8.7   THE COLLABORATIVE EMERGENCE OF RESOURCES

The question of how the local interactional resources that mediate sequential small-group interaction are related to large-scale socio-cultural context as well as to individual learning is an empirical question in each case. These connections across levels take place in many ways. It is likely that they often involve mechanisms that are not apparent to participants. In the following, we explore how such connections can occur thanks to interactional resources.

In his study of how social institutions can both affect and be affected by small-group interactions, Sawyer (2005, p. 210f) argues that we can conceptualize the interactions between processes at different levels as forms of *collaborative emergence*: "During conversational encounters, interactional frames emerge, and these are collective social facts that can be characterized independently of individuals' interpretations of them. Once a frame has emerged, it constrains the possibilities for action." The frames that emerge from small-group interactions can take on institutional or cultural-level powers to influence actions at the individual unit. This interplay among levels involves both *ephemeral* emergents and *stable* emergents. Sawyer's theory of emergents suggests a relationship among different kinds of resources along the lines pictured in Figure 8.6.

While Sawyer's analysis addresses a broad "sociology of social emergence," it can be confined and adapted to the concerns of CSCL. What is most relevant in his theory is the view of emergence arising out of the subtle complexities of language usage and small-group interaction—rather than from the law of large numbers, the interaction of simple rules or the chaotic behavior of non-linear relationships. He thereby rejects the approaches of most popular theories of emergence for CSCL and shifts the focus to the discourse at the small-group unit of analysis.

The vast variety of interactional emergents form an intermediate level of analysis between the level of individuals and the level of community structures, providing a dynamic and processual understanding of social structures and infrastructures. Analysis focused on these emergent artifacts can deconstruct the reifying processes of emergence that span from the group level to both the individual and the social.

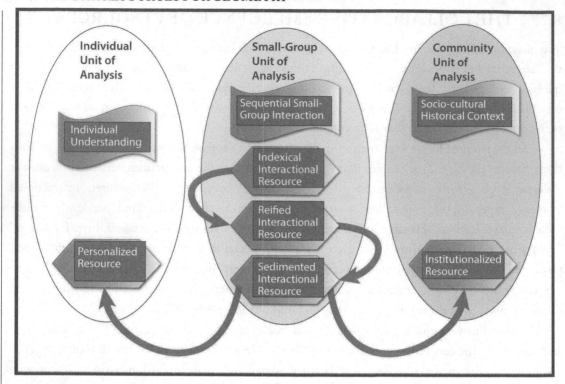

Figure 8.6: A diagram of emergent interactional resources bridging levels of analysis through reification, sedimentation, personalization, and institutionalization.

The small-group interaction represented in the center of Figure 8.6 can be theorized as being based on an "indexical ground of deictic reference" (Hanks, 1992). This means that the "common ground" (Clark & Brennan, 1991)—which forms a foundation for mutual understanding of what each other says in conversation—consists of a shared system of *indexical-reference resources*, such as deictic pronouns, which are used to point to unstated topics or resources. The coherence of the interaction and its comprehensibility to the group participants is supported by a network of references, each of which is defined indexically, that is by a pointing within the on-going discourse context ("here," "it," "now," "that point"). Interactional resources, which can be indexically referenced in the interaction, can typically only be understood within their discourse context, but they facilitate meaning making within that context.

Interactional resources can undergo a process like Rabardel's instrumental genesis (Rabardel & Beguin, 2005; Rabardel & Bourmaud, 2003). They may initially be constituted as an object of repeated discussion—an interaction frame (Goffman, 1974)—which we might call a *reified resource*, something capable of being picked out as having at least an "ephemeral-emergent" existence. Through repetition within a group discussion, a term or the use of an object might take on a settled significance within the group's current work. Over time, continued usage can result in a *sedimented resource*, something whose existence has settled into a longer-term "stable-emergent" form, which retains its meaning across multiple group interactions.

A sedimented resource is susceptible to being taken up by a larger community as an *institutionalized resource* within a structured network of such resources, as in Latour's social-actor networks (Latour, 2007), contributing to the socio-cultural-historical context surrounding the interaction. Thus, the institutional resource not only references the social context, but also partially reproduces it in a dialectical relationship of mutual constitution by contributing a new element or revitalizing an old set of resources.

On the other hand, interactional resources at various degrees of reification can also be taken up into the individual understanding of community members as *personalized resources*, integrated more or less into the intra-personal perspective of one or more group members. The personalization of previously inter-personal resources by individuals renders them into resources that can be referenced in activities of individual understanding—corresponding to processes of micro-genesis in Vygotskian internalization.

The various components of this view of interactional resources have been hinted at in previous theoretical contributions grounded in empirical examples. The progressively emergent character of resources can be seen in the logs of virtual math teams, as phrases and actions proposed by one participant are taken up repeatedly and come to have a meaning for the group.

The term "reification" goes back to Hegel's dialectical philosophy of mediation (Hegel, 1807/1967)—as discussed in Chapter 3. Sfard (Sfard, 2000; 2008; Sfard & Linchevski, 1994) applied it to the formation of mathematical concepts. Husserl (1936/1989) argued that the ideas of the early geometers became "sedimented" in the cultural heritage of the field of geometry. Livingston (1999) differentiated discovering a mathematical proof from presenting the proof; a transformational process takes place, in which the byways of exploration and possibly even the key insights are suppressed in favor of conforming to the "institutionalized" template of formal deductive reasoning. Netz (1999) documented the important role of a controlled (restricted and reified) vocabulary to the development, dissemination and learning of geometry in ancient Greece. Analogously, Lemke (1993) argued that learning the vocabulary of a scientific domain such as school physics is inseparable from learning the science. Vygotsky (1930/1978, esp. pp. 56f) noted that the micro-genetic processes of "personalizing" a group practice into part of one's individual understanding—which he conceptually collected under the title "internalization"—are lengthy, complex, non-transparent, and little understood. These seminal writings name the processes of *reification*, *sedimentation*, *institutionalization*, and *personalization* of interactional resources; their empirical investigation remains as a major task for future CSCL research.

According to the foregoing discussion of resources as products of collaborative emergence, we can see that resources are neither pre-existing objects given in advance of their involvement in group interactions nor completely arbitrary creations *ex nihilo* of the group interaction. Their nature is discovered by the group in its attempts to reference or index the resource in different ways, some of which work and some of which do not work. One cannot say that the nature of the resource already existed prior to or independent of the group's exploration. Neither pure realism about an existent world nor pure idealism about a free subject captures the whole picture. The character of a resource is created through a constrained process of creative discovery.

To understand this concept of resource, one must overcome the traditional categories of beings. Resources are not necessarily physical tools, like hammers. They can be verbal expressions, social practices, or any type of object, physical, mental, linguistic, etc. What is important is the kinds of processes that they can be involved in and the sorts of transformations they undergo. A resource is an analytic term, much as group cognition is an analytic stance. Group cognition does not imply a certain number of human bodies acting in a certain way, but a methodological perspective on the unit of analysis. Analogously, a resource is not necessarily a fully defined physical object like a hammer, textbook, or drawing. Rather, it can be anything that can emerge in interaction, be repeatedly taken up, progressively articulated, reified into an identifiable object, passed down to new contexts of use, and recognized as having taken on a certain social persistence and mediating role.

As the theory of affordances (Dohn, 2009) emphasizes, a resource is associated with certain potentialities that are manifested in response to relevant approaches. The same tension exists in Rabardel's theory of instrumental genesis, where a designed technical instrument (such as a software interface) continues to evolve as users adapt it to their practices and adapt their understanding to it. Similarly, the theory of enactment in sense-making processes in organizations involves an interplay between the actors and the available resources: "The external environment literally bends around the enactments of people, and much of the activity of sense-making involves an effort to separate the externality from the action" (Weick, 1988).

> Resources are not necessarily physical tools.... What is important is the kinds of processes they can be involved in and the sorts of transformations they undergo. A resource is an analytic term, much as group cognition is an analytic stance.

The classic philosophic debate between idealism and realism is related to the Cartesian division between mind and body. In Heideggerian terms, the analysis should not start from a thinker opposing a world, but from a unity of human being-in-the-world. Through the gradual development of understanding, the possibilities given by the past are created in the present in terms of our future-oriented projects.

In the interaction example at the beginning of this chapter, three students explore hexagons in a grid of lines. The drawing provides a resource for the collaborative work involving patterns of hexagons. But the resource only gradually takes shape and becomes useful to them as they collaboratively explore it, sharing different ways of looking at it visually, marking it up graphically, talking about it in text chat and representing it symbolically in algebra. As the group works out what is and is not possible in the drawing, the drawing emerges as an effective resource, which supports the group in its mathematical work.

The group made use of many resources, including mathematical terminology, computer skills, visual capabilities and the drawing. Most of these were inherited from the past as elements of their individual skilled being-in-the-world or of their group's already established intersubjective shared understanding. Their group project of solving a math problem as given in the session instructions (but still needing to be understood, negotiated, explained, shared, enacted, evolved) oriented their group-cognition effort toward a future. Within these temporal dimensions, the group established and maintained a co-presence, which allowed them to collaborate effectively. We should be able to see similar processes in other examples of collaborative interaction.

8.8 RESEARCH ON ARTIFACTS

Among the theories influential in CSCL—such as activity theory, distributed cognition, and actor-network theory—*artifacts* play a central role as "mediators" of thought and action. The construct of interactional resource is intended to play a similar role in the theory of group cognition.

In the foundations of activity theory, Vygotsky (1930/1978) conceives of artifacts as including language as well as tools. In the seminal study of distributed cognition, Hutchins (1996) analyzes how the complex of navigational tools, naval procedures for trained teams of people, and specialized language work together to accomplish cognitive tasks like ship navigation. He even analyzes discourse data to show how an indexical term ("total") becomes reified within a dyad's interaction to take on significance that could have led to intra-personal and/or institutional usage (p. 342). In a witty essay, Latour (1992) shows how a common mechanical door-closer artifact can act to fill the role of an individual person (a doorman), to participate in the politics of a group and to enforce institutional rules. He also argues (Latour, 1990) that an inscription artifact like a map on paper—a stable emergent that he refers to as an "immutable mobile"—can traverse levels from a local discussion in ancient Asia to the social niveau of imperial Europe. However, studies like these have not often been duplicated in the CSCL literature.

Reviews of CSCL research show that few papers in this field have bridged multiple levels of analysis (Arnseth & Ludvigsen, 2006; Jeong & Hmelo-Silver, 2010). Yet, the desired CSCL research agenda (Krange & Ludvigsen, 2008; Stahl, Koschmann & Suthers, 2006; Suthers, 2006) calls for a study of representational artifacts and other resources that traverse between individual, small-group and community processes to mediate meaning making. The preceding sketch of a theory of emergent forms of evolving resources could be taken as a refinement of the research agenda for the field of CSCL: a hypothesis about how levels in the analysis of learning are connected; and an agenda for exploration.

Table of Rockets

An early attempt within CSCL to analyze the role of artifacts and resources appeared in (**Stahl, 2004**). The analysis was grounded in a half-minute interaction among four students working with a computer simulation of model rockets. The excerpt involved the students coming to understand how to interpret a textual resource: a table of rocket components arranged to facilitate comparisons among differently configured rockets.

At first, none of the students could see the designed affordance of the table, but after the half minute, they could all see the shared artifact as a resource for their scientific discourse. The interaction analysis of this excerpt showed how aspects of the table artifact were brought in as resources for the group discourse, as were shared and repeated words like "same" and "different." The words of one student were reused in the interaction by others in order to orient him to a new, shared understanding of the co-attended-to table.

The resource that emerged for the group's subsequent practice was a sophisticated understanding of the organization of the table (**Stahl, 2006**, Ch. 12 & 13). This locally achieved understanding was congruent to a standard scientific understanding, which the instructor had assumed in designing the table and offering it as a resource for the group task.

Here we can see the use of interactional resources connecting ideas from novice-individual and scientific-community planes in the small-group discourse, which led to a significant advance in the group's meaning-making ability. The table of rocket components was one such resource, which went through a process of instrumental genesis for the students, situated in their scientific problem-solving activity. The use of terms like "same" and "different"—introduced into the discourse by one member and then picked up by others as indices pointing to the problematic issue—became reified resources for the group. Interestingly, sameness and difference are fundamental concepts for mathematical discourse (aka thinking) according to Sfard (**2008**) (see also **Stahl, 2008**).

8.9 RESOURCES FOR COLLABORATION AND FOR MATHEMATICS

The idea of viewing interactional resources as central to mathematical discourse around dynamic geometry was proposed by Öner (2013). Building on an earlier analysis of mathematical learning (Çakir, Zemel & Stahl, 2009), she argued that rather than focusing on the "coordination of interaction," collaborative activity should be analyzed in terms of the "coordinated use of resources." Participants rely on two major categories of resources when working on a geometry problem within a computer-based dynamic-geometry environment: (1) mathematical and tool-enabled resources (math-content-related) and (2) collaboration resources (relational or social). Öner proposed a focus on the coordination of these resources—which, she argued, characterize collaborative dynamic-geometry problem solving—for understanding what goes on in such productive math learning.

The combination of social and content resources brought to bear on geometric problem solving often bridges levels. Social resources—such as greetings, invitations to speak, checks on discourse direction, even insults—may function to cohere the group out of its individual members, drawing upon community standards and institutional routines. Uses of math resources—such as manipulating visual representations, referencing recent findings, expressing relationships symbolically—move fluidly between individual perceptual behavior, group problem-solving sequences and the cultural stockpile of mathematical knowledge. Perhaps the incessant traversal of levels is particularly visible in collaborative math discourse because of its explicit use of multiple layers of reality involved in mathematical work: a physical drawing, the intended figure, a narrative description, a symbolic expression, the conceptualization, and the abstract mathematical object.

Öner's methodological proposal is to track both the math-content-related and the social/collaborative/relational resources used by students solving dynamic-geometry problems. Math resources may come from graphical, narrative, and symbolic representations or expressions of the math problem or from previous math knowledge of culturally transmitted concepts, theorems, procedures, symbolisms, etc. Social resources include communication practices, such as the rules of conversational discourse (transactivity, sequentiality, shared attention, argumentation, turn taking, repair, etc.).

Öner cites a number of distinctions drawn in the CSCL literature for contrasting social/collaborative/relational resources with content-related resources:

- an inter-personal-relations space vs. a content space (Barron, 2000);

- building a joint problem space (JPS) vs. solving a problem (Roschelle & Teasley, 1995);

- temporal dimensions of the JPS vs. diachronic content (Sarmiento & Stahl, 2008);

- text chat vs. shared-whiteboard graphics (Çakir, Zemel & Stahl, 2009);

- project discourse vs. mathematical discourse (Evans et al., 2011); and

- spatio-graphical observation (SG) vs. technical reflection (T) (Laborde, 2004).

The "space" that a group builds up and shares is a structured set of resources gathered by the group (JPS, indexical field, common ground). The resources are "indexical" in the sense that they are only defined within (and thanks to) this constructed space of the specific problem context. Through their discourse, the group compiles these resources as potentially relevant to the problem. In turn, the resources help to define the emergent problem.

Öner generated data to explore the interaction of the contrasting dimensions by having two people work together face-to-face in front of a shared computer using Geometer's Sketchpad. They collaborated on the inscribed triangles problem (see Chapter 7 and Figure 8.7). She selected this problem because its solution required a mix of spatio-graphical observation and technical reflection involving mathematical theory—a mix of SG and T resources, to use the distinction she adopted from Laborde. She uses this distinction among resources to structure her analysis. In doing so, she shows how these various resources bridge the different units of analysis. Resources of *individual* perception (during dragging of geometric objects on the computer screen) feed into the *group* problem solving, just as do references to classical theorems passed down through *cultural* institutions. They make possible and stimulate the group interaction. This analysis provides examples of interactional resources at work in a CSCL setting.

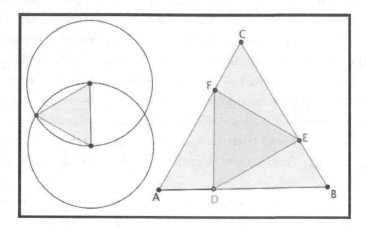

Figure 8.7: Constructing an equilateral triangle and an inscribed triangle.

By analyzing both social and content resources, Öner shows how interrelated these can be (Öner, 2013). For instance, at one point one student says, "now two isosceles, oops, equilateral triangles are formed here." This utterance is deeply indexical. It is pointing to the "here" and "now" of the geometric construction. The student is narrating his work, intersecting two circles to locate the vertices of the desired equilateral triangle (see Figure 8.7). The method he is using refers back over 2,500 years to Euclid's first proposition, which teaches this construction. It also notes that one could use either of two potential intersections to construct alternative triangles. This leads his partner to see first one of the intersection points and then the other. Öner notes that the two students collaboratively accomplished this construction; they collectively recalled the procedure in the doing of it, which they had performed in the past but forgotten. She also emphasizes that this utterance includes a self-repair, in which the speaker substitutes a correct term ("equilateral") for an incorrect one—a move she considers social. Repairs are conversational moves aimed at avoiding or correcting potential misunderstandings. The utterance is a resource that is used to foster co-presence, attending to the graphical resource of the computer figure. The repair conversational method is a resource for correcting a mistake and avoiding confusion; it is part of constructing the utterance as meaningful. The graphical resource contains two intersection points of the circles; the point used as a vertex of the triangle is immediately salient, whereas the other intersection point only gradually comes into view. The repaired utterance and the constructed figure work together to further the mathematical collaboration of the dyad. The effect of the resources is quite complicated and could be analyzed in much greater depth from different perspectives.

This raises a methodological point. Should the quoted utterance be analyzed, categorized, or coded as a social resource or as a mathematical one? What is the resource here? Is it the generic conversational resource of self-repair as a "member method" (Garfinkel, 1967), is it the word "equi-lateral" in the shared language, or is it the geometric concept of equilateral polygon? Is it a conversational move, linguistic term, or mathematical concept? This is a matter of what unit of analysis an analyst has chosen, because one could characterize it in any of these ways. Alternatively, one could argue that the interactional resource that exists here spans multiple levels of analysis, providing an object for analysis at the conversational, linguistic and mathematical levels of the interacting group, the speaking individual and the cultural conceptualization.

Öner succeeds in analyzing how her students collaborated on their geometry problem by focusing consistently on the interplay between social and content resources. This is a proposal for one way of filtering out some of the complexity of what takes place with interactional resources. It may be that we can often follow the movement of discourses across different levels by keeping our eyes on consequential resources. However, other CSCL researchers interpret the theme of resources differently from Öner. This leads them to different insights about their data. It may be that we can use the concept of resource as a boundary object (Star, 1989) to bring together the disparate theoretical voices and the multiple levels of analysis. Too often, analysts seem to talk at cross-purposes, emphasizing differences when they might well be seeing the same phenomenon from different angles.

8.10 REFERENTIAL RESOURCES FOR A MATH PROBLEM

A recent article (Zemel & Koschmann, 2013) analyzing VMT data takes an ethnomethodological look at the role of resources, representations, referential practices and indexical properties in mathematical problem-solving interactions. The paper by Zemel and Koschmann illustrates the importance of tracking the use of resources, and it emphasizes that it is the on-going specification-in-use that determines the significance of a given resource. It also adopts a concern with representations, and makes explicit the extent to which representational practices—how the representation was built and worked with—contribute to the problem clarification and problem solution.

In theoretical terms, the analysis by Zemel and Koschmann (2013) further develops the discussion of *indexical reference resources* by Hanks (1992). It considers two virtual math teams who were presented with the same problem statement involving combinatorics. The two groups identified completely different sets of "indexical properties," which allowed them to formulate implicitly, share collaboratively and solve mathematically the "same" problem, which, however, they specified quite differently. In the first team, one student specified a "given" stair-step pattern of squares in terms of two symmetric sets of lines. Each set of lines followed the pattern: 1, 2, 3,…, n, n. In the second team, a student specified the problem initially as: "the nth pattern has n more squares than the (n-1)th pattern."

Ethnomethodologists are keen to observe the work that people do to accomplish what they do. Both teams engaged in intricate coordination of text understanding, sequential drawing, retroactive narrative and symbolic manipulation to make sense of the problem statement they faced and to arrive at a mathematical solution. The work involved in this can be characterized as discovering, proposing and negotiating successive determinations of indexical properties of the problem they are working on. The indexical properties are ways in which the team members can reference aspects of the problem, such as in terms of sets of lines arrayed in specific identifiable patterns.

These indexical properties are tied to the local problem-solving context of the respective team. They specify the problem for the team in practical terms, which allow the team to make progress in both understanding and solving the problem. This approach is appropriate for what Rittel (Rittel & Webber, 1984) called "wicked problems." These are non-standard problems, for which the approach to problem solving is not obvious and turns out to be a matter of coming to understand the problem itself.

One can imagine a student logging into VMT and entering a completely unknown territory. Initially, he was not familiar with the online environment, had never seen the kind of problem statement that was displayed, did not know the other team members and was unclear about what was expected of him. He spotted (visually) an interesting symmetry in the problem and started by stating it as an initial specification about how to view (perceptually and conceptually) the problem. Then he started to draw the problem, so specified, on the shared whiteboard. The student in the other team entered a similarly unknown territory. She started drawing the pattern for N=4, as suggested in the text. In so doing, she developed some copy-and-paste practices, which she presented (in the sequentiality of her drawing process as well as in her accompanying description) as tentatively mathematically relevant.

Of course, no student starts in a world devoid of meaning and has to make sense out of nothing. He comes to the VMT environment—regardless of how unfamiliar it may appear to him at first—with a lifetime (however brief) of experience with social interaction, perception of drawings, skill with computer software and mathematical practices. In addition to this dimension of bringing along his past, he is oriented toward some future projects. He came to the VMT chat room with some motivations and expectations. He intended to solve some kind of math problem and he had some notion of possibilities for going about doing such a thing. For instance, his initial idea to break the figure into two symmetric parts and to look at each part as a pattern that could be expressed as a numeric sequence was probably based on past experience or previous practice that he situated in the local group context from a personal or institutional source. While resources have to be situated, adapted, enacted, and evolved within the local discourse context in order to function as specific and effective resources, they are generally brought in as potentialities for group use as resource from an individual or community source.

Starting from *individual* suggestions of indexical properties by a member of their team, each group developed a growing shared indexical ground of deictic reference. The work of building that space of possible references led the *group* to make sense of a problem and to discover a path to a solution in mathematical terms. The indexical ground itself is a set of shared interactional resources that allows the team to refer to their object of concern in mutually intelligible ways. By gradually moving from purely deictic terms like "it" or "this," to mathematical terms or abstract symbols, the indexical resources incorporated cultural knowledge and contributed to a less locally situated store of understanding that could be relevant in a larger classroom or *culture* of school mathematics (including standardized tests). The analysis of how these groups successively and collaboratively re-specify their referential resources suggests approaches to studying how groups make sense of problems and artifacts whose indexical properties are initially unknown or underspecified. This is a foundational concern for CSCL, as "a field of study centrally concerned with meaning and the practices of meaning making in the context of joint activity, and the ways in which these practices are mediated through designed artifacts" (Koschmann, 2002).

8.11 TOWARD A THEORY OF RESOURCES

This chapter explored the proposal that *interactional resources* play important roles in traversing the levels of individual learning, group cognition and community knowledge. In the process, it clarified three prerequisites of effective collaborative learning: co-presence, group cognition, and intersubjective shared understanding. Then it developed a number of perspectives on resources as emergent and enacted artifacts.

The different ideas discussed here and the theories referenced along the way show that there are many ways to conceptualize, analyze and theorize resources. One can conceive of the resources as interactional resources, indexical-reference resources, ephemeral emergents, immutable mobiles, social and content resources, structuring resources, representational resources, framing resources, cognitive resources, level-traversing, or boundary-spanning resources.

Resources do not just take the form of physical artifacts and linguistic terms; they can also take the form of practices. For teaching dynamic geometry, among the most important resources are the practices of dragging objects, constructing figures and building dependencies. These practices may be acquired at the group level through guided collaboration. Community-level math content—the culture of doing mathematics and the effective practices of mathematics—can be introduced into group activities, for instance in the form of scaffolded resources defining topics of discussion and exploration. Through participation in group practices that emerge in the interaction in which they participate, individuals can then develop the corresponding personal skills.

> For teaching dynamic geometry, among the most important resources are the practices of dragging objects, constructing figures and building dependencies.

For instance, Chapter 7 provided examples of practices being developed and moving across levels. The practice of constructing an equilateral triangle and the practice of using the compass tool to copy segment lengths both played major roles in the work by researchers, teachers, and students on the inscribed triangles problem. Each of these practices is rooted in established knowledge of the mathematics community: specifically Euclid's Propositions 1 and 2. These practices are also well known in the GeoGebra developer and user communities, where they are associated with specific software tools and have been illustrated in YouTube videos. The WinterFest curriculum, documented in Chapter 10, has been carefully designed to convey knowledge of these practices and to engage students in experiences with them. The groups whose chats were analyzed all adopted these two practices. The individuals in the groups demonstrated that they understood and could take advantage of these practices.

In an analysis of a VMT group working a few years ago, Medina, Suthers, and Vatrapu (2009) traced how several practices involving chat and drawing actions had emerged from the interaction of the virtual math team. The analysis showed that these practices had been introduced in various ways, but had been absorbed into the work of the group. They also demonstrated that each of the members of the team in the end had adopted these practices as interactional resources that they could bring to collaborative mathematics efforts.

The theory of interactional resources developed in this chapter is quite tentative. It probably raises more questions than it answers. However, it may serve to suggest the importance of providing materials of many kinds to learners, such that the learners can turn them into effective interactional resources to guide their group and individual absorption of community knowledge. Chapter 9 will specify some principles for the design of resources for collaborative dynamic geometry and Chapter 10 will present some of the resources that are currently used by groups of students in the VMT Project's WinterFest.

CHAPTER 9

Pedagogy: Designing Geometry

Chapter Summary

Based on the preceding analyses of interaction during cycles of design-based research and on the theoretical considerations concerning interactional resources, a number of design principles are discussed for a pedagogical approach to dynamic geometry. These principles focus on providing resources for collaboration, exploration, construction, proof, geometry content and math discourse.[4]

In order to support translating Euclid, the VMT Project is developing a socio-technical system to support group cognition among online teams of math students focused on discourse about dependencies in dynamic-geometry constructions. The following analysis of a pilot trial in an early cycle of the project's design-based-research approach reveals barriers to group success from both software and mathematics issues, and demonstrates that participants "cycled" between these types of issues. The Project responded by developing a curriculum to address the uncovered technical and cognitive issues—in addition, of course, to improving the software. This chapter presents the findings of the early pilot study and the curriculum-design criteria that emerged from subsequent cycles of re-design, prototyping, testing, and analysis.

9.1 DESIGN-BASED RESEARCH CYCLES OF TRIALS

Chapters 5 and 6 discussed some of the technical issues in developing the VMT collaboration environment and in transforming GeoGebra from a single-user application to a multi-user client integrated with VMT. However, when developing a socio-technical system, in addition to the technical development, we need to guide the group-cognitive work by providing helpful resources and scaffolding group practices. In designing resources for learning, we have to remember that the users will enact what we design to serve as effective resources based on their own circumstances and actions; designed artifacts are not resources until they are put into use concretely.

To get a realistic sense of how groups of students will interact within the environment using the resources or affordances we design into the environment, we need to conduct pilot tests throughout our design process. In order to try out our system in naturalistic settings as part of our socio-technical, design-based-research approach—as well as to provide a basis for eventual deployment—we have developed relationships with two teacher-professional-education schools, where we deploy our system with practicing math teachers. However, arranging to test innovative software

---

[4] Rachel Magee and Christopher Mascaro contributed to an earlier draft of this chapter.

and disruptive curriculum in school classrooms is a time-consuming, expensive, and difficult process. The software has to already be robust and easy to use, the curriculum has to be well conceived and aligned with the institutional curriculum, teachers have to be prepared, school authorities need to give permission, and IRB procedures have to be followed.

In our preliminary research stages, we have run informal pilot tests with available teams, such as groups of VMT project team members or groups of college students studying the software development process. This can give us very fast feedback on things we are considering incorporating without subjecting young students to untested materials. In one of these early tests, we used teams of masters-level HCI students. Our findings showed that these students encountered significant problems due to a lack of preparation for using the technology and for engaging in the mathematics. As a result of the analysis of these sessions—as discussed below—we realized that we would have to carefully craft a curriculum, which the teachers taking our professional-development training could follow and then adapt for their own classrooms. This curriculum would need to incorporate not only math lessons, but also tutorials about the VMT-with-GeoGebra technological environment.

We started to sketch out a curriculum based on existing best practices and theories. We were fortunate that the Common Core State Standards for Mathematics (CCSSI, 2011) had recently been released and adopted by most states in the U.S. This provided an up-to-date, research-based outline of content for a geometry course, which was widely accepted. We also looked at progressive geometry textbooks and training materials for GeoGebra and Geometer's Sketchpad.

As we reflected on the results of the initial trials analyzed below, we realized that there were still many problems to be addressed. These involved design issues in extending VMT, making GeoGebra multi-user, supporting collaboration around the activities, teaching the deep conceptual ideas in geometry, taking advantage of computer-supported dynamic math, and promoting significant math discourse. We ran several cycles of additional trials within our research group and with available college students. In each cycle, we revised the curriculum, revised the software, ran the trial, and analyzed the behaviors. Generally, there were clear lessons from each trial, which led to the next cycle.

Gradually, a set of design criteria for the curriculum was formulated and allowed to evolve. In this chapter, we report findings from the early session without curriculum to identify challenges faced by technologically adept individuals when attempting to engage in significant math discourse within the GeoGebra environment. Then we review some of the lessons for the technology and some of the aspects of the discourse that we believe are important. Based on these lessons, we then developed a curriculum based around online, small-group activities. This chapter discusses the criteria for the design of that curriculum, as it emerged from testing of trial curriculum drafts. The next chapter will present some of the activities we subsequently designed.

We will focus here on the curriculum design because, from a socio-technical standpoint, the curriculum plays a central role of mediating between the people and the technology. It tells the people what activities they should be engaging in while communicating through and working within the technology. It also models for them how to talk about math. For an online course, in which there is no teacher present to orchestrate activities and interaction, the textual curriculum provides the major scripting of collaborative sessions and the primary scaffolding of the group cognition.

9.2 A TRIAL WITHOUT CURRICULAR RESOURCES

In Fall 2011, we held an hour-long chat with four groups of information-science graduate students taking a course on CSCL using the VMT environment. In these chats, the groups met online and attempted to solve a geometry problem within the GeoGebra environment. The students had used the VMT environment to perform collaborative writing exercises in previous weeks, but had not previously used GeoGebra. These students were enrolled in majors related to technology, suggesting that they were engaged rather than nervous about technology use. As part of the exercise, there was no explicit introduction to the GeoGebra tool or further instructions other than the assigned problem.

We were interested in analyzing these groups' interactions and their strategies for navigating a new online collaborative environment. Two research assistants examined each log independently, using a thematic-analysis approach to reveal themes that were typical stages of conversation. The stages that emerged in the analysis included: social niceties, problem identification, technical discourse, math discourse, design suggestions, and future planning. While these are separate stages of conversation, we found that each group moved back and forth between *technological* and *mathematical* discourse; we termed this behavior "cycling."

We examined the logs further, using our initial categories as a guide to analyze this process of cycling. In our subsequent look, we identified the cyclical behavior triggered by individual statements distinctly indicating technical issues (involving software usage issues or software problems) versus mathematical issues and discourse (involving attempts to understand, represent and solve the geometry problem). By examining the chat logs we were able to observe phases of group interaction, how technology affects each phase and how the technology can both facilitate and inhibit successful completion of the task in an online environment new to group members.

Analysis of the group chat logs illustrated the presence of a variety of stages of conversation by the members of the groups in the context of the problem-solving task. Each of the chats begins with an orientation, including the exchange of social niceties and resolution of unrelated issues, typically lasting two to three lines per group member.

Following the orientation stage, the groups formulated the problem by either explaining it in the chat to the other group members or by referring to the posted problem in another tab. This typically involved a statement to orient the group:

Quick summary – we have to work thru the problem (see topic). Summarize the process in the Summary tab and post a few sentences on the wiki too. We good? (Group 1, line 16)

This quote illustrates some of the important characteristics of this type of focusing statement, including a description of what the speaker is going to do with the statement, instruction and then a leading question to ensure the team is on the same page.

Table 9.1 illustrates the different stages identified in the chat logs of the four groups and the different places in the discussion in which math discourse began. This varied for each group, and even when groups did not start with technical issues, they arose very quickly.

Table 9.1: Stage identification of each of the groups				
	Group 1	Group 2	Group 3	Group 4
Opening Stages	Orientation; Problem Identification			
Intermediate Stages	Role Assignment	Math Discourse	Technical Issues	Technical issues
	Technical Issues	Technical Issues	Math Discourse	Role Assignment
	Math Discourse	Design Suggestions	Math Confusion	Math Discourse
			Technical Issues	Use of Alternative Tools
			Technical Confusion	
Concluding Stages	Summarization of task/experience; social niceties; next steps			

Once Group 3 reached math discourse, they experienced confusion about the mathematical concepts, compounded by technical issues with the tool that further confused the participants in the group and degraded the quality of math discourse:

I'm trying to figure out how to delete this line… I kind of messed up… do you still see a line on the screen? (Group 3, line 24-25)

This quote highlights a number of issues that were common across multiple groups: not knowing how to delete an object (an option expected by participants), and group members being unsure that they were looking at the same objects as their fellow group members.

Both Group 1 and Group 4 achieved significant math discourse as each of the team members attempted to solve the problem, but did so with the help of outside tools. Group 1 used PowerPoint. Group 4 experienced confusion because the VMT environment did not display the same screen to all group members, so one emailed a screenshot to share the solution. This indicates that use of familiar tools or tools that work intuitively enables groups to more quickly reach effective math discourse that achieves a solution.

9.3 OVERCOMING TECHNOLOGICAL BARRIERS

The technological tool of multi-user GeoGebra—while providing many opportunities and options—often raised barriers for users. Barriers could be as simple as not being able to undo an action. However, even simple barriers stopped the groups from engaging in fluid math discourse and sometimes even went unresolved as the individuals found ways to work around issues. One example of this is the issue of not being able to easily rename an object. The mathematical problem these groups were attempting involved constructing an angle ABC (see Figure 9.1).

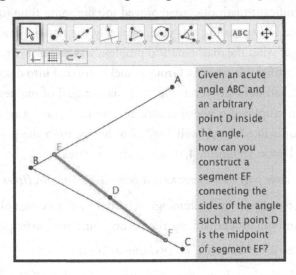

Figure 9.1: Task for groups of graduate students.

Groups began playing with the system by adding objects to their GeoGebra screen. However, each group discovered that they were unable to simply rename the points on their screen, and the names they needed (e.g., A, B, and C) were already in use by the system, although the objects they developed later in the process were better suited to solving the problem. This meant that their refined objects were confusingly named (for example, J, K, and L), making math discourse about the objects in relation to the problem statement more complicated:

> *One thing we can state is how the lettering got messed up… I think that is helping to confuse us. (Group 3, lines 58–59)*

Each group experienced this issue, and because of their lack of familiarity with the system, none were able to fix this problem. Other barriers were easier for the groups to creatively work around.

Because of the nature of the work, as groups overcame tool issues and moved into math discourse, new mathematical objectives (e.g., renaming a point, adding a ray) resulted in a return to the tool and often the discovery of a new technological barrier. Even in the face of such issues with the tool, multiple groups managed to achieve effective math discourse that led to solutions. Each successive cycle of math discourse and tool use also led to difficulty with the mathematical concepts at hand, which we will now discuss.

9.4   DISCOURSE ABOUT MATH DIFFICULTIES

The goal of these chats for the students was to experience a new CSCL software tool, but also to engage in mathematical discourse around the visualization and solution of a geometry problem. Reaching a stage of significant math discourse proved to take some time for most groups, despite the fact that they were actively pursuing this goal. Typically, the first approach involved developing a shared understanding of what the mathematical problem was, which we termed "problem identification" in our stage-identification process. Groups quickly entered into discussion of technological issues with the tool, but had difficulty returning to the larger goal of mathematical discourse.

Participants often employed a question structure to encourage a return to math discourse, and usually included words like "okay," "well," or "so" to bridge from the previous topic, which was typically a technological issue. In Group 4, one participant states:

> *Ok, we are on the same page now… we need a point in the middle. (lines 179–180)*

In an attempt to move past the technological barrier of not being able to effectively rename objects and establish common ground among the participants, one participant transitioned with:

> *Well, anyway, do we all at least see i, j, k? (Group 4, line 83)*

In addition to bridging words, participants also employed explicit questions to reorient the group, for example:

> *Can i start by drawing two lines to create an angle? (Group 3, line 22)*

These structures serve to call attention to a reorientation and to give other participants the opportunity to request a pause in that reorientation to ensure they share understanding with the rest of the group.

Reorienting questions also served to highlight an understanding gap, pulling the group back into a math discussion to provide an explanation or confirm an understanding. One example of this math-question reorientation comes from Group 2:

> *If you try to construct a line EF trying to connect AB and BC, wouldn't that mean A=C. (line 94)*

The use of reorienting statements rotates through group members, indicating that it was not always the same participant to return the group to math discourse. Talking about technological issues could quickly grab the attention of the group, but these reorienting statements were effective at refocusing the group's attention on the mathematical issues.

When groups returned to this higher level of math discourse, there were a variety of approaches employed by individuals. Multiple participants displayed something akin to math anxiety, highlighting their lack of experience or inability:

I haven't done geometry in a long time… I'll need the hints. (Group 1, line 18)

Often, members of the group shared in their confusion, as evidenced by Group 3's experience with making the decision to look at the hints during a series of math discourse. The group looked at the hints as a whole, but each member admitted to being more confused after doing so, imagining that it could be their unfamiliarity with math causing the issue:

I'm not sure if its cause I haven't done these types of problems in a while or the hints just aren't that good. (Group 3, line 95)

However, Group 1 and Group 4 were able to achieve math discourse and a solution, notably, with the use of familiar outside technologies.

9.5 CYCLES OF PROBLEMS

The analysis of this pilot trial revealed cycles of problems, with the groups having to go back and forth between confronting technical problems with the software and cognitive problems with the mathematics. The cyclic nature of the alternation between technical and mathematical difficulties may have been an artifact of the task and the preliminary state of the software prototype. Although the task was to work on a geometry construction, within the online environment software problems intervened and distracted the group. Groups tried to quickly get around the technical problems and cycle back to the math. There, they found themselves poorly prepared to tackle a geometry problem. Both the technical and the cognitive problems were consequences of the situation of pilot-test participants in a design-based-research project. The socio-technical goal of the project was still in the distant future and the necessary supports for the participants were not yet in place. Thus, the subjects met with many difficulties. The point is to learn from the pilot trial: what are the most important social and technical features to be developed next?

> The experiences of the groups highlight interesting aspects of group-cognitive processes and how tool and math skills can hinder the ability to solve the problem by otherwise competent users.

The experiences of the groups highlight interesting aspects of group-cognitive processes and how tool and math skills can hinder the ability to solve the problem by otherwise competent users. Clearly, while math discourse was a goal of each group, it proved difficult to achieve in the face of tool issues and feelings of math anxiety. When faced with a technical issue, the individuals blamed the tool for the inability to solve the problem, because they felt they were technically competent in general:

> I'm an IT consultant and have to deal with various software programs meaning I'm familiar with how software should be designed and navigating my way around…this was definitely tough. (Group 4, lines 310–313)

On the other hand, when faced with a mathematical concept that they were not familiar with, members of the groups blamed themselves for not being mathematically focused:

> My High School Math teachers are furious with me right now I can feel it. (Group 3, line 96)

This dichotomy between technical ability and mathematical inability was identified in each log. While this is an interesting case in our specific dataset pertaining to mathematically oriented online-learning contexts, we suspect that this phenomena may be evident in other collaborative-learning situations. Working to learn both content and the technology used to deliver that content can be overwhelming and may distract from the conceptual intent of the lesson. These difficulties are evident in our analysis as triggers of cycling and may be applicable to many technologically mediated learning situations. Because of these identified issues, it is important to build technological familiarity into any educational groupware environment to overcome technological issues early in the process. We find that in the face of tool adversity individuals defaulted to tools they were comfortable with such as PowerPoint, paper/pencil, or screenshot/email. The use of familiar tools allowed the members of the groups to focus on the actual math discourse and problem solving, and isolate negative effects of the prototype tool on their productivity.

One of the most striking elements of our analysis is the concept of *cycling* in the group process between *tool* issues and *math* discourse, including math anxiety, confusion and solutions. Our observations in this environment indicate that there was a salient presence of software functionality issues that, when coupled with gaps in knowledge, derailed mathematical discourse. This derailment and interest in getting back on task led to cycling. Although each group experienced cycling, the groups that were most successful were able to quickly manage technological barriers and return to math discourse for the majority of their chat.

In the future, it seems clear that reducing tool issues and increasing the time available for math discourse is key for productive computer-supported collaborative mathematical problem solving. While we are not arguing that all technological systems will include these barriers, the experience of technological confusion does seem to be a common occurrence for, at least, new users of technological systems. As highlighted by one of the participants:

> The issue with our first attempts was the usability of the tools—and lack of familiarity of the capabilities available within GeoGebra. (Group 1, line 109)

An increase in familiarity with the system may reduce cycling.

In addition to our analytical findings, each of the groups had recommendations for ways to improve the technology and the process of group math problem solving in the VMT-with-GeoGebra environment. These ranged from calls for an undo option to hopes for a primer or tutorial to alleviate some of the early technological issues. In Group 2, one individual thought they missed a tutorial because of difficulty with the system:

Was there a tutorial on GeoGebra that we were supposed to read first? (Group 2, line 91)

The ability for individuals to get exposure to the core functionality of the GeoGebra environment may allow for more comfort with the tool, which may facilitate better math discourse between the group members and make the GeoGebra tool more transparent.

9.6 CURRICULUM DESIGN CRITERIA

In response to the analysis of the GeoGebra use sessions, we drafted a set of dynamic-geometry curricular activities, interspersed with tutorials of the technology features. Curriculum activities were designed to promote collaborative learning, particularly as exhibited in significant mathematical discourse about geometry. Collaborative learning involves a subtle interplay of processes at the individual, small-group and classroom levels of engagement, cognition and reflection. Accordingly, the activities are structured with sections for individual work, small-group collaboration and whole-class discussion. It is hoped that this mixture will enhance motivation, extend attention and spread understanding.

The curriculum is designed to provide a systematic pathway to skills in a number of dimensions simultaneously. It is hoped that building up the required skill sets systematically, without assuming many skills initially, may avoid the math anxiety that students feel when they get stuck. In addition, the collaborative approach allows students to support each other, filling in for each other's deficits.

The *goal* of the set of activities is to improve skills in collaborative and mathematical discourse, exploring dependencies, geometric construction, analytic explanation and domain content for math teachers and students:

1. to engage in significant mathematical *discourse*; to collaborate on and discuss mathematical activities in supportive small online groups;

2. to collaboratively explore mathematical phenomena; to make mathematical phenomena visual in multiple representations; and to vary their parameters through dynamic *dragging*;

3. to *construct* mathematical diagrams—demonstrating a practical understanding of their structure;

4. to design *dependencies* in geometric figures to establish desired relationships;

5. to notice, wonder about and form conjectures about mathematical relationships; to justify, *explain,* and prove mathematical findings; and

6. to understand core concepts, relationships, theorems, and constructions of basic high-school *geometry.*

The working hypothesis of the project is that these goals can be furthered through activities that specify an effective combination of:

1. collaborative experiences in mathematical activities with guidance in collaborative, mathematical and accountable geometric *discourse*;

2. exploring (e.g., by *dragging*) dynamic-mathematical diagrams and multiple representations;

3. *constructing* geometric figures;

4. designing *dependencies* in dynamic-mathematical constructions;

5. *explaining* conjectures, justifications, and proofs; and

6. engagement in well-designed activities around basic high-school geometry *content.*

In other words, the activities seek a productive synthesis of the six areas of: communication, exploration, visualization, design, and mathematical skills applied in the domain of beginning geometry. They operationalize "deep conceptual learning" of mathematics in terms of these measurable outcomes:

1. the quality and quantity of significant mathematical *discourse* in collaborative interactions;

2. involvement in group *explorations* of mathematical objects and representations, including noticing and wondering;

3. effective *constructions* of mathematical objects with specified characteristics;

4. establishment of robust dynamic *dependencies* among geometric objects;

5. articulation of *explanations*, justifications, and proofs of conjectures; and

6. engagement with *geometric* notions of congruence, symmetry, dependencies, relationships, transformations, and deduction.

The set of activities is designed to provide a hands-on educational experience in basic geometry to math teachers and students, taking them from a possibly novice level to a more skilled level, from which they can proceed more effectively without such designed, scaffolded activities. By providing activities on different levels for each of the dimensions, we hope to help math teachers and students to increase their relevant skills—in different ways for different people.

Our focus has centered increasingly on facilitating and supporting lessons involving geometric dependencies. GeoGebra allows one to construct systems of inter-dependent geometric objects. Students have to learn how to think in terms of these dependencies. They can learn through visualizations, manipulations, constructions and verbal articulations. These can all be modeled and these skills can be developed gradually; our pilot study indicates that for successful math discourse to be achieved, supporting these skills must be an explicit priority of the socio-technical system.

Our design work is guided by socio-technical implications of continuing pilot studies as the technology and pedagogy of our project co-evolve. We are countering the problems that caused negative cycling of technical and cognitive distractions by improving the software and testing the curriculum. The curriculum integrates tutorials about using the VMT and GeoGebra interfaces with carefully structured sequences of dynamic-geometry activities for virtual math teams. The activities systematically build up the background knowledge, group practices, and problem-solving orientation needed for engaging in significant mathematical discourse.

The set of activities should gradually increase student skill levels in each of these dimensions. The design starts out assuming relatively low skill levels and gradually increases the level of skill expected.

1. The *discourse* begins with having students greet each other online and then negotiate about who will do what, when in the online environment. Students are then asked to comment on their noticings and wonderings. Later, they are to make conjectures. Finally, they are expected to explain things to each other, make sure that everyone understands, and produce presentations of group findings. Practices developed in collaborative work eventually contribute to individual skills.

2. The *exploration* begins with being introduced to software widgets and tools. It goes on to increasingly complicated geometric drawings. Then, students are expected to construct geometric objects themselves and in small groups. Finally, they are given open-ended scenarios and encouraged to figure out how to explore unknown mathematical territory.

3. *Construction* skills gradually grow from dragging existing objects, to constructing with step-by-step instructions, to figuring out how to construct objects with specific dependencies, to defining their own construction tools, to constructing objects of their own design in open-ended micro-worlds. The skill level progresses from novice to a reasonable command of GeoGebra's geometry tools. A transition to GeoGebra's algebra connection (analytic geometry) is provided at the end, opening up GeoGebra's multiple representations of geometric diagrams, analytic geometry graphs, spreadsheet data, 3-D transformations, and a computer algebra system.

4. *Dependencies* are stressed as a key to understanding dynamic geometry. They frequently provide the goal of a construction, the means to building a relationship or the insight for a proof.

5. *Proof* in geometry is introduced slowly, with a focus on noticing and wondering. This is followed by formulation of text-chat-based explanations and multi-media documentation of findings. The explanations gradually entail increased levels of justification, finally approaching formal proofs, without ever reaching the completely formalized version of two-column proof.

6. The *geometry* content starts by covering most of the activities in Book I of Euclid's *Elements* (300 BCE), but translated into and implemented in the computer-supported collaborative-learning medium of multi-user dynamic geometry. It incorporates most of the initial standards for high-school geometry in the new *Common Core Standards* (2011), including congruence, symmetry, and rigid transformations. The fundamental features of triangles are examined first, and then students are encouraged to explore similar features for quadrilaterals. For instance, students are involved in designing hierarchies of kinds of triangles or quadrilaterals based on alternative representations and dependencies of congruence, symmetry and rigid transformations. Finally, a sampling of creative objects, micro-worlds, and challenge problems are offered for student-centered exploration.

There is a theoretical basis for gradually increasing skill levels in terms of both understanding and proof in geometry. Here "understanding" and "proof" are taken in rather broad senses. The van Hiele theory (see deVilliers, 2003, p. 11) specifies several levels in the development of students' understanding of geometry, including:

1. *recognition*: visual recognition of general appearance (something looks like a triangle);

2. *analysis*: initial analysis of properties of figures and terminology for describing them;

3. *ordering*: logical ordering of figures (a square is a kind of rectangle in the quadrilateral hierarchy); and

4. *deduction*: longer sequences of deduction; understanding of the role of axioms, theorems, and proofs.

The implication of van Hiele's theory is that students who are at a given level cannot properly grasp ideas presented at a higher level until they reach that level. Thus, a developmental series of activities pegged to the increasing sequence of levels is necessary to effectively present the content and concepts of geometry, such as, eventually, formal proof. Failure to lead students through this developmental process is likely to cause student feelings of inadequacy and consequent negative attitudes toward geometry.

Citing various mathematicians, deVilliers (2003) lists several roles and functions of proof, particularly when using dynamic-geometry environments.

1. *Communication*: Proof as the transmission of mathematical knowledge.

2. *Explanation*: Proof as providing insight into why something is true.

3. *Discovery*: Proof as the discovery or invention of new results.

4. *Verification*: Proof as concerned with the truth of a statement.

5. *Intellectual challenge*: Proof as the self-realization/fulfillment derived from constructing a proof.

6. *Systematization*: Proof as the organization of various results into a deductive system of axioms, major concepts and theorems.

In his book, deVilliers suggests that students be introduced to proof by gradually going through this sequence of levels of successively more advanced roles of proof through a series of well-designed activities. In particular, the use of a dynamic-geometry environment can aid in moving students from the early stages of these sequences (recognition and communication) to the advanced levels (deduction and systematization). The use of dragging geometric objects to explore, analyze and support explanation can begin the developmental process. The design and construction of geometric objects with dependencies to help discover, order and verify relationships can further the process. The construction can initially be highly scaffolded by instructions and collaboration; then students can be guided to reflect upon and discuss the constructed dependencies; finally, they can practice constructing objects with gradually reduced scaffolding. This can bring students to a stage where they are ready for deduction and systematization that builds on their exploratory experiences.

The set of activities can be used as is, following the given sequence. Alternatively, a classroom instructor, workshop facilitator or group of learners can select activities and adapt them to local circumstances and interests. Although they build on specific knowledge explained in previous activities, the activities are each self-contained. While they are designed for a small group of learners to progress through them using the VMT-with-GeoGebra collaboration environment, the activities can be adapted for other approaches.

9.7 PRACTICES AS RESOURCES

As discussed above in Chapter 8, the key resources for learning may not be physical artifacts, but can, for instance, be practices. The most important learning outcome may not be the ability to reproduce factual knowledge, but the skill to engage in certain social or domain-specific practices. The Common Core standards include a set of recommended mathematical practices for proficient students. The goals of our curricular design of dynamic-geometry resources align closely with those practices.

The following set of practices state the main skills that we want to instill. They integrate math and discourse skills. They are specifically oriented to dynamic geometry and its unique strengths.

1. *Visualize*: View and analyze constructions of geometric objects and relationships.

2. *Drag*: Explore constructions of geometric objects through manipulation.

3. *Discourse*: Notice, wonder, conjecture, strategize, discuss relationships in constructions and how to investigate them further.

4. *Dependencies*: Discover and name dependencies among geometric objects in constructions.

5. *Construction*: Construct dependencies among objects, and define custom tools for doing so.

6. *Argumentation*: Build deductive arguments, and explain and prove them in terms of the dependencies.

7. *Math Accountability*: Listen to what others say, solicit their reactions, re-voice their statements, re-state in math terminology and representations.

8. *Collaboration*: Preserve discourse, reflect on it and organize findings; refine the statement of math knowledge; build knowledge together by building on each other's ideas.

These practices can be placed in rough isomorphism with the Common Core math practices.

1. Make sense of problems and persevere in solving them: (b).

2. Reason abstractly and quantitatively: (c).

3. Construct viable arguments and critique the reasoning of others: (g).

4. Model with mathematics: (a).

5. Use appropriate tools strategically: (e).

6. Attend to precision: (f).

7. Look for and make use of structure: (d).

8. Look for and express regularity in repeated reasoning: (h).

It may be possible to organize, present, and motivate our course activities in terms of these practices. Then pedagogy could be discussed in terms of how to promote and scaffold each of these; formative assessment (including group portfolio construction) could also be structured according to these practices.

The next chapter will illustrate the foregoing principles of design with examples from the current curriculum of dynamic-geometry activities.

CHAPTER 10

Practice: Doing Geometry

Chapter Summary

To provide a concrete example of human-centered geometry, a number of sample activities are presented here for student groups to engage in collaborative dynamic mathematics. They include the basic exploration of triangles and quadrilaterals—largely translated from Euclid's Elements—as well as the concepts of congruence, symmetry, and transformation. They build sequentially, emphasizing student exploration, hands-on construction, awareness of dependencies, explanation of reasoning and collaborative mathematical discourse at every stage.

A sample curriculum in dynamic geometry has been designed, based on the principles in Chapter 9. It consists of 20 topics. Gradually, these topics guide groups of students through a series of interactive experiences intended to encourage them to develop practices that provide a shared understanding of dynamic geometry. Each topic consists of three or more tabs within the VMT interface. Each of these tabs is a multi-user GeoGebra environment in which the group can work.

10.1 A CURRICULUM OF RESOURCES

Figure 10.1 shows a VMT chat room, pre-loaded with a topic. Notice that there are six tabs and the students are currently working in the tab entitled "Objects." They are discussing point 13 in the list of instructions. They have created a couple of objects in the GeoGebra tab in addition to the objects that were provided. They created a circle with a radius, LM. One student asks the others what they notice, in accordance with point 13. Another says she noticed, "no matter where the radius is, it will be the same length." Other students agreed. Then the group decided to move to the next tab.

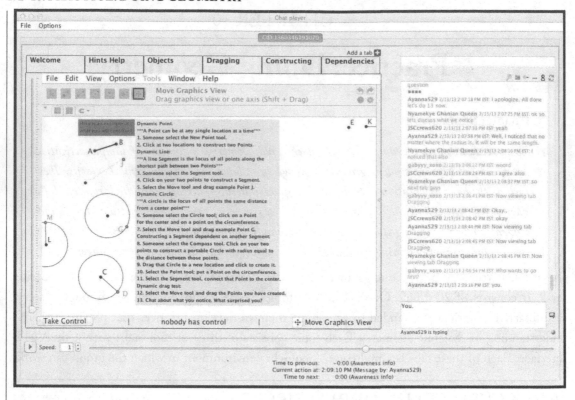

Figure 10.1: A VMT chat room for Topic 1 as viewed in the VMT Replayer.

10.2 BUILDING UP GEOMETRY FROM AN INTUITIVE STARTING POINT

The first topics allow students to explore the elements of dynamic geometry: the point, line, circle, and polygon. They can drag them, create new ones, and explore their behavior and dependencies. In an initial warm-up exercise (Figure 10.2), they are introduced to the elements and encouraged to drag them.

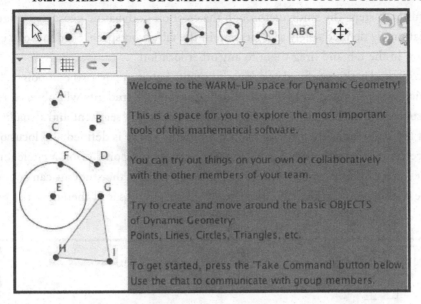

Figure 10.2: The Warm-up tab, "Warm Up."

In the first stage of the first session (tab A of Topic 1), they are stepped through a collaborative approach to using the GeoGebra tools (Figure 10.3). The second tab provides some advice on using the VMT tools.

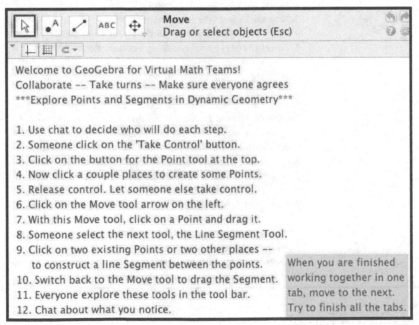

Figure 10.3: Topic 1, tab A, "Welcome."

The third tab steps the students through the creation of dynamic geometry (Figure 10.4). A *point* is operationally defined solely as a location in the tab's workspace. Students can create points at any location in the tab and drag them to any other location.

A line *segment* is then defined as a locus of points between any two end points. By dragging point J—which is constrained to stay on an existing segment—students will observe a visual locus of the path covered. They can physically drag the point along the segment and visually observe the formation of the segment as the path of a point. Similarly, a *circle* is defined as a locus of points the same distance from a center point. Again, a student can drag a point G on a circle and observe a display of the locus of points traversed. Taking this a step further, the students can connect the center of a circle with a point on the circumference to create a radius and then drag the point around the circumference to observe the behavior of the radius.

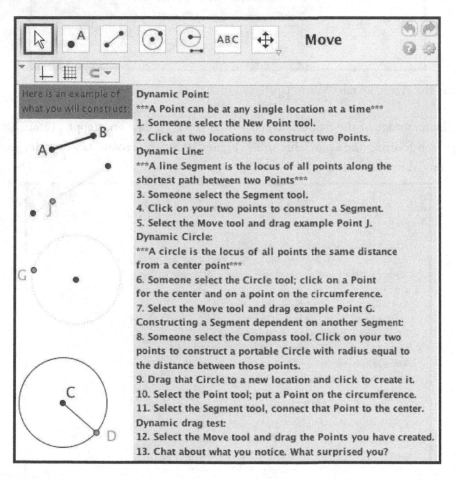

Figure 10.4: Topic 1, tab C, "Objects."

In this way, one can see the objects of dynamic geometry built up from the simple point. Moreover, the student is already exposed to some basic notions of dynamic geometry, such as that a point can be constrained to remain on a segment or a circle and that all radii of the circle are the same length by definition of the circle as a locus of points the same distance from the center.

One can see the objects of dynamic geometry built up from the simple Point.

The fourth tab (Figure 10.5) provides further experience with dragging and constructing points that are constrained to stay on a segment or are dependent upon the point of intersection of two lines. This introduces from the start the concepts of constraint and dependence as central to dynamic geometry. Students may not fully comprehend these concepts right away, but the terms are introduced into the discourse vocabulary, where they can be played with and mature.

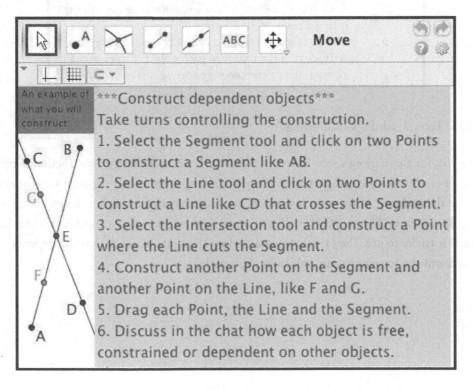

Figure 10.5: Topic 1, tab D, "Dragging."

The next tab (Figure 10.6) explores an aspect of these terms. First, it has the students contrast the results of copy-and-paste with dynamic-geometry construction. They see that there is a dependency maintained between segment AB and segment CD, but not with the copy-and-pasted segment A1B1. Further, the terms "constrained" and "dependent" are differentiated by distinguishing "partially constrained" from "completely dependent."

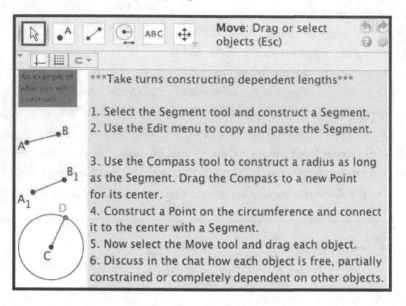

Figure 10.6: Topic 1, tab E, "Constructing."

Finally, for those groups who have time for a sixth tab, a challenge construction is presented. A central operation in dynamic geometry is copying a length from one segment to another, maintaining the dependence of the new length on the old, even if the original length is changed by dragging. In this tab (Figure 10.7), students must copy two lengths using GeoGebra's compass tool, which is tricky to use. They are instructed to drag all points to check that the dependencies are maintained and the lengths dynamically adjust properly.

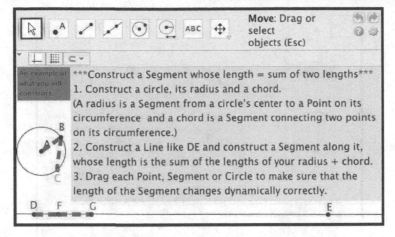

Figure 10.7: Topic 1, tab F, "Dependencies."

10.3   THE DEPENDENCIES OF TRIANGLES

Much of Euclid's geometry is implicit in his first proposition, the construction of an equilateral triangle. In dynamic geometry, many of the fundamental resources of dynamic dragging, dynamic construction and dynamic dependencies can be experienced by working on this construction. Topic 2 focuses on this. The first tab (Figure 10.8) steps the students through the construction, including dragging to check the dependencies and then discussing the dependencies among the distances between the three points, and hence the lengths of the equal sides. The mastery of this construction—including a shared understanding of its design rationale—signifies an initial level of expertise in dynamic geometry.

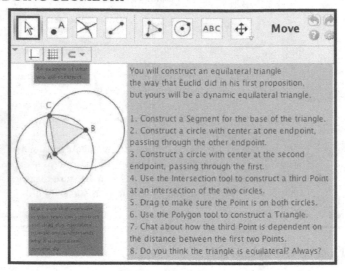

Figure 10.8: Topic 2, tab A.

The second and third tab (Figure 10.9) provide an extension of the equilateral-triangle construction to make explicit some of the relationships inherent there. This will lead to constructions in Topic 3 involving perpendiculars and bisectors. The exploration of various constraints and dependencies in this construction are related to the same constraints in different kinds of triangles.

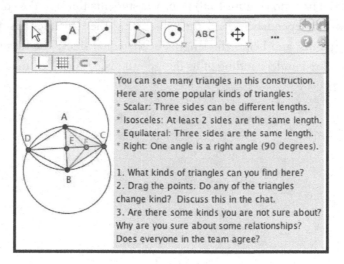

Figure 10.9: Topic 2, tab C.

The fourth tab (Figure 10.10) displays a variety of triangles, with built-in (invisible) constraints. The students can drag the triangles and their vertices to see how they are each constrained and to see which can be made to overlay others

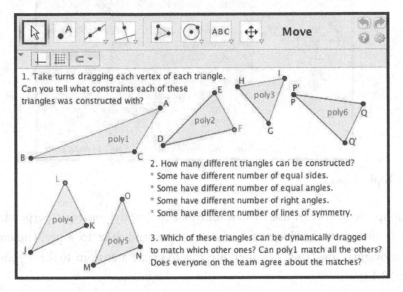

Figure 10.10: Topic 2, tab D.

10.4 DESIGNING CUSTOM TOOLS

As part of having the students build up dynamic geometry themselves, Topic 3 has them create their own custom tools before giving them access to the corresponding GeoGebra tools. It has them construct perpendicular bisectors and perpendiculars through a given point. It then leads them through the creation of a custom tool that encapsulates their construction (Figure 10.11).

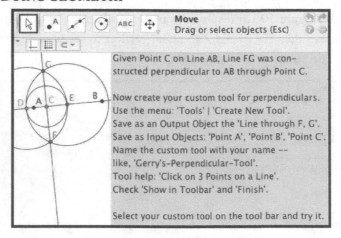

Figure 10.11: Topic 3, tab B.

The group members can use this custom tool to quickly construct perpendiculars to lines. Applying their custom tool twice, they construct a perpendicular to a perpendicular, which is a parallel to the original line. They can then use this to create a custom tool for generating parallel lines (Figure 10.12).

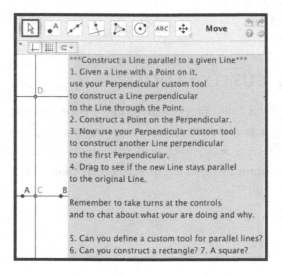

Figure 10.12: Topic 3, tab C.

10.5 THE HIERARCHY OF POSSIBLE TRIANGLES

Topic 4 encourages the students to think about all the different kinds of triangles that are possible—given three line segments joined at three vertices. They create custom tools for generating right triangles using their perpendicular tool, for instance. Then they are asked to organize the variety of differently constrained triangles into an inheritance hierarchy (Figure 10.13). This introduces a systematic view of the phenomena.

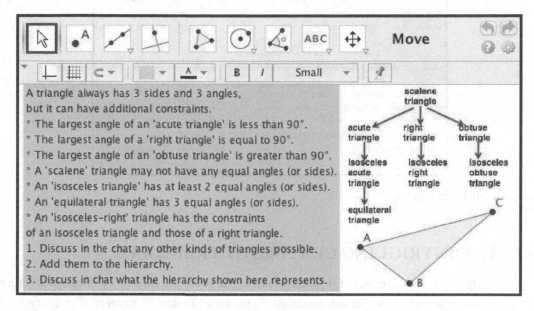

Figure 10.13: Topic 4, tab C.

10.6 DISCOVERING DEPENDENCIES

The exercise involving inscribed equilateral triangles has been found to be a fruitful one because of how strongly it involves the detection of dependencies and the attempt to re-construct them—thus integrating exploratory dragging, analyzing dependencies, and designing constructions. Accordingly, Topic 5 starts with that exercise in the first tab (see Section 7.3). Its second tab extends the problem to inscribed squares. This is then generalized to N-sided regular polygons inscribed inside each other, illustrated with inscribed regular hexagons (Figure 10.14). The challenge is stated to come up with a general conjecture for all inscribed regular polygons and even to prove the conjecture. If students do not figure out the key to the inscribed triangles in tab A, they are encouraged to explore the figures in the other tabs so that they might see the dependency that is common to them all. This Topic introduces a mathematical sense of generality of dependencies and the connection of this to proof.

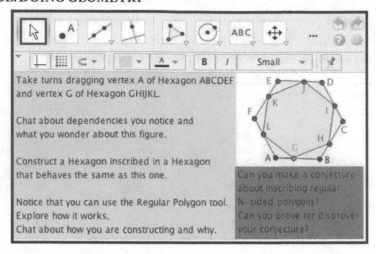

Figure 10.14: Topic 5, tab C.

10.7 THE INTRIGUING CENTERS OF TRIANGLES

As we already saw in Chapter 4, the incenter of a triangle possesses interesting properties (due to the dependencies designed into its construction). There are a number of "centers" that are typically studied in geometry. They are useful for constructing an inscribing or a circumscribing circle, for instance, or for locating a point such that the sum of the paths from there to the sides or to the vertices is minimal (Figure 10.15).

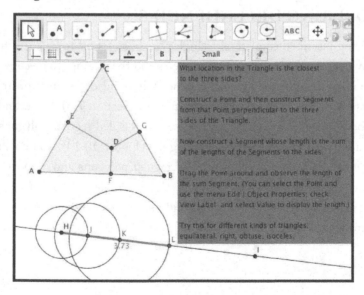

Figure 10.15: Topic 6, tab C.

In Topics 6 and 7, students construct custom tools for the incenter, circumcenter, centroid, and orthocenter. They can then easily construct Euler's segment and explore the associated nine-point circle (Figure 10.16).

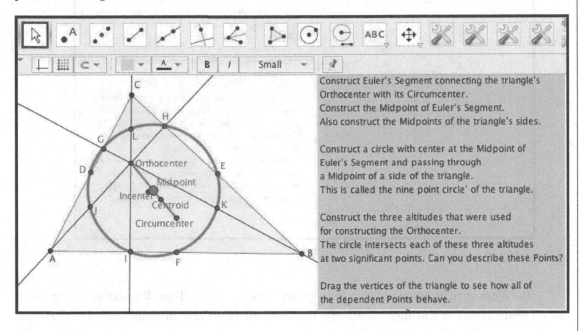

Construct Euler's Segment connecting the triangle's
Orthocenter with its Circumcenter.
Construct the Midpoint of Euler's Segment.
Also construct the Midpoints of the triangle's sides.

Construct a circle with center at the Midpoint of
Euler's Segment and passing through
a Midpoint of a side of the triangle.
This is called the nine point circle' of the triangle.

Construct the three altitudes that were used
for constructing the Orthocenter.
The circle intersects each of these three altitudes
at two significant points. Can you describe these Points?

Drag the vertices of the triangle to see how all of
the dependent Points behave.

Figure 10.16: Topic 7, tab D.

10.8 TRANSFORMATIONS, SYMMETRIES, AND PROOFS

The rigid transformations of an object (e.g., a triangle) are introduced in Topic 8, including the possibility of sequences of transformations. Students are encouraged to explore the use of GeoGebra's transformation tools. Transformations are then used to introduce the concept of symmetry. The ideas of rigid (i.e., area preserving) transformations and symmetry are then used to motivate the conjecture that the area of a triangle is one-half the area of the rectangle that contains it (Figure 10.17). It is suggested that a proof could follow from a consideration of the dependencies.

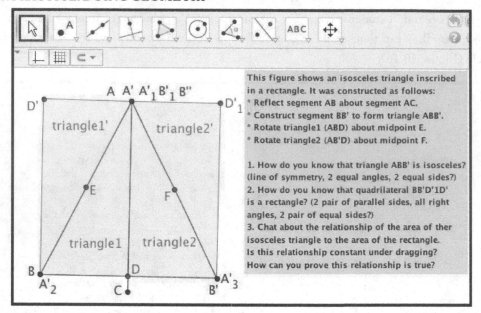

Figure 10.17: Topic 8, tab C.

The ideas of rigid transformations and symmetries are used in Topic 9 to derive and/or prove several propositions of Euclidean geometry. These include that the sum of the angles in a triangle equal a straight line (Figure 10.18). This is generalized to a conjecture about the sum of the angles in an N-sided polygon.

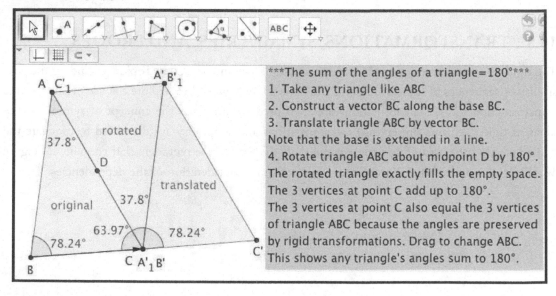

Figure 10.18: Topic 9, tab A.

10.9 VISUALIZING SIMILARITY AND CONGRUENCE

The dilation transformation is introduced in Topic 10. It is one way to construct similar triangles. Another way is to copy the angles so corresponding vertices of an original triangle and a constructed copy have the same size angles (Figure 10.19). The students can consider the relationship of these two different approaches to similarity of triangles.

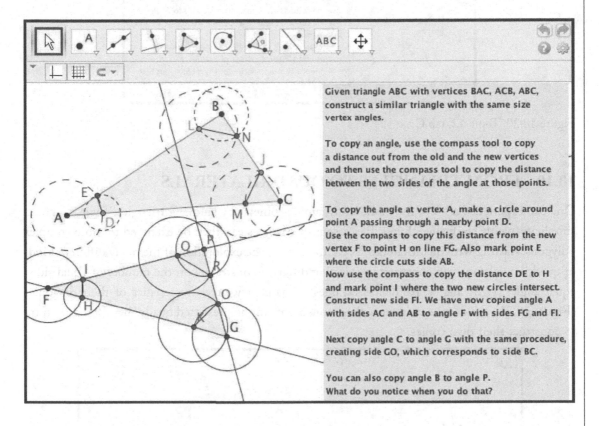

Figure 10.19: Topic 10, tab B.

Topics 11 and 12 are devoted to giving students a hands-on visualization of why certain combinations of equal sides and angles produce congruent or similar triangles. This includes the standard rules of SAS, SSS, ASA. The last case considered is the tricky one of SSA (Figure 10.20). The construction with the SSA constraint almost determines that the constructed triangle will be congruent to the original, but there is sometimes a second possibility. It is hoped that students will internalize the figures constructed in these tabs to understand why certain combinations of constraints guarantee congruence, rather than simply memorizing the list of acronyms.

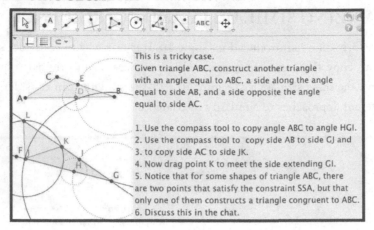

Figure 10.20: Topic 12, tab C.

10.10 FROM TRIANGLES TO QUADRILATERALS

One can experience a lot of the basics of dynamic geometry by studying triangles. Their structural simplicity avoids confusing clutter. The lessons of triangles can then be extended to more complex polygons, starting with quadrilaterals. Topic 13 involves the exploration of the many different kinds of quadrilaterals one can construct by selecting different constraints on the number of equal sides, equal angles, right angles, parallel sides, lines of symmetry, or characteristics of their diagonals (Figure 10.21). Students can identify these constraints in the presented quadrilaterals and then try to construct their own copies.

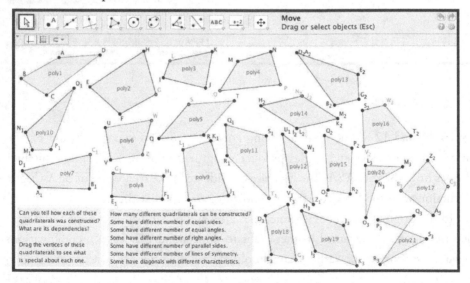

Figure 10.21: Topic 13, tab A.

Like triangles, quadrilaterals seem to have mysterious properties. One is that connecting the midpoints of an arbitrary quadrilateral produces a parallelogram with half the area of the original figure. In Topic 14, the students are stepped through a proof explaining this (Figure 10.22).

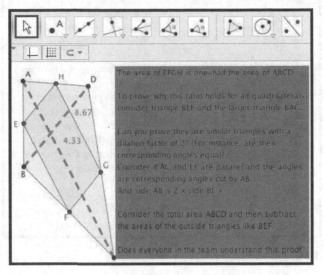

Figure 10.22: Topic 14, tab B.

Then the students are asked to explore whether there is an incenter of quadrilaterals that behaves like the incenter of a triangle (Figure 10.23); interestingly, the answer is that it is only similar under certain constraints on the quadrilateral.

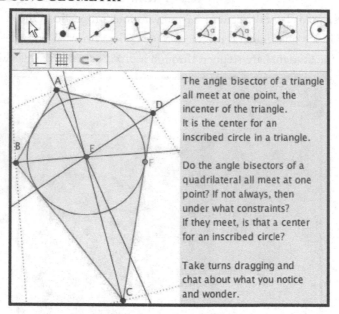

The angle bisector of a triangle all meet at one point, the incenter of the triangle.
It is the center for an inscribed circle in a triangle.

Do the angle bisectors of a quadrilateral all meet at one point? If not always, then under what constraints?
If they meet, is that a center for an inscribed circle?

Take turns dragging and chat about what you notice and wonder.

Figure 10.23: Topic 14, tab C.

The hierarchy of triangles was relatively simple. Now that systematic approach is applied to the more complex zoo of differently constrained quadrilaterals (Figure 10.24). In traditional geometry, there are several names for kinds of quadrilaterals and it is difficult for students to remember the names and the corresponding definitions. In Topic 14, it becomes clear that many distinct kinds of quadrilaterals exist that have no special name. Furthermore, there are certain kinds that can be defined in multiple ways, in terms of different sets of constraints. Working out and debating the structure of a hierarchy of quadrilaterals can be a rich exercise.

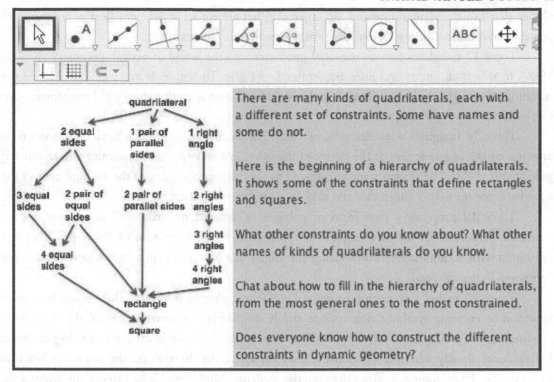

Figure 10.24: Topic 14, tab D.

10.11 ADVANCED TOPICS

The initial topics are designed to introduce teams of students to dynamic geometry and to give them a sense of the core resources of dynamic dragging, dynamic constructing, and dynamic dependencies. Ties are made to materials from Euclidean geometry. This introduction should prepare groups and individual students to use the technology of dynamic mathematics to explore further realms of mathematics. As a taste for this, students are offered a number of problems to solve or open-ended micro worlds to explore.

> This introduction should prepare groups and individual students to use the technology of dynamic mathematics to explore further realms of mathematics.

Topic 15 provides some challenge problems that can be explored using dynamic geometry. Some of these came from Math Forum's Problem of the Week.

Topic 16 provides a series of explorations of rigid transformations and their possible compositions. The students are asked to pretend that they are designing a factory operation using machines that can translate, rotate and flip objects. What are the most efficient fleet of machines to purchase and use, assuming various physical and economic constraints?

Topic 17 translates transformational geometry into the world of taxicab geometry (Krause, 1986), in which all points and lines are confined to a grid. The students are asked to redefine the meaning of triangle, circle and distance in this world and then to explore how rigid transformations can be carried out and composed.

Topic 18 imagines a jeweler with two identical squares of gold for a broach. She wants to attach a corner of one square at the center of the other in a way that will maximize the amount of gold that is visible. The students are encouraged to consider special cases of the arrangement of the squares, come up with a conjecture and explain why their conjecture is true.

Topic 19 proposes a new form of polygon: a "crossed quadrilateral" that looks like an hourglass. Students are asked to explore its properties, such as the sum of its angles. They are presented with an argument for measuring the angles in a way that maintains properties from the "uncrossed" quadrilateral.

Topic 20 makes a transition to using GeoGebra's algebra interface. This view allows construction by entering symbolic descriptions and it also displays numeric values of objects. First, a construction of a tangent to a circle from a point outside the circle is carried out using the tools the students already understand. Then the students are shown how to do the same construction using the algebraic approach. From here on, the students should be able to explore the wide range of functionality available in GeoGebra on their own. Meanwhile, they may have internalized an approach to mathematical thinking that includes emphasis on exploratory inquiry, construction design, and understanding of dependencies.

10.12 AN INTRODUCTORY TRAJECTORY

The sequence of topics presented in this chapter is designed to accomplish multiple goals. It introduces students to collaborative dynamic geometry at a technical level by guiding them in the use of the VMT and GeoGebra software tools. It does this by providing heavily scaffolded exercises in constructing basic geometric objects and discussing them with team members. These exercises familiarize the student with the elemental structure of dynamic geometry: how points can be located and moved; how lines (segments, rays, infinite lines, vectors, circles) connect points; how points can be confined to lines or intersections; how hierarchies of dependencies determine the possible movements or behaviors of dynamic-geometry objects. Simultaneously, small-group chats about what team members notice and wonder begin to instill effective collaboration practices, such as taking turns controlling the construction, recognizing the contributions of others, assuming helpful roles, directing work on given tasks, summarizing findings, repairing misunderstandings, negotiating differences of opinion, focusing attention on mathematical issues, providing innovative perspectives, proposing creative approaches.

Exploration of dynamic construction begins with Euclid's first two propositions: constructing an equilateral triangle and copying a segment length. These are both transformed into their dynamic analogues. Careful study of these two examples reveals the core of dynamic geometry. To be dynamically equilateral, a triangle must not only have equal side lengths and equal angle measurements. The sides must remain equal to each other even when one of the sides is dynamically dragged to be longer or shorter and the angles must remain equal to each other even when a vertex is dynamically dragged to change the orientation of the angle. This introduces the notion of dependency—that one side's length is dependent upon that of another side (due to both being constructed as radii of the same or congruent circles). Similarly, when copying a segment it is not sufficient to duplicate its current length since that might change. It is necessary to ensure that its length changes in accordance with any dynamic change in the length of the original segment. This involves constructing a sequence of dependencies connecting the two segments. Incredibly, Euclid's ancient construction methods for non-dynamic geometry suffice for dynamic geometry—given the dependency mechanisms of a software system like GeoGebra.

Once students acquire a feel for working collaboratively with dynamic geometry, they can begin to explore the standard themes of geometry. Traditionally, this begins with the characteristics of triangles, the simplest closed figure composed of lines. Students can construct isosceles and right triangles and discuss how these are just some of the possible special cases of three-sided polygons. They can investigate various "centers" of triangles and different ways of establishing congruence of triangles. Already at this point, the notion of deductive proof enters. Many proofs—as well as many problem-solving strategies—rely on identifying congruent triangles and proving congruence. The GeoGebra topics on congruence emphasize visualizing in dynamic constructions (and discussing in chat) the dependencies that establish congruence of triangles. This is intended to bring together different senses of proof (visual, intuitive, explanatory, conceptual, systematic) to support each other.

At the core of the establishment of congruence in dynamic geometry are the relationships of dependency. To the extent that students and groups can visualize (construct and drag) and understand (discuss) these dependencies, they in effect prove them. Some researchers of dynamic geometry have argued that students who demonstrate that a conjecture is always true by dragging the relevant figure through many cases lose their motivation for developing a traditional formal proof. Other researchers counter that there are different levels of proof and that students must progress through them, including the levels supported by dynamic dragging. These views are focused on dragging rather than on construction and dependencies. The approach of the topics in this chapter is aimed at orienting the students and groups to construction as a design process for establishing dependencies. To establish the dependencies that guarantee that, for instance, two triangles are congruent is to prove that the triangles are congruent. This conception of proof contrasts to the formalist sense of axiomatic deduction, which has grown in geometry over the millennia. The conception of proof through the establishment of dependencies is central to dynamic geometry and provides the student with a visual and conceptual understanding of why a conjecture is true, allowing the group to engage in significant mathematical discourse about the conjecture.

Following the investigation of triangles, the topics move to other areas of basic geometry, as defined by the Common Core standards, such as quadrilaterals and transformations. From here on, the topics are presented more as open-ended explorations, where the student groups can negotiate how to proceed. The goal is to encourage the groups to work like mathematicians exploring a new area of mathematics. The groups are encouraged to decide for themselves what the most interesting questions or conjectures are, how to investigate them, and what to conclude.

The final topic connects the geometry interface of GeoGebra with the algebra interface, exposing the student to more of the power of GeoGebra for supporting a wide range of mathematical work. The hope is that students at his point will be able to adopt GeoGebra as a flexible toolkit for their future work in mathematics. In addition, they may have come to appreciate the power of collaborative learning in mathematics and will continue to engage in small-group interaction—whether online or face-to-face—around stimulating topics in mathematics.

The goal of these topics is not to present a full course on dynamic geometry, but to equip students with the tools and more importantly the orientation to visualize, construct, and articulate relations of dependency as they study mathematics in the future.

CHAPTER 11

Design-Based Research: Human-Centered Geometry

Chapter Summary

What can be concluded about the research presented in this book? Has it succeeded in translating Euclid? The design-based research effort to develop a CSCL approach to dynamic geometry requires continued exploration of history, philosophy, mathematics, technology, collaboration, research, theory, pedagogy, and practice to effectively translate Euclid's geometry into a form appropriate to a perspective of human-centered informatics.

What is the measure of a task like translating Euclid? There can be no question of complete and final success in such an enterprise. Did the first geometers succeed? Did Euclid succeed? We can say that the Greek geometers founded an intellectual pursuit that changed the world. We can say that Euclid compiled the most influential book of mathematical, rational, scientific thinking. However, we can only make these judgments from two millennia after the fact. Furthermore, it is still true that even among students exposed to many hours of training in geometry, a sizable proportion of them seem to have totally missed the point and failed to value the experience.

11.1 DESIGN-BASED RESEARCH

The effort in the Virtual Math Teams Project to translate Euclid into an approach that stresses creative discovery adopted a design-based research approach. This posits that one can strive to keep improving the form of geometry education being designed. It accepts that one will never reach a final product. Of course, the project may end at some point—for instance, when funding runs out—but the effort will never reach a final goal state.

It is clearly unreasonable to expect that any specific, fixed form of geometry education will meet every student's needs under all conditions and in all respects. There will always be some students who catch on more quickly or who excel at certain aspects of geometry study and others who do not have the nutritional fortitude, the psychological self-discipline, the external motivation, the support system, the linguistic skills, etc. There is an infinity of conditions within which students could be situated as they enact collaborative dynamic geometry. No one design, however refined, can work in all these settings for all these unique people.

Traditional summative assessments, structured to measure simple causal relationships, are not the most appropriate measures of success in an undertaking like ours. Standard experimental design assumes that conditions are fixed, controlled, and well understood. They assume that goals are simple, independent, specified in advance and unproblematically measurable. However, the conditions in which collaborative dynamic geometry might be used if it is widely adopted are as unpredictable now as the math classroom you knew in high school would have been to Euclid. If it is successful, it will be because the spirit of our research will have been taken up by a community of educators distributed around the world and will be reinterpreted by teachers, parents, mentors, team coordinators, support groups and teams of learners in diverse settings. It will be adapted and evolved in ways we cannot foresee.

11.2   FORMATIVE ASSESSMENT

This is not at all to eschew assessment. Rather, it is to focus on situated formative assessment. The analysis of the triad of students in Section 7.3 provides an initial example. Here, we looked at how three students worked together using certain features of a specific version of the VMT-with-GeoGebra technology, on a given topic statement in their concrete motivational context. Rather than trying to measure how the students did against some preconceived expectations, we tried to understand what they accomplished on their own terms. Of course, we brought to our reading of the logs some guiding interests, such as a concern for geometric relationships of dependency.

A positive reading of the analysis of the student team's work might point to their demonstration that they could construct an equilateral triangle using what they had previously learned and that they figured out on their own how to construct a square. They also succeeded in the task of re-creating the inscribed triangle. Not only did they describe what they did and provide some insightful reflections on why their solution was valid, but they also demonstrated a firm grasp of the insights into the solution procedure by immediately applying the same procedures to construct the inscribed square. Furthermore, the team worked collaboratively: each member explained what she was doing during the key GeoGebra actions, everyone confirmed that they understood each step and they took turns with the steps so that the major accomplishments were done by the group as a whole. They discussed relationships among geometric objects in terms of restrictions, constraints and dependencies—sighting a number of forms of evidence.

The quality of their collaborative discourse is probably the most important indicator of success. The VMT Project is based on the theory that learning mathematics is largely a matter of becoming more proficient at talking about mathematics. The centrality of discourse is the motivation for adopting an approach of collaborative learning—learning as a group that talks (or chats) together about math. The stated goal of the Project is to increase "significant math discourse." To assess Project success is to analyze in various ways the quantity and quality of significant math discourse in the virtual math teams. Quantitative statistics comparing groups to each other and computing trends within individual groups can provide rough indications (see Section 6.5). However, closer qualitative analysis—such as detailed interaction analysis of chat and GeoGebra logs—is needed to provide closer understanding of changes in discourse practices.

The example of the team in Section 7.3 seems to provide some indication that, at least in this instance, the intent of the project was in some ways achieved. Of course, this initial analysis is but a small first step. It raises many more questions than it answers. It calls for further analyses.

- Would closer analysis of the same log—for instance, looking into the long sequences of GeoGebra actions during which there was no chat—confirm or contradict the positive impression?

- How did the other groups in the same class with the same preparation and the same topic statement do?

- How did other student groups from different classes, with different teachers and at other ages do?

- If the students continue to experience collaborative dynamic geometry for a significant period of time this year and then take a traditional geometry course next year, how will this experience affect their ability to visualize and conceptualize geometry then?

- How will this experience affect the participants' scores on standard math tests? (Does this question make sense, given that this experience was a tiny fraction of the students' math study and that the tests do not look for what we are trying to instill?)

> How will this experience affect the ability to visualize and conceptualize geometry later?

- How will their learning of geometry in this experience compare to that of students who spend the same amount of time learning geometry a different way? (Again, does this question make sense, given that such a "comparison" could never be comparable with different students and other tasks and resources?)

These questions call for much more research to be done before any significant educational claims can be made. However, we are not really aiming to make claims about the current state of our approach. We are aiming for a vision of the future, one we know we are not very near. We are interested in using our analyses of the current state in order to improve that state, not to institutionalize it. That is the nature of design-based research (DBR) in computer-supported collaborative learning (CSCL). Both DBR and CSCL are future-oriented, visionary, evolutionary, and emergent. That is why they go together well. The purpose of this book is not to claim that Euclid has been translated successfully, but to suggest a long and winding path for pursuing the translation.

11.3 ISSUES FOR THE FUTURE

Furthermore—as the chapters of this book should have indicated—the set of questions requiring further inquiry is not restricted to the preceding sort of learning questions. Rather, there are questions of history, philosophy, mathematics, technology, collaboration, research, theory, pedagogy, and practice which have just been touched on in the VMT Project and which continue to morph as we address them.

History: How should one translate the classic-education approach of Euclid's geometry into the contemporary vernacular of social networking, computer visualization and discourse-centered pedagogy? The "contemporary" forms of these dimensions have been rapidly changing during our project. It is impossible for a research project to keep pace with them and to re-conceptualize its approach adequately. How can we incorporate social networking motivations and the connectivity of massively multiplayer online games (MMOG), massive open online courses (MOOC), FaceBook, YouTube, etc.? What benefits can teachers and students get from new learning analytic and visualization tools? What new insights are available into discourse forms like accountable talk or the role of insults in group cohesion among teens that might help our effort?

Philosophy: If the plight of geometry is part of a larger world-historical dialectic of enlightenment, in which reification and individualization accompany rationalization and socialization, then what are the larger counter-trends and what do they imply for geometry education? Post-cognitive theory has reached into human-computer interaction through activity theory, distributed cognition, actor-network theory and group cognition. What new inspiration and implications can we draw from these sources?

Mathematics: Dynamic mathematics is an active field, with developments happening in theory and practice. For instance, the GeoGebra software has frequent new releases. The GeoGebra user community is growing rapidly, spreading into hundreds of countries. How can the efforts of one small research project keep up with this global phenomenon and feed into it with a perspective that emphasizes collaborative learning?

Technology: Of course, both commercial collaborative software and affordable hardware platforms change continuously. Should we consider porting our software to the iPad and other tablets, to the more affordable Chromebook, to increasingly more powerful and ubiquitous smart phones? Do we need to rethink our client-server architecture in order to scale up beyond what a central server can handle? Our system has been designed to support research; at what point should it be redesigned to support independent usage?

Collaboration: The analysis of co-presence, intersubjective shared understanding, and group cognition are not well developed. We need to understand them much better and to consider much more extensively how they can be supported in our technology, pedagogy, and curricular resources. More generally, we need many more studies of collaborative mathematics. When the VMT Project began, we did not even know that math could be done collaboratively, let alone that collaborative learning could be a powerful form of math education. Now we are exploring collaboration with dynamic geometry—and doing so in an online setting where there is not necessarily much institutional support or teacher involvement. Although we have gained a sense that this is do-able, we are also still discovering the difficulties that this can present to schools, teachers and students.

Research: The VMT software has been instrumented to capture every detail of the interactions of virtual math teams. As the system becomes more complicated—with GeoGebra tabs, shared whiteboards, wiki pages, web browser tabs—it becomes more difficult for the software to capture everything coherently and to present it to analysts in meaningful formats. As more student teams work in the system, it becomes a daunting task to maintain an overview and to find the best excerpts for specific kinds of examination, the best sessions for specific kinds of comparisons or the best corpora for specific kinds of quantitative analysis. We need more tools to assist with this, but above all, we need to conduct more analyses now that we are generating rich data.

Theory: The theory presented in this book is clearly currently "under construction." It emerged largely out of specific analyses of brief excerpts of interaction in student teams—guided, of course, by perspectives from post-cognitive philosophies and theories prevalent in CSCL and HCI. The refinement of this theory requires more analysis of what is taking place in VMT sessions of collaborative dynamic geometry. In particular, we need to analyze instances of creative discovery in the chats and GeoGebra activities; this will clarify what could be meant by a human-centered informatics. Theory is an essential element of the DBR iterative cycles. Theory drives the design of a next refined approach and directs the questions used to analyze the results of the latest intervention. Out of the deepened understanding gained by a new experience of a trial, the theory is developed further. For instance, the theory of group cognition emerged from the design-based research reported in (Stahl, 2006) and was significantly expanded by the research reported in (Stahl, 2009) and elsewhere. This research profited from rich experiences involving designed supports for collaborative-learning discourse. The theory of resources proposed in Chapter 8 similarly arose from recent studies of VMT-with-GeoGebra, such as that in Section 7.3. The current experimental collaborative-learning environment is instrumented to capture small-group enactment of complex configurations of resources, including the tools of VMT-with-GeoGebra and the topics of the dynamic-geometry curriculum. In this setting, the development of theory may be the most important product of DBR. Greek geometry's real contribution to the world was not to produce propositions for generations of students to memorize, but to promote rational discourse in the culture at large.

> The development of theory may be the most important product of DBR. Greek geometry's real contribution to the world was to promote rational discourse.

Pedagogy: The principles for the design of the topics presented to student teams arose largely from rethinking previous presentations of geometry and dynamic geometry, from Euclid to the Common Core Standards. They were translated in order to emphasize a human-centered perspective of creative discovery centered on geometric dependencies. Now it should be possible to investigate how well this is working through detailed analysis of team logs. Are the student groups experiencing their discoveries as products of their own work or as otherworldly truths? What suggestions for refining the pedagogy can be gleaned from analysis of actual data from teams enacting the resources provided?

Practice: Similarly, analysis of the data now starting to be generated can drive revision of the curriculum of topics. The sequence of topics was designed to achieve certain goals. The early topics introduced the basic paradigm of collaborative dynamic geometry: taking turns, chatting about what one is doing, making sure everyone on the team understands, dragging figures, creating objects. There was an attempt to show how all of geometry is built up step-by-step and tool-by-tool from the atomic point and the act of dragging. Students are guided to construct their own tools and to understand the basics of geometry in terms of how they can construct things. They are encouraged to see explanations of how things work in terms of dependencies—and to gradually come to understand the nature of dependencies in dynamic geometry. Finally, the scaffolded development of higher-level skills should allow groups to explore open-ended micro-worlds with considerable latitude. Now, we can start to see if these goals are being achieved. Analyses of how different teams enact the topics will provide a concrete source of detailed ideas for improving the topics, revising the curriculum, and refining the approach. The latest phase of the project has produced logs of over 100 sessions of virtual teams of math teachers working on selected GeoGebra topics and logs of 280 hour-long sessions of teams of students, mainly working on the first five topics. Most of the student groups worked together for eight sessions. This provides a wealth of data on how teachers and students enact the designed resources and environment and how they start to engage in effective math discourse and collaboration. So far, the only extended analyses of these logs are those in Chapter 7. The formative analysis of these complex interactions is the next major task of the project.

11.4 HUMAN-CENTERED GEOMETRY

This book has tried to provide a sense of how DBR can work in a CSCL project and to offer a vision of the potential translation of Euclidean geometry into an exciting experience of human-centered collaborative dynamic geometry. It has taken a number of chapters on diverse topics, but the aim has been to present a coherent, though multi-faceted argument, providing a model of concrete research proposing a way forward for a specific educational domain. The evolution of geometry learning has been underway for a long time. Perhaps the reflections in the preceding pages will contribute to its continuing dynamic.

What is an appropriate way to teach geometry today? This book opened with the following question: How should one translate the classic-education approach of Euclid's geometry into the contemporary vernacular of social networking, computer visualization, and discourse-centered pedagogy? Current socio-cultural theories of learning suggest that students learn best through active, student-centered, collaborative learning (Sawyer, 2006). They propose that to learn mathematics is to start to participate in the community or culture of mathematics: to engage in the discourse practices of mathematical activity oneself. In addition, there is pressure to instruct students in so-called 21st century skills, including social networking and computer-based inquiry. For instance, the international PISA tests, which measure the math skills of children in hundreds of different countries, will be adding evaluation of collaborative problem-solving skills in 2015. The research behind this book has tried to present an approach to geometry that responds to these complex and ever-shifting challenges.

The previous chapter presented illustrative topics for teams of students to explore in VMT-with-GeoGebra. These were not designed to comprise a traditional course in geometry. They do not attempt to address all the historic issues of geometry education in public schooling, such as those reviewed by Sinclair (2008). These problems are largely left to the teachers (potentially with professional development), who will have to decide how to integrate the topics into their classes or to encourage their use outside of class. The topics are meant just to provide an introductory experience in dynamic geometry, to train student visualization skills, collaboration practices, software literacy, and an orientation to mathematical relationships or dependencies. The hope is that such a preparation—whether it comes before or during or even after a traditional geometry course—will help the students to make sense of geometry and to engage in it more deeply, actively, collaboratively, and with greater understanding.

The focus on deeper understanding applies to the issue of proof in geometry as well. Proof is a central and highly contentious notion in geometry. As discussed in the conclusion to the previous chapter, proof in dynamic geometry can be considered closely aligned with the design of dependencies in dynamic construction. Research in dynamic geometry has persuasively argued that proof is quite different in dynamic geometry, that the processes of dragging and constructing mediate the conception of proof (Jones, 2000; Laborde, 2000; deVilliers, 2003, 2004). By focusing on the understanding of why a conjecture is true, the process of designing dependencies to construct a figure to behave as conjectured parallels the process of designing a corresponding proof. Furthermore, because the focus on dependencies leads to explanation, it is likely to be more motivating than a formal deductive approach. The use of dynamic-geometry environments that tends to reduce student motivation to explicitly prove conjectures is the kind of use that is limited to dragging and does not involve the student in designing, discussing, and constructing dependencies. Accordingly, the approach advocated in this book has focused on dependencies as central to the study of dynamic geometry. To reduce the use of dynamic geometry to dragging is counter-productive.

Dependencies have an interesting ontological ambiguity. They can be experienced as objective barriers, which constrict our freedom to drag objects at will, or they can be experienced as tools, which allow us to impose our agency and rules on the objects that we design. In dynamic geometry, we discover pre-existing dependencies as we drag figures and we create new dependencies as we construct interrelated objects. Given a specific figure in GeoGebra, we can discover that it consists of two triangles that are constrained to be inscribed and equilateral. Then we can design and construct two new triangles such that they are similarly constrained to be inscribed and equilateral. Before dragging the first pair of triangles, we could not know that they were dynamically inscribed and equilateral; before properly constructing the second pair of triangles, they were not dynamically inscribed and equilateral. The world does not simply exist for us to passively observe; neither can we create it without encountering any constraints. We must engage in creative discovery—both in dynamic geometry and in the world at large. Perhaps if students collaborate in a human-centered mathematics environment they will be better prepared to work together in a socially constructed but highly constrained shared world.

Author Index

Bibliography

Ackerman, M., Halverson, C., Erickson, T., & Kellogg, W. (2008). *Resources, co-evolution and artifacts: Theory in CSCW*. London, UK: Springer. 138

Adorno, T. W., & Horkheimer, M. (1945). *The dialectic of enlightenment* (J. Cumming, Trans.). New York: Continuum. 28, 37, 38

Alexander, C. (1964). *Notes on the synthesis of form*. Cambridge, MA: Harvard University Press. 21

Andriessen, J., Baker, M., & Suthers, D. (Eds.). (2003). *Arguing to learn: Confronting cognitions in computer-supported collaborative learning environments*. Dordrecht, Netherlands: Kluwer Academic Publishers. Computer-supported collaborative learning book series, vol 1. 11

Arnseth, H. C., & Ludvigsen, S. (2006). Approaching institutional contexts: Systemic versus dialogic research in CSCL. *International Journal of Computer-Supported Collaborative Learning*. 1(2), 167-185. DOI: 10.1007/s11412-006-8874-3. 147

Arvaja, M. (2012). Personal and shared experiences as resources for meaning making in a philosophy of science course. *International Journal of Computer-Supported Collaborative Learning*. 7(1), 85-108. DOI: 10.1007/s11412-011-9137-5. 138

Barab, S. (2006). Design-based research: A methodological toolkit for the learning scientist. In R. K. Sawyer (Ed.), *The Cambridge handbook of the learning sciences*. (pp. 153-170). Cambridge, UK: Cambridge University Press. 35

Barron, B. (2000). Achieving coordination in collaborative problem-solving groups. *Journal of The Learning Sciences*. 9(4), 403-436. DOI: 10.1207/S15327809JLS0904_2. 149

Barrows, H. (1994). *Practice-based learning: Problem-based learning applied to medical education*. Springfield, IL: SIU School of Medicine. 11

Bereiter, C. (2002). *Education and mind in the knowledge age*. Hillsdale, NJ: Lawrence Erlbaum Associates. 11

Boaler, J. (2008). *What's math got to do with it? Helping children learn to love their most hated subject: And why it is important for America*. New York: Viking. 9, 11

Bransford, J., Brown, A., & Cocking, R. (Eds.). (1999). *How people learn: Brain, mind, experience, and school*. Washington, DC: National Research Council. Web: `http://books.nap.edu/html/howpeople1/`. 10, 11

Brown, A. (1992). Design experiments: Theoretical and methodological challenges in creating complex interventions in classroom settings. *The Journal of the Learning Sciences*. 2(2), 141-178. DOI: 10.1207/s15327809jls0202_2.

Brown, A., & Campione, J. (1994). Guided discovery in a community of learners. In K. McGilly (Ed.), *Classroom lessons: Integrating cognitive theory and classroom practice*. (pp. 229-270). Cambridge, MA: MIT Press. 11

Çakir, M. P., & Stahl, G. (2013). The integration of mathematics discourse, graphical reasoning and symbolic expression by a virtual math team. In D. Martinovic, V. Freiman & Z. Karadag (Eds.), *Visual mathematics and cyberlearning*. New York: Springer. Web: `http://GerryStahl.net/pub/visualmath.pdf`. 130, 135

Çakir, M. P., Zemel, A., & Stahl, G. (2009). The joint organization of interaction within a multimodal CSCL medium. *International Journal of Computer-Supported Collaborative Learning*. 4(2), 115-149. Web: `http://GerryStahl.net/pub/ijCSCL_4_2_1.pdf`. DOI: 10.1007/s11412-009-9061-0. 132, 135, 148, 149

CCSSI. (2011). High school -- geometry. In Common Core State Standards Initiative (Ed.), *Common core state standards for mathematics*. (pp. 74-78). 103, 156, 166

Cekaite, A. (2009). Collaborative corrections with spelling control: Digital resources and peer assistance. *International Journal of Computer-Supported Collaborative Learning*. 4(3), 319-341. DOI: 10.1007/s11412-009-9067-7. 138

Clark, H., & Brennan, S. (1991). Grounding in communication. In L. Resnick, J. Levine & S. Teasley (Eds.), *Perspectives on socially-shared cognition*. (pp. 127-149). Washington, DC: APA. 144

Cobb, P., Yackel, E., & McClain, K. (2000). *Symbolizing and communicating in mathematics classrooms: Perspectives on discourse, tools, and instructional design*. Mahwah, NJ: Lawrence Erlbaum Associates. 11

Descartes, R. (1633/1999). *Discourse on method and meditations on first philosophy*. New York: Hackett. 38

deVilliers, M. (2003). *Rethinking proof with the Geometer's Sketchpad*. Emeryville, CA: Key Curriculum Press. 12, 166, 167, 199

deVilliers, M. (2004). Using dynamic geometry to expand mathematics teachers' understanding of proof. *International Journal of Mathematics Education in Science & Technology*. 35(4), 703-724. DOI: 10.1080/0020739042000232556. 12, 199

Dewey, J. (1938/1991). Logic: The theory of inquiry. In J. A. Boydston (Ed.), *John dewey: The later works, 1925-1953*. (Vol. 12, pp. 1-5). Carbondale, IL: Southern Illinois University Press. 29

Dillenbourg, P., Baker, M., Blaye, A., & O'Malley, C. (1996). The evolution of research on collaborative learning. In P. Reimann & H. Spada (Eds.), *Learning in humans and machines: Towards an interdisciplinary learning science*. (pp. 189-211). Oxford, UK: Elsevier. 42, 134

Dohn, N. B. (2009). Affordances revisited: Articulating a Merleau-Pontian view. International *Journal of Computer-Supported Collaborative Learning*. 4(2), 151-170. DOI: 10.1007/s11412-009-9062-z. 45, 136, 146

Dourish, P. (2001). *Where the action is: The foundations of embodied interaction*. Cambridge, MA: MIT Press. 34, 41

Dreyfus, H. (1991). *Being-in-the-world: A commentary on Heidegger's Being and time, division I*. Cambridge, MA: MIT Press. 34

Ehn, P. (1988). *Work-oriented design of computer artifacts*. Stockholm, Sweden: Arbetslivscentrum. 34, 41

Euclid. (300 BCE/2002). *Euclid's elements* (T. L. Heath, Trans.). Santa Fe, NM: Green Lion Press. 8, 14, 23, 26, 65, 166

Evans, M. A., Feenstra, E., Ryon, E., & McNeill, D. (2011). A multimodal approach to coding discourse: Collaboration, distributed cognition, and geometric reasoning. *International Journal of Computer-Supported Collaborative Learning*. 6(2), 253-278. 1271. DOI: 10.1007/s11412-011-9113-0. 131, 149

Floyd, C. (1992). Software development and reality construction. In C. Floyd, H. Zuellinghoven, R. Budde & R. Keil-Slawik (Eds.), *Software development and reality construction*. (pp. 86-100). Berlin, Germany: Springer Verlag. 41

Furberg, A., Kluge, A., & Ludvigsen, S. (2013). Students' conceptual sense-making with and of science diagrams in computer-based inquiry settings. *International Journal of Computer-Supported Collaborative Learning*. 8(1). DOI: 10.1007/s11412-013-9165-4. 138

Gadamer, H.-G. (1960/1988). *Truth and method*. New York: Crossroads. 3

Gadanidis, G., Graham, L., McDougall, D., & Roulet, G. (2002). On-line mathematics: Visions and opportunities, issues and challenges, and recommendations. (white paper on-line working meeting). Presented at the Fields Institute for Research in Mathematical Sciences Mathematics, Ontario: University of Toronto. 14

Gallese, V., & Lakoff, G. (2005). The brain's concepts: The role of the sensory-motor system in conceptual knowledge. *Cognitive Neuropsychology*. 21(3-4), 455-479. DOI: 10.1080/02643290442000310. 132

Gardner, H. (1985). *The mind's new science: A history of the cognitive revolution*. New York: Basic Books. 135

Garfinkel, H. (1967). *Studies in ethnomethodology*. Englewood Cliffs, NJ: Prentice-Hall. 151

Garfinkel, H., & Sacks, H. (1970). On formal structures of practical actions. In J. Mckinney & E. Tiryakian (Eds.), *Theoretical sociology: Perspectives and developments*. (pp. 337-366). New York: Appleton-Century-Crofts. 126, 137

Gleick, J. (2011). *The information*. New York, NY: Vintage. 21

Goffman, E. (1974). *Frame analysis: An essay on the organization of experience*. New York: Harper & Row. 144

Goodwin, C. (1994). Professional vision. *American Anthropologist*. 96(3), 606-633. DOI: 10.1525/aa.1994.96.3.02a00100. 64, 102, 131

Goodwin, C., & Heritage, J. (1990). Conversation analysis. *Annual Review of Anthropology*. 19, 283-307. DOI: 10.1146/annurev.an.19.100190.001435. 141

Greeno, J. G., & Goldman, S. V. (1998). *Thinking practices in mathematics and science learning*. Mahwah, NJ: Lawrence Erlbaum Associates. 11

Guribye, F. (2005). *Infrastructures for learning: Ethnographic inquiries into the social and technical conditions of education and training*. Unpublished Dissertation, Ph.D., Department of Information Science and Media Studies, University of Bergen. Bergen, Norway. 42

Hall, R., & Stevens, R. (1995). Making space: A comparison of mathematical work in school and professional design practices. In S. L. Star (Ed.), *The cultures of computing*. Oxford, UK: Blackwell Publishers. 11

Hanks, W. (1992). The indexical ground of deictic reference. In A. Duranti & C. Goodwin (Eds.), *Rethinking context: Language as an interactive phenomenon*. (pp. 43-76). Cambridge, UK: Cambridge University Press. 131, 144, 151

Healy, L., Hölzl, R., Hoyles, C., & Noss, R. (1994). Messing up. *Micromath*. 10(1), 14016. 12

Hegel, G. W. F. (1807/1967). *Phenomenology of spirit* (J. B. Baillie, Trans.). New York: Harper & Row. 39, 132, 145

Heidegger, M. (1927/1996). *Being and time: A translation of Sein und Zeit* (J. Stambaugh, Trans.). Albany, NY: SUNY Press. 34, 40, 131, 132, 136

Heidegger, M. (1935/2003). Der Ursprung des Kunstwerkes. In M. Heidegger (Ed.), *Holzwege*. Frankfurt a. M., Germany: Klostermann. 136

Heidegger, M. (1938/1999). *Contributions to philosophy (from enowning)* (P. Emad & K. Maly, Trans.). Bloomington, IN: Indiana University. 25

Heidegger, M. (1950/1967). Das Ding. In *Vorträge und Aufsätze ii.* (pp. 37-60). Pfullingen, Germany: Neske. 137

Heidegger, M. (1979). *On time and Being* (J. Stambaugh, Trans.). New York: Harper & Row. 28, 33

Hölzl, R. (1996). How does "dragging" affect the learning of geometry. *International Journal of Computers for Mathematical Learning.* 1(2), 169–187. DOI: 10.1007/BF00571077. 12

Hölzl, R., Healy, L., Hoyles, C., & Noss, R. (1994). Geometrical relationships and dependencies in Cabri. *Micromath.* 10(3), 8-11. 12, 123

Hoyles, C., & Jones, K. (1998). Proof in dynamic geometry contexts. In C. M. a. V. Villani (Ed.), *Perspectives on the teaching of geometry for the 21st century.* (pp. 121-128). Dordrecht: Kluwer. 12

Husserl, E. (1929/1960). *Cartesian meditations: An introduction to phenomenology* (D. Cairns, Trans.). The Hague, Netherlands: Martinus Nijhoff. 65, 137

Husserl, E. (1936/1989). The origin of geometry (D. Carr, Trans.). In J. Derrida (Ed.), *Edmund Husserl's origin of geometry: An introduction.* (pp. 157-180). Lincoln, NE: University of Nebraska Press. 22, 36, 132, 145

Hutchins, E. (1996). *Cognition in the wild.* Cambridge, MA: MIT Press. 21, 29, 36, 138, 147

Hutchins, E., & Palen, L. (1998). Constructing meaning from space, gesture and speech. In L. B. Resnick, R. Saljo, C. Pontecorvo & B. Burge (Eds.), *Discourse, tools, and reasoning: Situated cognition and technologically supported environments.* Heidelberg, Germany: Springer Verlag. 36

Jeong, H., & Hmelo-Silver, C. (2010). *An overview of CSCL methodologies.* Paper presented at the 9th International Conference of the Learning Sciences. Chicago, IL. Proceedings pp. 921-928. 147

Johnson, D. W., & Johnson, R. T. (1989). *Cooperation and competition: Theory and research.* Edina, MN: Interaction Book Company. 10

Jones, C., Dirckinck-Holmfeld, L., & Lindström, B. (2006). A relational, indirect, meso-level approach to CSCL design in the next decade. *International Journal of Computer-Supported Collaborative Learning.* 1(1), 35-56. DOI: 10.1007/s11412-006-6841-7. 42

Jones, K. (1996). *Coming to know about 'dependency' within a dynamic geometry environment. Paper presented at the 20th Conference of the International Group for the Psychology of Mathematics Education.* University of Valencia. Proceedings pp. 3: 145-152. 12, 123

Jones, K. (1997). *Children learning to specify geometrical relationships using a dynamic geometry package.* Paper presented at the 21st Conference of the International Group for the Psychology of Mathematics Education. University of Helsinki, Finland. Proceedings pp. 3: 121-128. 12

Jones, K. (2000). Educational Studies in Mathematics. 44(1/2), 55-85. Web: http://www.jstor.org/stable/3483205. 199

Kant, I. (1787/1999). *Critique of pure reason.* Cambridge, UK: Cambridge University Press. 38, 45

Kapur, M., & Bielaczyck, K. (2012). Designing for productive failure. *Journal of the Learning Sciences.* 21(1), 45-83. DOI: 10.1080/10508406.2011.591717. 35

Kapur, M., & Kinzer, C. (2009). Productive failure in CSCL groups. *International Journal of Computer-Supported Collaborative Learning.* 4(1), 21-46. Web: `http://dx.doi.org/10.1007/s11412-008-9059-z`. DOI: 10.1007/s11412-008-9059-z. 35

Karlsson, G. (2010). Animation and grammar in science education: Learners' construal of animated educational software. *International Journal of Computer-Supported Collaborative Learning.* 5(2), 167-189. DOI: 10.1007/s11412-010-9085-5. 138

Koschmann, T. (2002). *Dewey's contribution to the foundations of CSCL research. In G. Stahl (Ed.), Computer support for collaborative learning: Foundations for a CSCL community: Proceedings of CSCL 2002.* (pp. 17-22). Boulder, CO: Lawrence Erlbaum Associates. 153

Koschmann, T., Glenn, P., & Conlee, M. (1997). Analyzing the emergence of a learning issue in a problem-based learning meeting. *Medical Education Online.* 2(1). Web: `http://www.utmb.edu/meo/res00003.pdf`. DOI: 10.3402/meo.v2i.4290. 11

Koschmann, T., Stahl, G., & Zemel, A. (2004). *The video analyst's manifesto (or the implications of Garfinkel's policies for the development of a program of video analytic research within the learning sciences).* Paper presented at the International Conference of the Learning Sciences (ICLS 2004). Los Angeles, CA. Proceedings pp. 278-285. Web: `http://GerryStahl.net/pub/manifesto2004.pdf`. 138

Krange, I., & Ludvigsen, S. (2008). What does it mean? Students' procedural and conceptual problem solving in a CSCL environment designed within the field of science education. *International Journal of Computer-Supported Collaborative Learning.* 3(1), 25-51. DOI: 10.1007/s11412-007-9030-4. 147

Krause, E. (1986). *Taxicab geometry: An adventure in non-euclidean geometry.* New York: Dover. 10, 190

Laborde, C. (2000). Dynamic geometry environments as a source of rich learning contexts for the complex activity of proving. *Educational Studies in Mathematics.* 44, 151–161. DOI: 10.1023/A:1012793121648. 12, 199

Laborde, C. (2004). The hidden role of diagrams in pupils' construction of meaning in geometry. In C. H. J. Kilpatrick, & O. Skovsmose (Ed.), *Meaning in mathematics education.* (pp. 1-21). Dordrecht, Netherlands: Kluwer Academic Publishers. 149

Lakatos, I. (1976). *Proofs and refutations: The logic of mathematical discovery.* Cambridge, UK: Cambridge University Press. 11, 23, 37

Lakoff, G., & Núñez, R. (2000). *Where mathematics comes from: How the embodied mind brings mathematics into being.* New York City: Basic Books. 45, 66, 129

Latour, B. (1990). Drawing things together. In M. Lynch & S. Woolgar (Eds.), *Representation in scientific practice.* Cambridge, MA: MIT Press. 138, 147

Latour, B. (1992). Where are the missing masses? The sociology of a few mundane artifacts. In W. E. Bijker & J. Law (Eds.), *Shaping technology/building society.* (pp. 225-227). Cambridge, MA: MIT Press. 138, 147

Latour, B. (2007). *Reassembling the social: An introduction to actor-network-theory.* Cambridge, UK: Cambridge University Press. 36, 138, 145

Latour, B. (2008). The Netz-works of Greek deductions. *Social Studies of Science.* 38(3), 441-459. DOI: 10.1177/0306312707087973. 6, 25

Lave, J., & Wenger, E. (1991). *Situated learning: Legitimate peripheral participation.* Cambridge, UK: Cambridge University Press. 11, 135

Lemke, J. L. (1993). *Talking science: Language, learning and values.* Norwood, NJ: Ablex. 11, 145

Linell, P. (2001). *Approaching dialogue: Talk, interaction and contexts in dialogical perspectives.* New York: Benjamins. 138

Livingston, E. (1999). Cultures of proving. *Social Studies of Science.* 29(6), 867-888. DOI: 10.1177/030631299029006003. 10, 11, 27, 28, 66, 145

Lockhart, P. (2009). *A mathematician's lament: How school cheats us out of our most fascinating and imaginative art forms.* New York, NY: Belevue Literary Press. 9, 11

Lonchamp, J. (2012). An instrumental perspective on CSCL systems. *International Journal of Computer-Supported Collaborative Learning.* 7(2), 211-237. DOI: 10.1007/s11412-012-9141-4. 138

Long, P. O., McGee, D., & Stahl, A. M. (Eds.). (2009). *The book of Michael of Rhodes: A fifteenth-century maritime manuscript.* Cambridge, MA: MIT Press. 21

Looi, C.-K., So, H.-j., Toh, Y., & Chen, W. (2011). CSCL in classrooms: The Singapore experience of synergizing policy, practice and research. *International Journal of Computer-Supported Collaborative Learning*. DOI: 10.1007/s11412-010-9102-8. 42

Maher, C. A., Powell, A. B., & Uptegrove, E. B. (Eds.). (2010). *Combinatorics and reasoning: Representing, justifying and building isomorphisms*. New York: Springer. DOI: 10.1007/978-0-387-98132-1. 11

Marx, K. (1858/1939). *Grundrisse der Kritik der politischen Oekonomie (Rohentwurf)*. Frankfurt, Germany: Europische Verlagsanstalt. 132

Marx, K. (1867). *Das Kapital: Kritik der politischen Oekonomie* (Vol. I). Hamburg, Germany: Otto Meisner. 40

McDougall, D., & Karadag, Z. (2008). *Tracking students' mathematical thinking online: Frame analysis method*. Paper presented at the 11th International Congress on Mathematical Education. Monterrey, Nuevo Leon, Mexico. 14

Medina, R., Suthers, D. D., & Vatrapu, R. (2009). Representational practices in VMT. In G. Stahl (Ed.), *Studying virtual math teams*. (ch. 10, pp. 185-205). New York: Springer. Web: `http://GerryStahl.net/vmt/book/10.pdf`. DOI: 10.1007/978-1-4419-0228-3_10. 131, 138, 154

Mercer, N., & Wegerif, R. (1999). Is "exploratory talk" productive talk? In K. Littleton & P. Light (Eds.), *Learning with computers: Analyzing productive interaction*. (pp. 79-101). New York: Routledge. 131

Merleau-Ponty, M. (1945/2002). *The phenomenology of perception* (C. Smith, Trans. 2nd ed.). New York: Routledge. 132

Merleau-Ponty, M. (1955). *Visible and invisible*. Evanston, IL: Northwestern University Press. 65

Merleau-Ponty, M. (1961/1964). Eye and mind (C. Dallery, Trans.). In J. M. Edie (Ed.), *The primacy of perception*. (pp. 159-190). Evanston, IL: Northwestern University Press. 65

Michaels, S., O'Connor, C., & Resnick, L. B. (2008). Deliberative discourse idealized and realized: Accountable talk in the classroom and in civic life. *Studies in the Philosophy of Education*. 27(4), 283-297. DOI: 10.1007/s11217-007-9071-1. 11, 103

Morris, R. (Ed.). (1986). *Studies in mathematics education: Teaching of geometry*. (Vol. 5). Paris, FR: UNESCO. 29

Moss, J., & Beatty, R. (2006). Knowledge building in mathematics: Supporting collaborative learning in pattern problems. *International Journal of Computer-Supported Collaborative Learning*. 1(4), 441-465. DOI: 10.1007/s11412-006-9003-z. 11

Nancy, J.-L. (2000). *Being singular plural* (R. Richardson, Trans.). Palo Alto, CA: Stanford University Press. 35

Netz, R. (1999). *The shaping of deduction in Greek mathematics: A study in cognitive history.* Cambridge, UK: Cambridge University Press. 6, 22, 65, 66, 145

Noss, R., Healy, L., Hoyles, C., & Hölzl, R. (1994). *Constructing meanings for construction.* Paper presented at the 18th Conference of the International Group for the Psychology of Mathematics Education. Lisbon, Portugal. Proceedings pp. III: 360- 367. 12

Öner, D. (2013). Analyzing group coordination when solving geometry problems with dynamic geometry software. *International Journal of Computer-Supported Collaborative Learning.* 8(1). DOI: 10.1007/s11412-012-9161-0. 58, 94, 148, 150

Ong, W. (1998). *Orality and literacy: The technologizing of the world.* New York: Routledge. 28

Overdijk, M., Diggelen, W., Kirschner, P., & Baker, M. (2012). Connecting agents and artifacts in CSCL: Towards a rationale of mutual shaping. *International Journal of Computer-Supported Collaborative Learning.* 7(2), 193-210. DOI: 10.1007/s11412-012-9143-2. 138

Papert, S. (1980). *Mindstorms: Children, computers and powerful ideas.* New York: Basic Books. 9, 11

Pappus of Alexandria. (340). *Synagoge [mathematical collection].* Alexandria, Egypt. 27

Piaget, J. (1990). *The child's conception of the world.* New York: Littlefield Adams. 28

Plato. (340 BCE/1941). *The republic* (F. Cornford, Trans.). London, UK: Oxford University Press. 24, 38

Plato. (350 BCE/1961). Meno. In E. Hamilton & H. Cairns (Eds.), *The collected dialogues of Plato.* (pp. 353-384). Princeton, NJ: Princeton University Press. 24

Polanyi, M. (1966). *The tacit dimension.* Garden City, NY: Doubleday. 130

Powell, A. B., & Dicker, L. (2012). *Toward collaborative learning with dynamic geometry environments.* Paper presented at the 12th International Conference on Mathematical Education. Seoul, Korea. 12

Powell, A. B., Francisco, J. M., & Maher, C. A. (2003). An analytical model for studying the development of mathematical ideas and reasoning using videotape data. *Journal of Mathematical Behavior.* 22(4), 405-435. DOI: 10.1016/j.jmathb.2003.09.002. 11

Powell, A. B., & López, J. A. (1989). Writing as a vehicle to learn mathematics: A case study. In P. Connolly & T. Vilardi (Eds.), *The role of writing in learning mathematics and science.* (pp. 157-177). New York: Teachers College. 11

Rabardel, P., & Beguin, P. (2005). Instrument mediated activity: From subject development to anthropocentric design. *Theoretical Issues in Ergonomics Science.* 6(5), 429–461429–461461. DOI: 10.1080/14639220500078179. 45, 144

Rabardel, P., & Bourmaud, G. (2003). From computer to instrument system: A developmental perspective. *Interacting with Computers.* 15, 665–691. DOI: 10.1016/S0953-5438(03)00058-4. 144

Reis, Z. A., & Karadag, Z. (2008). *A proposal for developing online collaborative environment for learning mathematics.* Paper presented at the World Conference on Educational Multimedia, Hypermedia and Telecommunications. VA. Proceedings pp. 5123-5128. AACE. 14

Resnick, L., O'Connor, C., & Michaels, S. (2007). *Classroom discourse, mathematical rigor, and student reasoning: An accountable talk literature review: LearnLab*, Pittsburgh Science of Learning Center. Web: `http://www.learnlab.org/research/wiki/images/f/ff/Accountable_Talk_Lit_Review.pdf`. 103

Ritella, G., & Hakkarainen, K. (2012). Instrumental genesis in technology-mediated learning: From double stimulation to expansive knowledge practices. *International Journal of Computer-Supported Collaborative Learning.* 7(2), 238-258. DOI: 10.1007/s11412-012-9144-1.138

Rittel, H., & Webber, M. M. (1984). Planning problems are wicked problems. In N. Cross (Ed.), *Developments in design methodology.* (pp. 135-144). New York: John Wiley & Sons. 152

Rogoff, B. (1995). Sociocultural activity on three planes. In B. Rogoff, J. Wertsch, P. del Rio & A. Alvarez (Eds.), *Sociocultural studies of mind.* (pp. 139-164). Cambridge, UK: Cambridge University Press. 42, 134

Roschelle, J., & Teasley, S. (1995). The construction of shared knowledge in collaborative problem solving. In C. O'Malley (Ed.), *Computer-supported collaborative learning.* (pp. 69-197). Berlin, Germany: Springer Verlag. 149

Sarmiento, J., & Stahl, G. (2007). *Bridging and persistence in sustained, collaborative problem solving online.* Paper presented at the Hawaii International Conference on System Sciences (HICSS 2007). Hawaii, HI. Web: `http://GerryStahl.net/pub/hicss07`. DOI: 10.1109/HICSS.2007.110. 131

Sarmiento, J., & Stahl, G. (2008). *Extending the joint problem space: Time and sequence as essential features of knowledge building.* Paper presented at the International Conference of the Learning Sciences (ICLS 2008). Utrecht, Netherlands. Web: http://GerryStahl.net/pub/icls2008johann.pdf. 131, 149

Sartre, J.-P. (1968). *Search for a method* (H. Barnes, Trans.). New York: Random House. 132

Sawyer, R. K. (2005). *Social emergence: Societies as complex systems.* Cambridge, UK: Cambridge University Press. DOI: 10.1017/CBO9780511734892. 143

Sawyer, R. K. (Ed.). (2006). *Cambridge handbook of the learning sciences.* Cambridge, UK: Cambridge University Press. 10, 11, 29, 199

Scardamalia, M., & Bereiter, C. (1996). Computer support for knowledge-building communities. In T. Koschmann (Ed.), *CSCL: Theory and practice of an emerging paradigm.* (pp. 249-268). Hillsdale, NJ: Lawrence Erlbaum Associates. 11

Schatzki, T. R., Knorr Cetina, K., & Savigny, E. v. (Eds.). (2001). *The practice turn in contemporary theory.* New York: Routledge. 135

Schegloff, E. A. (2007). *Sequence organization in interaction: A primer in conversation analysis.* Cambridge, UK: Cambridge University Press. DOI: 10.1017/CBO9780511791208. 140

Scher, D. (2000). Lifting the curtain: The evolution of the Geometer's Sketchpad. *The Mathematics Educator.* 10(1). 57

Scher, D. (2002). *Students' conceptions of geometry in a dynamic geometry software environment.* Unpublished Dissertation, Ph.D., School of Education, New York University. New York. Web: `http://GerryStahl.net/pub/GSP_Scher_Dissertation.pdf`. 11, 29

Schön, D. A. (1983). *The reflective practitioner: How professionals think in action.* New York: Basic Books. 41

Schwarz, B. B. (1997). Understanding symbols with intermediate abstractions: An analysis of the collaborative construction of mathematical meaning. In L. B. Resnick, R. Saljo, C. Pontecorvo & B. Burge (Eds.), *Discourse, tools, and reasoning: Essays on situated cognition.* (pp. 312-335). Berlin, Germany: Springer. 11

Sfard, A. (2000). Symbolizing mathematical reality into being—or how mathematical discourse and mathematical objects create each other. In P. Cobb, E. Yackel & K. McClain (Eds.), *Symbolizing and communicating in mathematics classrooms: Perspectives on discourse, tools, and instructional design.* (pp. 37-98). Mahwah, NJ: Lawrence Erlbaum Associates. 37, 145

Sfard, A. (2008). *Thinking as communicating: Human development, the growth of discourses and mathematizing.* Cambridge, UK: Cambridge University Press. 11, 37, 93, 135, 148

Sfard, A., & Linchevski, L. (1994). The gains and the pitfalls of reification - the case of algebra. In P. Cobb (Ed.), *Learning mathematics: Constructivist and interactionist theories of mathematical development.* (pp. 87-124). Dodrecht, Netherlands: Kluwer. 37, 145

Silverman, J., & Thompson, P. W. (2008). Toward a framework for the development of mathematics content knowledge for teaching. *Journal for Mathematics Teacher Education.* 11(6), 499-511. DOI: 10.1007/s10857-008-9089-5. 10

Sinclair, N. (2008). *The history of the geometry curriculum in the united states*. Charlotte, NC: Information Age Publishing, Inc. 12, 29, 199

Slavin, R. (1980). Cooperative learning. *Review of Educational Research*. 50(2), 315-342. DOI: 10.3102/00346543050002315. 10

Stahl, G. (1975a). The jargon of authenticity: An introduction to a Marxist critique of Heidegger. *Boundary 2. III(2)*, 489-498. Web: `http://GerryStahl.net/publications/interpretations/jargon.htm`. 35

Stahl, G. (1975b). *Marxian hermeneutics and Heideggerian social theory: Interpreting and transforming our world*. Unpublished Dissertation, Ph.D., Department of Philosophy, Northwestern University. Evanston, IL. Web: `http://GerryStahl.net/publications/dissertations/philosophy`. 36

Stahl, G. (1976). Attuned to Being: Heideggerian music in technological society. *Boundary 2. IV(2)*, 637-664. Web: `http://GerryStahl.net/publications/interpretations/attuned.pdf`. 35, 36

Stahl, G. (2000). *A model of collaborative knowledge-building*. Paper presented at the Fourth International Conference of the Learning Sciences (ICLS '00). Ann Arbor, MI. Proceedings pp. 70-77. Lawrence Erlbaum Associates. Web: `http://GerryStahl.net/pub/icls2000.pdf`. 139

Stahl, G. (2002). *Contributions to a theoretical framework for CSCL*. Paper presented at the Computer support for collaborative learning: Foundations for a CSCL community. Proceedings of CSCL 2002. Boulder, CO. Proceedings pp. 62-71. Lawrence Erlbaum Associates. Web: `http://GerryStahl.net/cscl/papers/ch15.pdf`. DOI: 10.3115/1658616.1658626. 139

Stahl, G. (2004). Building collaborative knowing: Elements of a social theory of CSCL. In J.-W. Strijbos, P. Kirschner & R. Martens (Eds.), *What we know about CSCL: And implementing it in higher education*. (pp. 53-86). Boston, MA: Kluwer Academic Publishers. Web: `http://GerryStahl.net/cscl/papers/ch16.pdf`. 148

Stahl, G. (2006). *Group cognition: Computer support for building collaborative knowledge*. Cambridge, MA: MIT Press. Web: `http://GerryStahl.net/mit/`. 11, 15, 39, 42, 103, 133, 134, 135, 142, 148, 197

Stahl, G. (2008). Book review: Exploring thinking as communicating in CSCL. *International Journal of Computer-Supported Collaborative Learning*. 3(3), 361-368. DOI: 10.1007/s11412-008-9046-4. 11, 94, 135, 148

Stahl, G. (2009). *Studying virtual math teams.* New York: Springer. Web: `http://GerryStahl.net/vmt/book`. DOI: 10.1007/978-1-4419-0228-3. xxi, 15, 71, 126, 133, 140, 197

Stahl, G. (2010a). Group cognition as a foundation for the new science of learning. In M. S. Khine & I. M. Saleh (Eds.), *New science of learning: Cognition, computers and collaboration in education.* (pp. 23-44). New York: Springer. Web: `http://GerryStahl.net/pub/scienceoflearning.pdf`. 42, 133

Stahl, G. (2010b). *Marx and Heidegger.* Philadelphia. PA: Gerry Stahl at Lulu. 217 pages. Web: `http://GerryStahl.net/elibrary/marx`. 40

Stahl, G. (2011a). *How a virtual math team structured its problem solving.* Paper presented at the Connecting computer-supported collaborative learning to policy and practice: CSCL 2011 conference proceedings. Lulu: ISLS. Proceedings pp. 256-263. Web: `http://GerryStahl.net/pub/cscl2011stahl.pdf`. 132

Stahl, G. (2011b). Social practices of group cognition in virtual math teams. In S. Ludvigsen, A. Lund, I. Rasmussen & R. Säljö (Eds.), *Learning across sites: New tools, infrastructures and practices.* (pp. 190-205). New York: Routledge. Web: `http://GerryStahl.net/pub/cmc.pdf`. 126, 131

Stahl, G. (2013). Theories of collaborative cognition: Foundations for CSCL and CSCW together. In S. Goggins & I. Jahnke (Eds.), *CSCL@work.* (Springer CSCL Book Series). New York: Springer. Web: `http://GerryStahl.net/pub/collabcognition.pdf`. 133, 135, 140, 141

Stahl, G., Jeong, H., Sawyer, R. K., & Suthers, D. D. (2012). Workshop: Analyzing collaborative learning at multiple levels. Presented at the International Conference of the Learning Sciences (ICLS 2012), Sydney, Australia. Web: `http://GerryStahl.net/pub/icls2012workshop.pdf`. 135

Stahl, G., Koschmann, T., & Suthers, D. (2006). Computer-supported collaborative learning: An historical perspective. In R. K. Sawyer (Ed.), *Cambridge handbook of the learning sciences.* (pp. 409-426). Cambridge, UK: Cambridge University Press. Web: `http://GerryStahl.net/elibrary/global`. 9, 14, 93, 147

Stahl, G., Zemel, A., & Koschmann, T. (2009). *Repairing indexicality in virtual math teams.* Paper presented at the International Conference on Computers and Education (ICCE 2009). Hong Kong, China. Web: `http://GerryStahl.net/pub/icce2009.pdf`. xxi, 15, 131

Stahl, G., Zhou, N., Cakir, M. P., & Sarmiento-Klapper, J. W. (2011). Seeing what we mean: Co-experiencing a shared virtual world. In *Connecting computer-supported collaborative learning to policy and practice: CSCL 2011 conference proceedings.* (Vol. I, pp. 534-541). Lulu: ISLS. Web: `http://GerryStahl.net/pub/cscl2011.pdf`. 128, 131

Star, S. L. (1989). The structure of ill-structured solutions: Boundary objects and heterogeneous distributed problem solving. In L. Gasser & M. N. Huhns (Eds.), *Distributed artificial intelligence.* (pp. 37-54). San Mateo, CA: Morgan Kaufmann. 151

Stein, M. K., Engle, R. A., Smith, M. S., & Hughes, E. K. (2008). Orchestrating productive mathematical discussions: Five practices for helping teachers move beyond show and tell. *Mathematical Thinking and Learning.* 10(4), 313-340. DOI: 10.1080/10986060802229675. 84

Strijbos, J. W., & Stahl, G. (2007). Methodological issues in developing a multi-dimensional coding procedure for small group chat communication. *Learning & Instruction. Special issue on measurement challenges in collaborative learning research.* 17(4), 394-404. Web: `http://GerryStahl.net/vmtwiki/jw.pdf`. DOI: 10.1016/j.learninstruc.2007.03.005. 140

Suchman, L. (1987). *Plans and situated actions: The problem of human-machine communication.* Cambridge, UK: Cambridge University Press. 138

Suchman, L. A. (2007). *Human-machine reconfigurations: Plans and situated actions* (2nd ed.). Cambridge, UK: Cambridge University Press. 133

Sutherland, I. E. (1963). *Sketchpad: A man-machine graphical communication system.* Cambridge, MA: MIT Lincoln Labs. 57, 68

Suthers, D., Lund, K., Rosé, C. P., & Law, N. (Eds.). (2013). *Productive multivocality.* New York: Springer. CSCL book series. 135, 140

Suthers, D. D. (2006). Technology affordances for intersubjective meaning making: A research agenda for CSCL. *International Journal of Computer-Supported Collaborative Learning.* 1(3), 315-337. DOI: 10.1007/s11412-006-9660-y. 147

Suthers, D. D. (2007). *A framework for analyzing interactional processes in online learning.* Paper presented at the international conference on Computer Support for Collaborative Learning (CSCL 2007). New Brunswick, NJ. Web: `http://GerryStahl.net/vmtwiki/dan.pdf`. 140

Swetz, F. (1987). *Capitalism & arithmetic: The new math of the 15th century.* Chicago, IL: LaSalle University Press. 28

Teasley, S. D., & Roschelle, J. (1993). Constructing a joint problem space: The computer as a tool for sharing knowledge. In S. P. Lajoie & S. J. Derry (Eds.), *Computers as cognitive tools.* (pp. 229-258). Mahwah, NJ: Lawrence Erlbaum Associates, Inc. 131

van Aalst, J. (2009). Distinguishing knowledge-sharing, knowledge-construction, and knowledge-creation discourses. *International Journal of Computer-Supported Collaborative Learning.* 4(3), 259-287. DOI: 10.1007/s11412-009-9069-5. 11

Vygotsky, L. (1930/1978). *Mind in society.* Cambridge, MA: Harvard University Press. 11, 15, 41, 42, 93, 132, 134, 138, 140, 145, 147

Wegerif, R. (2007). *Dialogic, education and technology: Expanding the space of learning.* New York: Kluwer-Springer. 11

Weick, K. E. (1988). Enacted sensemaking in crisis situations. *Journal of Management Studies.* 25(4), 305-317. DOI: 10.1111/j.1467-6486.1988.tb00039.x. 146

Winograd, T., & Flores, F. (1986). *Understanding computers and cognition: A new foundation of design.* Reading, MA: Addison-Wesley. 34

Wittgenstein, L. (1921/1974). *Tractatus logico philosophicus.* London, UK: Routledge. 40

Wittgenstein, L. (1953). *Philosophical investigations.* New York: Macmillan. 40, 131, 132, 137

Zemel, A., & Koschmann, T. (2013). Online math problem solving as a process of discovery in CSCL. *International Journal of Computer-Supported Collaborative Learning.* 8(1). 102, 151

Zhou, N., Zemel, A., & Stahl, G. (2008). *Questioning and responding in online small groups engaged in collaborative math problem solving.* Paper presented at the International Conference of the Learning Sciences (ICLS 2008). Utrecht, Netherlands. Web: `http://GerryStahl.net/pub/icls2008nan.pdf`. 131

BIBLIOGRAPHY

Author's Biography

Gerry Stahl

My life began when I first encountered geometry in high school. From that moment on, I devoured books on mathematics, physics, and cosmology. I wondered, like Pythagoras, about the place of mathematical objects in the universe. This led me—via the logicians—to philosophy.

I could not wait to explore these topics as an undergrad at MIT. Once there, however, I became discouraged about the contemporary approach to math and physics education, as well as the militaristic uses being made of them. I turned increasingly to philosophy, moving away from positivism to its critique by 20th century continental thought. Upon graduation, I went to Heidelberg for a year to study German philosophy during the exhilarating 1960s, later spending two years at the Frankfurt School. Meanwhile, I completed a doctoral dissertation on Marx and Heidegger at Northwestern.

Back in Philadelphia, I briefly tried my hand at teaching remedial high school math at an urban public school. However, I soon found systems programming to be a less frustrating way to earn a living. I also engaged in union and community organizing, learning how to bring federal grants into the neighborhoods for local development. When the first personal computers appeared, I ran a service to help non-profit organizations computerize.

Eventually, I decided to fill in my computer science background at the University of Colorado in Boulder, where I earned a doctorate in artificial intelligence and cognitive science. My research work after graduation is documented in *Group Cognition* (MIT Press, 2006). Following a year abroad at a CSCW lab outside Bonn, I went to the College of Information Science at Drexel to teach HCI and CSCL in 2002. In collaboration with many colleagues, I started the VMT Project, which is reported on in *Studying Virtual Math Teams* (Springer, 2009).

My specialty is Computer-Supported Collaborative Learning. I founded the *International Journal of CSCL* and have been active in the CSCL Conference series. My most recent ideas, discoveries, and wonderings are brought together in *Translating Euclid*. Other writings are available in my e-Library at www.GerryStahl.net.